Late Harvest

Contributions in American Studies
Series Editor: Robert H. Walker

"Ezra Pound Speaking": Radio Speeches of World War II
Leonard W. Doob, editor

The Supreme Court: Myth and Reality
Arthur Selwyn Miller

Television Fraud: The History and Implications of the Quiz
Show Scandals
Kent Anderson

Menace in the West: The Rise of French Anti-Americanism
in Modern Times
David Strauss

Social Change and Fundamental Law: America's Evolving Constitution
Arthur Selwyn Miller

American Character and Culture in a Changing World: Some
Twentieth-Century Perspectives
John A. Hague, editor

Olmsted South: Old South Critic/New South Planner
Dana F. White and Victor A. Kramer, editors

In the Trough of the Sea: Selected American Sea-Deliverance
Narratives, 1610-1766
Donald P. Wharton, editor

Aaron Burr and the American Literary Imagination
Charles J. Nolan, Jr.

The Popular Mood of Pre-Civil War America
Lewis O. Saum

The Essays of Mark Van Doren
William Claire, editor

Touching Base: Professional Baseball and American Culture in the
Progressive Era
Steven A. Riess

Late Harvest

ESSAYS AND ADDRESSES IN AMERICAN LITERATURE AND CULTURE

Robert E. Spiller

 CONTRIBUTIONS IN AMERICAN STUDIES, NUMBER 49

GREENWOOD PRESS

WESTPORT, CONNECTICUT • LONDON, ENGLAND

Library of Congress Cataloging in Publication Data

Spiller, Robert Ernest, 1896-
    Late harvest.

    (Contributions in American studies; no. 49
ISSN 0084-9227)
    Bibliography: p.
    Includes index.
    1. American literature—History and criticism—
Addresses, essays, lectures.   2. United States—
Study and teaching—Addresses, essays, lectures.
I. Title
PS121.S55   810′.9   80-543
ISBN 0-313-22023-9 lib. bdg.

Library of Congress Catalog Card Number: 80-543
ISBN: 0-313-22023-9
ISSN: 0084-9227

First published in 1981

Greenwood Press
A division of Congressional Information Service, Inc.
88 Post Road West, Westport, Connecticut 06881
Printed in the United States of America

10 9 8 7 6 5 4 3 2 1

ACKNOWLEDGMENTS

Acknowledgment is made for material in copyright, reprinted by permission of the following:

"Biography of the American Scholar," copyright 1937 by National Council of Teachers of English, publisher of the *English Journal.*

"The Impossible Dream: Adventures in Editing American Literary Texts," copyright 1978 by Friends of the University of Pennsylvania Library, publisher of *Library Chronicle.*

"The American Literary Declaration of Independence," in part based on editorial material in *The American Literary Revolution, 1783-1837,* copyright 1967 by Doubleday and Co., Inc.

"The First Frontier" and "The Awakening of Literary Consciousness 1760-1830," from *The Roots of National Culture to 1830,* copyright, 1933, 1948 by The Macmillan Company, New York (Macmillan Publishing Co., Inc.).

"The Four Faces of Emerson," from *Four Makers of the American Mind,* edited by Thomas E. Crawley, copyright 1976 by Duke University Press.

"The Magic Mirror of American Fiction," from *Problems of International Literary Understanding* (Nobel Symposium No. 6), edited by Karl R. Gierow, copyright 1968 by Almqvist and Wiksell, Stockholm.

"The Cycle and the Roots: National Identity in American Literature," from *Toward a New American Literary History,* edited by Louis J. Budd, Edwin H. Cady, and Carl L. Anderson, copyright 1979 by Duke University Press.

"The Growth of American Literary Scholarship," copyright 1951 by Universitetsforlaget, Oslo, publisher of *Edda.*

"Those Early Days; American Literature and the Modern Language Association," copyright 1968 by The Macmillan Company, New York (Macmillan Publishing Company, Inc.).

"Unity and Diversity in the Study of American Culture: the American Studies Association in Perspective," copyright 1973 by the Trustees of the University of Pennsylvania, publisher of *American Quarterly.*

"American Studies Abroad: Culture and Foreign Policy," copyright 1966 by the American Academy of Political and Social Science, publisher of *Annals.*

CONTENTS

PREFACE

There comes a time when the clock stops, and the sun stands still in the heavens, and you ask, "Who am I?" All those wonders of childhood when you were a stranger in an amazing world — all those struggles of manhood when you were sharpening the tools without really knowing the job — all those years of sorrow and fulfillment, tragedy, and triumph — and now the evening. Who am I? What road have I followed?

Many people, with as deep and central a sense of mission as I have had during most of my professional life, have taken time out, at some point, to produce an ambitious work of research and creative biography or criticism. Perhaps I am at heart rather more of a teacher than a writer. With the exception of the *Literary History of the United States,* a couple of shorter volumes, and much editing, my work has taken the form of essays and addresses directed to fellow scholars, students, and colleagues who shared my interests. I seem to need the baffle of other minds to challenge me to formulate my researches and speculations into expression and action. Therefore, what I am professionally is related at every point to many other minds, and any consistent and central meaning in my life has come out of some kind of exchange with others, rather than merely from my own contemplations and actions.

And now, when I have reached that moment of pause that age provides, I am not tempted to undertake some long-deferred masterpiece, an autobiography, or a new project of research. Instead, I find myself rediscovering and rereading my own writings as they have appeared during the past half-century in journals and in cooperative works of editing and collaboration. I am researching my own past.

The outcome of this enterprise that has occupied my creative efforts of the past dozen years since retirement has been a series of four collections of essays, addresses, and reviews, some of them merely reprinted with commentary, some new essays of summary of one or another aspect of my past thought or actions.

As they have been planned one at a time, each of the volumes has its own focus, but each one leads to the next, and now with the collection, *Late Harvest*, they make a single story of professional growth. That is my excuse for making this fourth book more personal than the others by providing a semiautobiographical frame for the commentary, thereby at least partially answering the question, "Who am I?"

The first volume in the series, *The Third Dimension* (1965), contained the essays leading up to a new American literary history and concluded with the basic statement on philosophy and method, "The Province of Literary History," one of four commissioned by the Modern Language Association on "Aims and Methods of Literary Scholarship." All of these essays were written between 1929 and 1963. The book title was supposed to suggest that, in addition to its relevance to the time and place of its creation, a work of literary art exists in a third or historical dimension as well.

While reviewing my uncollected essays in preparation for this volume, I came to the realization that, since 1926 when I discovered that the novelist James Fenimore Cooper might well be more important as an international social critic than as a writer of romance, I had been fascinated by the possibilities in revisionist studies of the accepted images of major writers. Henry Adams' faults as a historian could be obscured by his brilliance as a literary symbolist, and Emerson and Franklin as earnest and striving human beings lost much of the starch from their public images. *The Oblique Light* (1968), which contains these and other similar portraits, was the result.

But there was still one source of uncollected work that I had not considered, namely, the hundreds of reviews I had published over the years in newspapers, general magazines, and scholarly journals. When I began to bring them together, I recognized a core of reviews of books dealing with theories of literary history that I had deliberately sought out and identified at the time of their appearance. It was as though unwittingly I had been preparing myself to bring together, in one major cooperative work, the wealth of scholarship and creative theory produced in my lifetime. The resulting collection of reviews, *Milestones in American Literary History* (1977), also contained my essay on how the *Literary History of the United States* had evolved, and it thus became a chapter in intellectual and professional autobiography, as in various ways the earlier books had also been.

Late Harvest is what its title suggests, a gathering of essays and addresses on aspects of my involvement in the renaissance of American studies from 1920 to 1979 that are recent or deal with aspects of the movement beyond my focus on American literary history. There are three clusters of essays. The first consists of discussions of factors that shaped my thinking early and formed the foundations of my scholarly career in its basic point of view and in the discovery of the bones and sinews of the work that lay ahead. The second is comprised of essays and addresses on the philosophical and architectural aspects of the general problem, most of them uncollected and at least one previously unpublished, which led to the culminating statement of my central theory of American literary history, "The Cycle and the Roots." These are best read in connection with *The Third Dimension* and *The Oblique Light*. The third cluster is related to the evolution of the American Studies Movement as such, at home and abroad, and to my own connections with the growth of the American Studies Association. A bibliography of my own writings is added to complete the record.

Because the essays in this book are arranged in the order of the ideas they express rather than in the order of their composition, the semi-autobiographical headnotes may create some problems of chronology by use of the flash-back; but a mental shuffle of the pages should present a coherent story on that level also. And because most of the essays were originally addressed to nonspecialized audiences, essential references to sources are incorporated in the text, and footnotes are avoided where possible. In some cases, however, circumstances have required full annotation.

Finally, I hope that this volume, taken with the other three collections of my writings, may define and document a consistent commitment to a single intellectual and human goal: the expression in historical criticism of the meaning of American literature and the culture of which that literature is the expression.

I • FOUNDATIONS

1 | BIOGRAPHY OF THE AMERICAN SCHOLAR

One day not long ago it came to me that the many and various strands of my professional life — miscellaneous and spontaneous as they seemed at the time — made sense when they were added together and put in order. There is an underlying consistency in much of our experience that we do not always recognize. To the extent that we are able to identify and respond to the guiding of the innermost self, we can move with confidence through the varieties of experience.

At the center of my thinking today on my professional life is the theory that literature is the expression, through the art of language, of the total culture of a people drawn together at a time and place. History provides the facts; art and philosophy provide the cultural pattern and meaning.

But I did not begin with any such focus of liberal studies on the nature and development of American culture. When I entered the University of Pennsylvania in 1913, the liberal arts program was emerging from a long tradition based on classical philology, with requirements in Latin and Greek and, for English majors, in Indo-Teutonic and related language disciplines. The study of science was based on physics, chemistry, and mathematics and was available in elective courses (beyond the required elementary courses) for the hardy; the study of the social sciences was struggling to find its disciplinary footing in economics and political science, whereas history, in all its branches, was presented as the chronological record of past events. In such a fluent situation it was possible to accept a

3

classical and historical base for an education that was an adventure in the unfolding world of modern thought. English literature became its core. The English department made only a token obeisance to the obsession of some institutions with an exhaustive drill in Teutonic and other related linguistic disciplines. My professors were already asking, each in his own way, what literature had to tell about the life of the people who wrote it. The Middle Ages provided a source of expression that could be applied to the fluent cultures of the modern world; the cafeteria offerings in the arts and the natural and social sciences were brief opportunities to broaden knowledge and to experiment tentatively with newly discovered ideas.

Up to this point my interest in American literature and life was limited to the field of my dissertation, the American in England from 1783 to 1835, out of which emerged the theme of the awakening of a national consciousness; but at Swarthmore College, where I first taught, there was almost no opportunity to teach American subjects. Frank Aydelotte had just come to the college as president, bringing with him an Oxford, Rhodes-scholar background. The revolutionary honors plan he introduced was based on the Oxford Modern Greats (English literature, history, and philosophy) and emphasized seminar study in depth instead of the familiar class and lecture method. The whole college — faculty and students alike — became absorbed in the aims and methods of higher liberal education, and my growing concentration on research and writing in the field of American literature was relegated for more than a quarter of a century to professional activity and scholarly production. By 1945 I was ready to pull these interests together and accept a university post where teaching, research, and writing became focused on a single course.

Thus the urgent need to realize my own identity, which I began to feel in my teens and which I carried through my college years and the early years of teaching, slowly and then fully became one with a conviction that the culture of which I was a part must be drawn into a fuller realization that it too has a unique identity. In this way my professional life gradually became focused first on the study of American literature and *then on the larger configuration of American civilization and culture. Many apparent inconsistencies in my course through life have thus become, in retrospect, but steps toward a single goal. In some sense, therefore, the lecture on "Biography of the American Scholar," which I prepared for the opening of honors work at Swarthmore on September 24, 1936, provides the pattern for the formative years of my own autobiography. It appeared in the English Journal 26 (October 1937): 637-47.*

Almost a century has passed since Emerson defined the American scholar as "man thinking" before the Phi Beta Kappa Society at Harvard in August, 1837. His address was but a chapter in the biography of the American man of letters whom he had in mind and whose education I should like to trace in swift outline from his first landing on these shores to what we hope is his maturity today. For the study of literature is not an isolated pursuit; it is but one means for the acquirement of a liberal education. What Emerson said of the man of letters may be translated by the philosopher or the physicist into his own idiom; and conversely, whatever may now be said of the history of liberal education in this country must apply specifically to the study of English if that study is to be of full cultural value.

When we consider our educational facilities today, it is hard for us to realize the problems with which our cultural pioneers were faced. A college, yes, but what should be taught? The philosophy of Aristotle or how to fight Indians? The principles of Euclid or the cultivation of corn? Certainly common sense dictated the latter sort of learning. There was no liberal education which could be of much service in the face of the realities of hostile savages, disease, and starvation. But the Puritans and their neighboring colonists were, for the most part, idealists, and they wished to preserve in their children the cultural traditions which they had inherited. The curriculum of their early colleges was based on that of the English academy: the classics, philosophy, mathematics, and of course theology, with little or no science, history, or recent literature. Here was a liberal education which had been tried and proven by generations of English schoolboys. It was a ready-made formula, the only one available. Arbitrarily transplanted as it was, it became the fixed pattern of American higher education, and there are probably people living today whose college courses were determined by it. Until almost the end of the last century it was taken for granted as the requisite of the cultured man. Traditionally known as the classical course, it was not limited to the study of Greek and Roman literature as such. Underlying it was an idealization of classical culture, but in centuries of English usage it has developed into an educational procedure remote from living experience in a new and undeveloped country. It had the merits of definite form, disciplinary aims, and ancient sanction. There was a security in it which our ancestors were loath to relinquish, even though the expanding and vital needs of American life have always found it too limited in its subject matter, too rigid in its form, and too sharp in its division between the life of thought and the life of action. The rebellion against it early found voice. In 1814 Jefferson wrote:

When sobered by experience I hope our successors will turn their attention to the advantages of education. I mean of education on the broad scale, and not that of the petty *academies*, as they call themselves, which are starting up in every neighborhood, and where one or two men, possessing Latin and sometimes Greek, a knowledge of the globes, and the first six books of Euclid, imagine and communicate this as the sum of science. They commit their pupils to the theatre of the world, with just taste enough of learning to be alienated from industrious pursuits, and not enough to do service in the ranks of science.

And John Trumbull, having just graduated from Yale, invoked an unusual muse in doggerel in "The Progress of Dulness" (1772-73):

> Kind headache hail! thou blest disease,
> The friend of idleness and ease;
> Who mid the still and dreary bound
> Where college walls her sons around,
> In spite of fears, in justice' spite,
> Assumst o'er laws dispensing right,
> Setts't from his task the blunderer free,
> Excused by dullness and by thee.

It was clear that liberal studies did not liberate the mind, that wholesome American youth was impatient for action in a world in which so much needed to be done and in which there was so little time for the contemplation of ultimates and the cultivation of the amenities. Fenimore Cooper was expelled from Yale for putting gunpowder in the keyhole of a friend's room and touching it off; Washington Irving was sent off to Europe as agent for his brothers' hardware firm; and birth in a log cabin became a more valuable asset for presidential aspirants than a degree from Harvard College. "In literature of the imagination," wrote Charles J. Ingersoll in 1823, "our standard is considerably below that of England, France, and Germany. . . . In the literature of fact . . . European preeminence is by no means so decided." The American world outside of the colleges was a world of action, engrossed in utilitarian pursuits as far removed as possible from the academic regime of the day. Even Franklin's practical wisdom had succeeded to only a slight degree in bringing the two together. Under his influence and that of other rationalists of the day, the emphasis on theology was lessened and certain of the early colleges timidly admitted a few courses in English literature, the modern languages, "natural philosophy," as the sciences were then called, and a new study, "political economy," which included most of what we now know as the social sciences. But the result was a compromise, a physical rather than a chemical union, donkeys' ears on an old horse. There was no educational formula which was adequate to the demands of the new country. Turn one way, and the educator was faced with principles and practices which had been handed down from civilizations long since dead or past their prime; turn the other, and he was confronted by the raw materials of existence in abundance, unformed to the uses and the spiritual enrichment of man. Franklin and Jefferson predicted the sort of liberal training that American thinkers should have, but the country was too young to put their theories into practice for more than a century.

Americans of truly contemplative mind soon began to realize that neither borrowed traditions nor exclusive concern with the practical present would serve to develop a native American culture. The genius of pure thought must find fields of exercise more immediate to actual experience, or it would be crowded out by utilitarian urgencies. In 1830 Ellery Channing wrote in his "Remarks on a National Literature":

It will be seen that we include under literature all the writings of superior minds, be the subjects what they may. We are aware that the term is often confined to compositions which relate to human nature, and human life; that it is not extended to physical science; that mind, not matter, is regarded as its main subject and sphere. But the worlds of matter and mind are too intimately connected to admit of exact partition. All the objects of human thought flow into one another. . . .

And Emerson seconded him in ridiculing "our devotion to the dead languages" as the single source of culture, and in making his plea for an American scholarship which was as keenly aware of the present as of the past.

It is difficult to say what sort of culture the American mind would have produced in the middle years of the last century, when Victorian England was ripening into full maturity, had not the Civil War and the frontier movement undermined our sense of security and once more confronted us with vast practical problems for which tradition provided no answer.

> Cheer up, brothers, as we go,
> O'er the mountains, westward ho. . . .

sang the elder Garland as Hamlin and his brothers, he tells us in *A Son of the Middle Border* (1917), joined heartily in the refrain:

> Then o'er the hills in legions, boys,
> Fair freedom's star
> Points to the sunset regions, boys,

and legions there were, poured into the uncharted mountain passes and the prairies of the west, while the east was tearing up her roots with war and the process of building up a civilization was beginning all over again. We can leave the historians and the economists to analyze for us the forces at work in these disrupting movements; but we can note in passing that the generation of American writers who reached their maturity in the forties produced little of significance after the passing of that decade, and we can see in the almost pathetic figure of Mark Twain the typical American, restlessly wandering over the world in search of the security that a matured culture alone could provide.

When the frontier was settled and the war forgotten — at least north of the Mason-Dixon line—America could once more turn her attention to the quest for culture which had been interrupted. It was not until the seventies and eighties that our literature flowed in the clearly marked channel of realism and our colleges were once more taking up the problem of defining a liberal course of study adequate to American ideals and needs. In that generation President Charles W. Eliot of Harvard stands out as the spokesman of the new order. In his inaugural address in 1869 he said:

It were bitter mockery to suggest that any subject whatever should be taught less than it is now in American colleges. The only conceivable aim of a college government in our day is to broaden, deepen, and invigorate American teaching in all branches of learning. It will be generations before the best of American institutions of education will get growth enough to bear pruning.

The spirit of the westward pioneer was in that statement; its keynote was expansion, exploration of the unknown, contempt for restraint or limitation. In an address on liberal education, delivered fifteen years later, he was more specific. Still a radical in his attack upon the classical curriculum, he urged that English, the modern languages, natural science, history, and political economy be granted places of equality with the traditional subjects. He concludes:

Liberal education is not safe and strong in a country in which the great majority of the men who belong to the intellectual professions are not liberally educated. . . . This sorry condition of things is doubtless due in part to what may be called the pioneer conditions of American society; but I think it is also due to the antiquated state of the common college curriculum.

As remedy he proposed the step which occurs to radical thinkers always when confronted by an intrenched and to them
undesirable order: destruction of the old, followed by unrestricted freedom for development of the new. In the specific
instance this step was the elective system of study, a plan which
opened the curriculum to all branches of knowledge from the
most theoretical and remote to the most practical and immediate. To the consequences those of us can best testify who
received our educations when the system had become practically universal in American colleges. We were held to the classical curriculum for a year or two and then were confronted by a
vast assortment of alluring courses offered by a diversified faculty. From these we chose, chiefly as fancy and convenience
dictated, until we had sat under lecturers for the number of
hours required for our Bachelor's degree.

In criticizing the elective system for its diversity, its utilitari-
anism, and its lack of form and purpose, we cannot wholly condemn the work of President Eliot. The era of disruption in
higher education for which he was so largely responsible was
necessary so that the practical needs of American life and the
theoretical training of the American mind could be brought
into closer harmony. The new freedom made a lasting contribution to American educational thought. The autocracy of the old
curriculum could never be reasserted; once and for all the principle that there is no single highroad to culture was established.
The modern literatures, history, and natural and social science
had established their right to a place in the liberal arts college.
As yet their aims were uncertain, their forms nebulous, their
methods confused. Jefferson's "education on a broad scale" was
an accomplished fact, but there was still much work to be done
before the new and purposive liberal arts college could emerge
from the confusion of unrelated knowledge which then characterized its curriculum.

The new disciplines were slow in asserting themselves, and
we may doubt that even today they are firmly established. Restlessness with the anarchy of the college course began to find
voice in the first decade of the present century. In 1908 Abra-
ham Flexner published his book, *The American College, a Criticism*. From a vantage point outside of, yet in close contact with,

the problem, he stated the case against the existing order—or perhaps one might better say the existing disorder. He wrote:

> Our college authorities are themselves far from happy. They dwell complacently on rapidly increasing numbers, splendid "plants," and unchecked flow of benefactions; but there is considerable uneasiness just below the surface. The pilots are apparently not sure as to whither to steer; at times they steer for several ports at once; again, for no particular port at all. . . . The elective system was in effect a profession of confidence in the actual capacity and probable seriousness of the average boy. It assumed that he possessed ability and might be led to develop purpose. Yet in the attempt to enlist his energy in congenial effort, the college finds itself forced to a low standard. A degree may be won with little or no systematic exertion. . . . The important thing is to realize that the American college is deficient, and unnecessarily deficient, alike in earnestness and in pedagogical intelligence; that in consequence our college students are, and for the most part, emerge, flighty, superficial and immature, lacking, as a class, concentration, seriousness and thoroughness.

Official statements of the day are even more revealing. "The college is without clear-cut notions of what a liberal education is and how it is to be secured," writes President Schurman of Cornell in his report for 1906-7, "and the pity of it is that this is not a local or special disability, but a paralysis affecting every college of arts in America." Not all administrators were as frank as this, but a Harvard committee of investigation found that the better students of that day were doing only three and a half hours of work a week for each of their courses. My own teaching experience would indicate that this condition or worse persisted at least until the recent past. Mr. Flexner's analysis of the causes of this state of affairs is explicit:

> The scheme fails for lack of sufficient insight; in the first place, because the preparatory school routine devised by the colleges suppresses just what the college assumes that it will develop [that is, initiative and earnestness in the student]; in the second place, because of the chaotic condition of the college curriculum; finally, because research has largely appropriated the resources of the college, substituting the methods of highly specialized investigation for the larger objects of college teaching.

His proposed solution may seem to us here today to be little more than an accomplished fact. First, the college must reassert itself by a divorce from the graduate school; second, far greater freedom from entrance requirements must be allowed the preparatory school so that students might early attain that capacity for self-development which can only come from dealing with immediate experience under guidance; finally, there must be no return to the discarded classical curriculum; rather, there must be an intelligent application of the elective system. He concludes:

> The youth chooses; he selects or is effectively assisted to select his status. The college must then organize for him the intermediate steps to his chosen end. For this purpose it is worse than useless to maintain a diffuse and practically endless course of study. A compact, related, and organized body of instruction in each of the fields which the college undertakes to cover must be substituted for the *disjecta membra* of the present catalogue.

When this is accomplished, "the college professor will not only offer courses, but teach."

When Mr. Flexner wrote, such theories were so far from existing conditions as to seem almost preposterous. As we scan the histories of the colleges and the universities during the following years, we discover few steps in the direction he indicated. Rather, small colleges, the last resorts of the old order, were moving in the direction of the university pattern: increasing their enrollments, adding specialized schools, admitting graduate students, accenting the flexibility and variety rather than the purpose and form of their curricula, and substituting lectures for more intimate methods of teaching.

As far as I have been able to discover, the introduction of the preceptorial system at Princeton in 1905 was the first significant move in a contrary direction, with the exception of a short-lived experiment at Michigan some years earlier. Woodrow Wilson, then its president, lavished the rhetoric for which he later became famous on coaxing several million dollars from his alumni in order that he might say to his undergraduates: "You will at a certain date, which may turn out for you to be a fateful date, be examined on the constitutional history of the United States. Now you can get up that subject in ways which you may discover for yourself, but if you don't get up that subject, we shall have the pain of parting company with you." "The new thing we are introducing," he told the alumni, "is the independent pursuit of certain studies by men old enough to study for themselves and accorded the privilege in their studies of having the counsel of scholars older than themselves."

The significant factor in Wilson's preceptorial was its emphasis upon the mastery of studies undertaken rather than on variety in the choice of study. It was a step in the direction we have since taken, courageous because counter to the dominant thought of the day.

I should like to trace the flow of such thought through the next two decades, particularly to give credit to President Meiklejohn's work at Amherst, for it was he who perhaps more than anyone else in the intervening years stressed the function of the liberal college as a training school in thinking for thinking's sake. "At Chicago," Professor Boynton of that university told a group of fellow Amherst alumni, "they know more; at Amherst they think more." But surely we have assembled enough evidence to suggest that Emerson's "man thinking" was beginning to be found in the colleges, hampered by neither conformity to an outworn formula or freedom so great as to lack direction and motive power.

But constructive thought on the subject was none too common when President Aydelotte of Swarthmore announced his program of honors work in his inaugural address of 1921. Ignoring his statement that "it is the task of our institutions of higher learning to *train* leaders," with all the implications of purpose and discipline that the word "train" implies, the popular mind caught at the greater freedom which he asked for the better students as an indication that the new program was one of further expansion and less form. "We could give these more brilliant students greater independence in their work," he said, "avoiding the spoon-feeding which makes much of our college instruction of the present day of secondary-school character," words which might have come from President Eliot a half-

century earlier, but with a different significance. "They talk a
lot about freedom around here," I once heard an early honors
student remark. "The only freedom that I can discover is the
freedom to work harder." Exactly that; but the distinction
between eclecticism in courses and self-reliance in study was
not always clear to students or to their instructors in these early
days.

President Aydelotte was among the first of American educators to realize that the liberal arts college needed redefinition,
and he has devoted his major energies to that task, first as a
teacher of English, later as an administrator. Bred in the university of his native state and in Harvard College, he had reason to
be fully aware of the virtues, the needs, and the shortcomings of
liberal education in America before, at the age of twenty-five,
he went to Oxford. The next three years served to establish in
his mind a liberal ideal which is neither English nor American,
although it is as ably defined by Newman in his *Idea of a University* (1873) as in any work I know:

Knowledge is capable of being its own end. . . . That alone is liberal
knowledge which stands on its own pretensions, which is independent of sequel, expects no complement, refuses to be *informed* (as it is
called) by any end, or absorbed into any art, in order duly to present
itself to our contemplation. The most ordinary pursuits have this specific character, if they are self-sufficient and complete; the highest lose
it, when they minister to something beyond them.

This is essentially what Emerson meant when he said in "The
American Scholar": "In this distribution of functions the
scholar is the delegated intellect. In the right state he is *Man
Thinking*. In the degenerate state, when the victim of society, he
tends to become a mere thinker, or still worse, the parrot of
other men's thinking." Newman had stirred Oxford to new life
in the forties by his reaffirmation of this classic ideal; Emerson
by it called his country to mental independence. It is the voice
of intelligence, perennially reborn.

So deep and lasting was Newman's influence that this ideal
was in the very Oxford air that the young American scholar
breathed in 1906. But whereas, in becoming adjusted to the spe-

cial needs of English liberal education, it had served to broaden the range of undergraduate study, in American education it would need to perform a contrary task. It must not only break down the high degree of technical specialization which had been reached in our graduate schools; its greater work was to provide correlation and form and purpose to the undergraduate college. It was to the latter task that Mr. Aydelotte addressed himself on his return as associate professor of English at Indiana University in 1908. While Presidents Schurman and Wilson were bemoaning the existing anarchy or seeking a panacea for the entire educational procedure, he undertook the work at his hand, the reformation of the freshman course in English. A few years later he wrote:

> To open the student's eyes to the world, to suggest to him some of the problems of education, of politics, of religion, and the methods of poetry and science in seeking for solutions—this is the function of the teacher of literature. We undertook to make [the student] realize that the world is a different place to each man—made what it is by the honesty and depth of his thought about it. We tried to start him thinking about the problems which confront him. We were not concerned so much that he should become a devotee of literature as that he should acquire a thoughtful attitude toward the world. The most important thing needed to make a student of literature or of any other subject is intellectual curiosity.

With a patience and fixity of purpose characteristic of his every step, he has been willing to watch his idea grow into an educational system embracing the whole liberal arts college, a system which could not have been formulated in advance because it has grown in the soil of American life and has been shaped by American needs. The cultivation of intellectual curiosity and the guidance of the awakened mind into channels suited to its own abilities and needs has become the working procedure of those American liberal colleges which are worthy of the name. They have become student-centered rather than subject-centered, and their work is more and more the integration, less and less the division, of knowledge.

We as Americans have had to learn over again and for ourselves the wisdom which was the life of Greek and later of
English culture. It could not be borrowed or transplanted. The
Greek mind was vital because it acquired its wisdom from the
experience of the Greek people. Even so brief a review as this of
the progress of the American people toward a mental life and a
culture of their own should at least suggest that we no longer
need to restrict our energies to the utilitarian pursuits of our
ancestors. For those of us who wish it and are able to meet it, the
life of thought is open. The ideal of the old classical curriculum
is ours, but it comes to us in a native form, not as a borrowed
formula. Our single task as students is the discovery of the significance of our own experience and, through it, that of the
experience of the American people and of humanity in the
present and in the past. We cannot afford to let ourselves be dis-
tracted by the great masses of people who are doing rather than
thinking if we are to be, in Emerson's phrase, "the delegated
intellect." Whether our subject of special interest be English,
the classics, or political science, it must be for each of us a vital
idiom of thought rather than an array of meaningless facts. Our
culture depends not so much on what we study as on the way in
which we think.

2 | THE WRITINGS OF JAMES FENIMORE COOPER

It is not often that the selection of a topic for a Ph.D. dissertation determines the direction, scope, method, and underlying philosophy of a professional career; but that is what happened to me. How little we really know about the seeming accidents of circumstance that may direct our course into unexpected and creative channels!

When the time came to choose a subject for my doctorate at the University of Pennsylvania, I wasted one year trying to shape my own speculations about English romantic poetry into acceptable form and then another year working on an uncongenial topic in Middle English drama. Finally, in desperation, I turned to Professor Arthur Hobson Quinn, most of whose survey courses in American literary types I had taken, and asked him for a topic. He suggested that the history of the travel essay in America "had not been done." "Where do I begin?" I asked, thinking of Irving, Emerson, and Henry James. "Begin at the beginning," he advised. That meant the year 1783 when the United States finally became a nation; and my first victims were, of course, Jefferson, Adams, and other early statesmen whose accounts of their travels and residences abroad were chiefly in the form of letters, journals, and reports rather than the familiar essay of travel. Thus I found myself embarked on a thorough investigation of the writings of all Americans who first visited England after independence, even though only a few of these writings—the imitative Addisonian essays of Franklin, Dennie, Freneau, and others—were in the form which Dr. Quinn had in mind. My point of view had shifted to what was essentially a

*problem in social psychology: not the study of a literary type
but an adventure into the wide world of international cultural
exchange and emergent nationalism. The result was my first
published book,* The American in England During the First Half
Century of Independence *(1926).*

*The dominant theme that finally shaped this book was the
inner conflict of the intelligent American who found himself in
England during these formative years divided between his deep
loyalty to the literary traditions of his inheritance and the drive
to extend his triumph of political independence into all parts of
his experience.* The Sketch Book *of Washington Irving was a
natural as an illustration of the sentimentality and nostalgia of
the wandering youth returning to his ancestral home; but the
contrary theme of criticism and rejection was not fully illustrated until I discovered the forgotten five volumes of* Gleanings in Europe *(including* Sketches of Switzerland*) by James
Fenimore Cooper.*

*This was probably, for me, the most important outcome of
the study. Here was a major author who stood at the very
threshold of an indigenous American literature, but whose
writings seemed to have been appreciated and studied for the
wrong reasons. Here was an "American Carlyle" rather than an
"American Scott," a social and political critic of comparative
national cultures rather than merely the writer of romances of
the wilderness, the Indians, and the sea.*

*To set this matter straight became my main scholarly activity
of the next decade. There was an immense amount of detailed
research and publication to be done—research that not only
trained me in a variety of methods but also opened my mind to
a much larger and more theoretical field of speculation.*

My first practical job was to get these Gleanings *republished
and understood. The* France *appeared in 1928; the* England *in
1930. Meanwhile I was off to Europe on a Guggenheim fellowship to do the basic research on Cooper's travels and to extend
the range of my larger concerns. The editing of other critical
prose works of Cooper led me into an in-depth study of the
techniques and methods of editing literary texts; the bibliography of the editions of the five volumes of travel developed into*

a definitive descriptive bibliography of the whole corpus of Cooper's works; and the study of the travels as critical prose became the biography, Fenimore Cooper: Critic of His Times.

The first professional American novelist thus taught me about both biography and bibliography. I have explained how I came to select as a topic for my dissertation the experience of the American traveler in England in the early years of independence and how this led to the discovery of Cooper as a social critic and student of comparative cultures. His five volumes of travels in Europe are hardly mentioned in the standard histories and biographies except as evidence of his bad temper and as a source for his biography. As writings, his critical prose was omitted from all editions of his collected works and had been virtually ignored until I wrote Fenimore Cooper: Critic of His Times *in 1931. The five travel books were listed in the bibliography of* The Cambridge History of American Literature *(1917), but copies were hard to find in even the major libraries. I finally located them in the subbasement of the Free Library of Philadelphia and in the private collection of W. R. Langfeld, an Irving scholar.*

I soon realized their importance and arranged for a new edition with the Oxford University Press. My first task was to obtain copies of my own, and I alerted a bookseller to follow the catalogues. Three editions of each of the five titles had been published at the time in English in Philadelphia (Carey), London (Bentley), and Paris (Baudry or Galignani), and translations had been made into French and German, but none of them had been reprinted since.

The next problem was to determine which editions were the first, and for this the title-page dates were of no help in most cases. Therefore, I turned to the book announcements in the current newspapers, as at that time booksellers usually listed themselves also as publishers. A startling fact emerged: It was obvious from studying styling changes that the American editions were usually printed first from the manuscript, but in almost every case the London edition was announced for an earlier date, with about two weeks' interval. A study of the copyright laws of the two countries provided an answer to this riddle. As I explain in my "Introduction," which follows, the differences in the copyright laws of the United States and England gave protection to American authors in both countries, a fact which, together with the cultural maturing of the Atlantic seaboard cities, undoubtedly made writing sufficiently profitable to encourage Cooper and other American authors to turn for the first time about 1820 to authorship as a profession. For its possibly far-reaching implications, this discovery would seem to be of the first importance to American literary history.

Meanwhile I had made a small collection of the five titles in all editions in English, and from the little I then knew about book collecting I realized that some sort of descriptive bibliography might be of value for reasons other than the establishment of text. It might even tell me something about Cooper I could not find out in any other way, but this never went beyond my own notes.

When I had a full year abroad, however, in 1928 to 1929, on a Guggenheim fellowship to follow Cooper's European experiences, the idea of extending this bibliography to cover his entire literary production developed logically as the best way to understand the man as writer. As I had had no training in bibliography, except as an exercise in title-listing, I turned to the specialists in the field: A. W. Pollard, R. B. McKerrow, and W. W. Greg—especially to the then standard manual, McKerrow's An Introduction to Bibliography for Literary Students *(1927). Much to my dismay, the detailed descriptions and collations of these scholars used a method and a terminology derived from the moveable-type, hand-press books of the fifteenth to the seventeenth centuries which would not apply to the newer stereotyped, rotary-press books of the early nineteenth. I found that I had to develop a revised system of notation, which I did with the help of Philip C. Blackburn of the New York Public Library.* A Descriptive Bibliography of the Writings of James Fenimore Cooper *(New York: R. R. Bowker Co., 1934) was a pioneer work of its kind and has served as something of a model for other American author bibliographies since. It was also a foundation work for the projected*

*complete edition of Cooper's writings recently initiated by
James F. Beard and the State University of New York Press.*

I

The bibliography of an author is the record of his literary life.
Through it we learn on what terms he met his public, and what
his public, both contemporary and future, thought of his work.
In inferences and conclusions the science of bibliography is as
rich as any other branch of literary research — richer than
many. Such study is especially fruitful in the case of an author
like James Fenimore Cooper, who threw so much of his mature
energy into writing. Having waited until the age of thirty
before starting, he scarcely paused until his death, thirty-two
years later, when he left part of his forty-eighth book in
manuscript. In addition, he published numerous pamphlets.
Something over forty of his contributions to periodicals and
collections have been identified, and there are doubtless many
more still undiscovered. One play by him was acted but never
published.

Such production meant continued and indefatigable work.
The best hours of each morning were devoted to filling long
folio sheets of fine paper in a hand which moved quickly and
seldom paused. His manuscripts are comparatively free from
alterations. After 1821, every move of the Cooper family was
influenced by the business needs of its head, and the main part
of its income was derived from the sale of rights to the books,
which were known to come as often as twice or three times a
year from his pen. Cooper was indeed a professional author.

It was not easy to make a success of the profession of authorship in America a century ago. Charles Brockden Brown had
tried it with but moderate success; and Washington Irving, in
Europe on other business, became, with the English edition of
The Sketch Book in 1820, our first distinguished as well as expatriate author. This was the year in which Cooper published his
first novel, an imitation of one of the thousands of English novels which were being reprinted in cheap editions and sold in
this country in such quantities that American competition was
practically futile. Our periodicals did little to encourage native

talent, and our reading public was still subservient to English taste and English judgment. No American of those days would deliberately become an author unless he were an idealist like Poe or an expatriate like Irving, or unless he were content with a small return for his labors. Cooper stumbled into authorship largely by accident, and no one was more surprised than he when his second novel, *The Spy*, was translated into foreign languages and accepted almost everywhere in Europe as the first authentic picture of American scenery and customs; but Cooper's character was such that, once an author, he could not be content until he had exhausted every possibility of financial as well as artistic success.

This is the story that his bibliography tells us. We learn that *Precaution* was privately printed in 1820 in New York, and that four years later *The Spy* was in its fourth edition in New York, its third in London, its second of a French translation in Paris, and its first of a German translation in Leipzig. The record goes on to chart Cooper's rising fame in the next few years when he devoted his best energies to the sea and the Indians; to supply the primary motive for his seven years' residence in Europe; to mark his turn from the historical romance to the novel of manners and to social criticism; to reveal heartlessly and in detail his declining popularity at the very time when his activity was increasing; and to follow him down to the year before his death when, unreconciled, he declared the decay of democracy in a final comment on "the ways of the hour."

The listing of Cooper's works in their various editions provides the best possible index to literary conditions in this country between 1820 and 1850. It reflects literary fashions in the decline of romanticism and the advent of the spirit of social reform; it reveals the highly unsatisfactory relationships between publisher, editor, author, and reader which handicapped our literary development for so many years; it makes its contribution of the first chapter in the history of international copyright law, still unfinished in so far as America is concerned; and it provides data upon which to determine the state of the public taste at home, as well as the popular attitude abroad toward the culture of the infant republic. Literary criticism is individual; it expresses the taste and judgment of trained and presumably discriminating minds. Bibliography is social; it reveals the taste of the public.

II

At the root of all bibliographic problems connected with the writings of Cooper lie the special and little understood factors which determined the circumstances of their publication. Differences in printing, format, and binding are often noted without consideration of their causes; and the priority of foreign over American editions is suggested without definite information as to the cases in which it occurred and the reasons for it.

In 1819-1820, when Cooper first turned to authorship, he had experimented with the life of a sailor, of a gentleman farmer, and of an owner of a sailing vessel, but he knew nothing of the business of printing and publishing. In his preface to the revised edition of *Precaution* he confesses frankly to his "precipitation and inexperience," but the book was, his daughter reports, "quite as successful as he had expected," and was promptly reprinted by Henry Colburn in London, probably without financial return to its author.

This experience revealed two things to Cooper. In the first place, he must himself supervise his manuscript through the hands of the stereotyper and printer. In the second, he must bargain with each of his publishers separately if he wished to make writing profitable. There was no doubt in his mind on this last point. He had a private income, chiefly derived from his wife's family, but at thirty, with a growing family of his own to support, a lucrative profession was essential. It is important always to remember that Cooper was interested in the business as well as in the art of writing.

He realized immediately that his central problem was the discovery of some way to overcome the disadvantages of a national, which was not offset by an international, copyright law. Publishers who were not required to pay royalties to writers of such established reputation as Walter Scott, Maria Edgeworth, and Lord Byron were not likely to risk their profits for the sake of an obscure American to whom they would have to pay royal-

ties. The fight must be taken to the source. An English reputation must be established first, and English publishers must be
made to pay for the right to issue American books. If this could
be accomplished, American authors would have a better instead
of a worse market than English authors. Irving alone attempted
to work out the problem with the result that he cleared £467 for
the English rights to *The Sketch Book* in 1820, and £3,150 for *The
Life of Columbus* in 1828.

The American copyright law of 1790 was explicit. An American author could copyright his book in the United States
regardless of the date of publication elsewhere, but authors
who were not citizens of the United States were allowed no
protection whatever. The only determining factor was citizenship, although prompt copyright entry was a valuable protection against pirates. The English law was vague in its statement
of its protection for the work of aliens. A revision in 1838 did
not clarify this point materially, and the rights of English publishers rested in a series of favorable court decisions until the
House of Lords decided in 1854, in the case of *Jeffreys vs. Boosey*,
that there existed under the law no such protection. The determining factor during Cooper's lifetime was prior publication in
England. Citizenship had nothing to do with the problem, for
any author, whether English or not, could obtain protection in
England by announcing his book there before its appearance in
any other country. He might take his case to court, and the
chances of being sustained in his rights were good.

Cooper did not learn how to take full advantage of this
unequal situation until he went to Europe in 1826. His first
business connections, after his initial experiment with author-
publishing (i.e., when the author takes the risks and the
publisher is little more than a distributor), were with Charles
Wiley, of New York. Wiley understood his problem, paid him
what he could for the right to print his next few novels, and
wrote to Irving, then in London, to negotiate with John Murray
for an English edition of *The Spy*. Irving's answer is a complete
revelation of the circumstances then attending English publication of American works. Murray was hostile to American authors;[1] Colburn, who had published *Precaution*, had expected

advance sheets of *The Spy* from his American agent; Whittaker had obtained such sheets and had won the race, issuing a handsome three-volume edition in 1822, at great profit to himself, but at none to anyone else.

Once more Cooper had learned a valuable lesson—to his cost. A friend, Benjamin W. Coles, of New York, was then in Europe, and Cooper named him as his personal agent in negotiations for his next novel, *The Pioneers*. He wrote to Irving that Halleck was taking abroad with him the first hundred pages, in advance sheets, and asked Irving to lend his experience to the negotiations by assisting Coles.[2] Coles, on Irving's advice, went directly to John Miller, and by June 1822 had a helpful report for Cooper.[3] *The Pioneers* was published, however, by Murray on a profit-sharing basis, on February 26, 1823, less than a month after its American appearance. Surviving records of the house show that Cooper's share of the returns totaled £134. Murray's reputation had helped to sell the book, but his lack of interest in it made dealing with him unsatisfactory. The Ettrick Shepherd remarked, "I suppose it will be worth its price, since it comes out of his shop,—for John's no that keen o' novels now-a-days!"[4] The problem of English publication was not yet solved, although the next three novels, *The Pilot*, *Lionel Lincoln*, and *The Last of the Mohicans*, were published by Miller on the same plan.[5]

Dissatisfaction with these arrangements, coupled with ambitious plans for his children's education, took Cooper to London and Paris in the summer of 1826; and he did not return to his own country again for seven years. What his first negotiations with Miller were, we do not know, or why they were not fruitful, but his next novel, *The Prairie*, appeared under the imprint of his original English publisher, Henry Colburn. His contract was again on a profit-sharing basis, but there was in it a new element.[6] For the first time, the author supervised the printing of a pre-first edition in English and sent advance sheets to his various publishers and translators, timing their arrival carefully so that he could reap the advantages of an actual copyright in the United States, a virtual copyright in England, and the right of prior publication in France and Germany. *The Prairie* and *The Red Rover* were thus printed first by H. Bossange in Paris,

The Wept of Wish-ton-Wish by Molini in Florence, and *The Water-Witch* by Walther in Dresden. In all these cases except the last, the London edition was the first to be *published*, and the Continental edition the first to be *printed*. *The Water-Witch* is the only genuine Continental first of the novels, having been issued in Dresden in English a month before its first London edition and about three months before the first American edition, a circumstance which called forth a protest from Cooper's regular German publisher, Duncker.[7] French and German translations were also made from these advance sheets and published by Charles Gosselin in Paris and by Duncker and Humblot in Berlin by contract with Cooper. These various authorized Continental editions should not be confused with those published by Baudry and Galignani, none of which are firsts, with the possible exception of the *Letter to Lafayette*.

Meanwhile Cooper had changed his American publisher as well. His friend, Charles Wiley, was in uncertain financial condition in 1826, and Cooper, with *The Last of the Mohicans*, transferred his business to Matthew Carey in Philadelphia.[8] Carey pirated regularly from the works of English authors by agreement with John Miller; but he was, at the same time, reasonably hospitable to the works of American authors. Cooper sold him the right to print and sell a definite number of copies of each work for a fixed sum. The author arranged for the stereotyping by Fagan, although the publishers usually paid for it, and he dealt with Carey through the latter's agent, Luther Bradish. Each new edition after the first meant a new contract, for Cooper retained ownership of the plates.

Between 1826 and 1843, Carey issued each of Cooper's works in two volumes, bound in cloth with paper labels, to sell at 75¢ to $1.00 per volume. By 1841, the market had become so bad that Lea and Blanchard, Carey's successors, experimented with a new printing of his novels in wrappers at 25¢ per volume. Dissatisfaction with these conditions led Cooper once more to return to the plan of author-publishing with *Afloat and Ashore* in 1844, but his protest was futile. With his next novel he accepted the inevitable; and Burgess, Stringer and Company, of New York, issued his works thereafter in wrappers at the 25¢

price until 1849, when he discovered G. P. Putnam, Irving's new publisher.[9] This meant a return to cloth-covered volumes and a revised uniform edition of the earlier titles, but Cooper did not live to profit materially by the change in fortune. He died two years later; and the Civil War sent more than one publisher into bankruptcy, among them Townsend, before the publishing business was again stabilized on a dignified basis.

In his later years, Cooper also attempted to follow the lead of Poe and the New England group in a vain effort to adapt his ability to the requirements of the literary monthly magazines which were then becoming so popular. *Jack Tier* and the *Lives of Distinguished Naval Officers* were published serially before their appearance in book form, and a number of shorter works first appeared in such journals.

He was more fortunate with his business affairs in England, although there too he suffered a constant decline in returns from the peak in 1830. In Richard Bentley, Colburn's successor, he found a man who was honest and conservative in his dealings and who was willing to pay promptly for the right of prior publication of American works in England. Nevertheless the amount received for each novel was decreased from £1,300 (1831), to £700 (1833), to £400 (1840), to £250 (1844), and finally, with *The Ways of the Hour* (1850), to £100. This decrease seems to be, in part at least, attributable to a decline in Cooper's popularity, but even the English book market was none too firm in the early days of Dickens and Thackeray. The same enemies of good books, the pirates and the periodicals, were forcing cheap paper-covered editions in England as they were in America. Bentley fought them both by threats and legal actions and by direct competition. He offered *Bentley's Miscellany* and the "Standard Novels" to the new market without sacrificing all quality in his productions, and his war with the pirates was constant. As early as 1839 we read that "The Master of the Rolls granted an injunction, at the instance of Mr. Bentley, to restrain some persons from publishing 'The Headsman'—the copyright of which so far as respects Great Britain and Ireland, has been purchased by Mr. Bentley."[10] And in the "Standard Novels" edition of *The Pathfinder* (1842), Bentley printed a notice of warning to public libraries that it was illegal for them to have pirated copies of Cooper's works on their shelves. The "conversation with Mr. Newby" of April 5, 1848, reveals the persistence of this English publisher in this just but losing cause.[11]

After his return from Europe in November, 1833, it was necessary for Cooper to decide whether to print his books first in England or the United States. Prior publication in England was essential under the terms of his understanding with Bentley, but his works could be put into type and printed in either country. He seems at first to have followed the obvious plan of printing in Philadelphia or New York and sending sheets to London. There is evidence of only one experiment with the reverse of this plan. The manuscript of *Italy* (1838) was mailed to Bentley, was temporarily lost in transit, and was finally recovered and printed first in London. This experience finally outweighed in Cooper's mind the superior reliability and care of English printers, for the remainder of his works seem to have been printed first in the U.S. and most of them published first in England from the American sheets.

A study of these facts will explain most of the variations in printing, format, and binding of Cooper's works in their various editions. They furnish a barometric record of his literary life. Supplemented by a similar set of facts for Irving and for Poe, they would write the history of international copyright— or the lack of it—during the period. They define textual differences. They explain the superior quality of all English firsts except those published by Miller. But perhaps most important of all, they formulate a simple rule of thumb as regards priority of issue of the various editions. Up to 1826, the American edition is, in every case, the first, both in printing and publication. From 1827 to 1830, the Continental edition is the first to be printed and the English edition is usually the first to be published. *Notions of the Americans* (1828) was both printed and published first in England. After 1831, with only a few exceptions, the American edition is the first to be printed and the English is the first to be published. . . .

It seems to be generally agreed that the date to be chosen for the determination of a first edition is that announced by the publishers as the day of publication, and not that when the printing and binding processes are completed. . . .

The story of how this bibliography came to be is the best form of acknowledgment of the aid of the many who have assisted in its compilation. . . . In order to edit Cooper's *Gleaning in Europe* for republication, I found it necessary to determine all the facts of their first issues. This involved a study of Cooper's method of publication both in America and in Europe, . . . and, in justice to the value of this material, I could not escape long hours in the British Museum and the Bibliothèque Nationale, collating and describing the volumes themselves.

NOTES

1. *Correspondence of J. F. Cooper* (New Haven, 1922), Vol. 2, pp. 89-90.

2. P. M. Irving, *Life and Letters of Washington Irving* (London, 1862-64), Vol. 2, pp. 54-55; and S. Smiles, *A Publisher and His Friends* (London, 1891), Vol. 1, p. 134.

3. *Descriptive Bibliography*, Appendix A.

4. "Noctes Ambriosianae," *Blackwood's Magazine* 13:609-10.

5. *Descriptive Bibliography*, Appendix A, and *Correspondence*, Vol. 1, pp. 95-97.

6. *Ibid.* Appendix B.

7. *Ibid.* Appendix C.

8. E. L. Bradsher, *Matthew Carey* (New York, 1911), pp. 84-85.

9. *Descriptive Bibliography*, Appendix E.

10. "Our Weekly Gossip." *The Athenaeum* 12 (October 1839):781.

11. *Descriptive Bibliography*, Appendix D.

3 | THE IMPOSSIBLE DREAM: ADVENTURES IN EDITING AMERICAN LITERARY TEXTS

Textual criticism follows logically from descriptive bibliography and is in a sense part of the same literary discipline. The life history of a work of literary art or of its author is written in the Book and the Word. All creative art is a continuing process and not a static artifact. The changes through which a work of art passes in its author's lifetime may be caused by conscious emendation or accidental circumstance of production, but in any case they record its life history. Chronology in a bibliography is established by a careful and comparative analysis of succeeding texts. Only in this way does an author come alive again as a writer.

For example: the 1855, 1860, and 1891 to 1892 editions of Leaves of Grass *show evidence of Whitman's alterations and through them the principal stages in his development; the New York edition of the novels of Henry James reflects a different author than the first editions; and the Emerson of the 1847 collected and revised* Nature, Addresses and Lectures *speaks, particularly in the "Divinity School Address," for the unspoken hurt that he felt from the attacks on him by the Unitarian establishment. All authorial changes in a text must therefore be examined and evaluated before a biography can be written. The textual critic has no choice but to attain the complete mastery of the textual history of the work to be studied.*

The selection of the text to be reprinted and the editor's treatment of it is another matter. There the editor must make choices. It is pretty well agreed that the text to be reprinted

must have had the approval of its author, which usually means
that it is the first edition or even the author's manuscript, if that
has survived. But an author may publish a major revision in a
few years, and then another, and perhaps finally a "deathbed"
edition, all of them approved by him in their turn. The question
no longer is, "What is the authorized text?" but rather "Which
of the several authorized texts is best for the purpose?" Even
when this is decided, the further question remains, "If one text
is reprinted verbatim, what should be done about the others;
should they be woven into the chosen text, relegated to the
textual notes, or omitted altogether?" When all this is settled,
the poor harassed editor has to decide whether to print an
unaltered original version, a corrected original version, or a
modernization — and by what principles that decision should
be determined. There is no question that an editor or a literary
scholar of any kind must know all that can be known about all
the authorized versions in order better to understand the work
of art and its author. In this the editor has no choice, but when
it comes to reprinting, choices are many.

This is the "impossible dream" of the editor who believes
that there is a perfect text to be reprinted or to be used as the
basis for his textual changes. It has haunted me all my working
hours, and it provoked the following address to various learned
groups in perhaps too light and careless a mood for such a sol-
emn subject. But it was well received by editors of both historical and literary texts and was finally published in The Library
Chronicle of the University of Pennsylvania, in volume 13
(Winter 1978):83-98.

The immediate provocation was the policy of the Center for
Editions of American Authors of the Modern Language Association. At first, apparently mild and harmless, this worthy project of the American Literature Section was undertaken to
provide authoritative texts of most of the major nineteenth-
century American authors. Under the first chairmanship of William M. Gibson, there was a liberal attitude toward all these
textual problems; and the individual editors were allowed to
solve them pretty much as they wished, with the approval of
the press that was doing the edition. But somewhere along the
line, the injection of foundation and federal subsidies into the

*project seemed to suggest more rigorous control by the central
committee, both in the selection of a text and in its treatment.
With a permanent home at the University of South Carolina
and with generous support from the National Endowment for
the Humanities, the Center for Editions of American Authors
was reorganized, with changes in personnel, and became much
more formal and authoritarian. With its "Statement of Editorial
Principles," derived largely from "The Rationale of Copy-text"
by W. W. Greg,* (Studies in Bibliography 3 *[1950-51]:22-35) and
"Some Principles for Scholarly Editions of Nineteenth-Century
American Authors" by Fredson Bowers* (Studies in Bibliography
17 [1964]: 223-38) it developed a system of "vetting" all texts
(i.e., submitting them for review and recommendation to a presumably impartial scholar) and awarding the Seal of the Center
to those that were approved. So powerful did this endorse-
ment become that few university presses would put an edited
text to press without it.*

*The good news is that the center fostered an impressive
library of commendable editions or partial editions. The bad
news is that its critics were often unfamiliar with the special
editorial problems presented by the author in question; and its
decisions in an uncomfortable number of cases were arbitrary,
uninformed, and destructive of the integrity of experienced
and mature scholars. In 1976 its subsidies were discontinued
and its work taken over by a new "Center for Scholarly Editions," which established a less rigid philosophy and procedure.*

Although the three-volume edition of The Early Lectures of
Ralph Waldo Emerson, *which I edited with Stephen E. Whicher
and Wallace E. Williams, was undertaken too early, and the
forthcoming edition of Cooper's* Sketches of Switzerland,
which I edited with James F. Beard and others for the new
Complete Works, *will be too late for CEAA consideration, I was
involved with CEAA as coeditor of the first volume of Emerson's* Collected Works *and as acting chairman of the editorial
board of the edition upon the death of Alfred H. Ferguson.*

*But that is another story. The most useful result of the experi-
ence for me was to prompt this declaration of independence.*

Like all literary scholarship, bibliography and textual criticism can be a creative discipline, and perhaps the most basic of all.

Like the Man of La Mancha, I have spent much of my life in pursuit of "The Impossible Dream." I have edited countless texts of American writers for all sorts of reprint volumes; and I have clung to the faith that there is one right way to do it. I have now reached the conclusion in my disillusioned old age that there is something quixotic about the whole enterprise, that much of it is a tilting at windmills, and that it doesn't matter much what you do just so you announce in a preface a reasonable procedure consistent with your main objectives and then stick to your own rules.

That would be the end rather than the beginning of my story were it not that few of my colleagues seem to agree with me. The quest for the perfect text has played so great a role in my career that I would like to ease my conscience at last by recalling some of the things that have happened to me on my journey and have helped me to gain, I hope, some perspective on the recent developments in textual scholarship. I refer of course to the Center for Editions of American Authors of the Modern Language Association and to its successor, the Center for Scholarly Editions.

I began editing texts almost as soon as I was through graduate school, where training in this technique had played no part in my professional education—why, I do not know. I had to find out how to do it the hard way, by doing. In spite of the fact that many of my teachers were receiving pocket money for editing editions of the classics, none of them seemed to have at hand any set of rules to pass on to me; so that when I undertook to do for the Oxford Press in 1928 an edition of James Fenimore Cooper's *Gleanings in Europe: France,* I made up my own rules.

Here was a book which had been hastily printed by the Carey firm in Philadelphia and, except for nearly simultaneous English and French editions, had not been reprinted since. A quick preliminary study revealed that the English edition had appeared first, although for reasons of the international copy-right situation at the time, it was probably set from sheets that were somewhat carelessly proofread by the author during a

short visit to Philadelphia in the summer heat, and that the
French edition (in English) was pirated from the English. There
were enough differences between the texts of these editions in
what have since come to be called "accidentals"—spelling,
punctuation, capitalization—to suggest that the English edition
had been "house-styled" by the publisher. I therefore chose to
reprint the American edition because it presumably had the
writer's authority; but what to do about obvious errors and
inconsistencies? I could leave them as they were, correct them
to modern usage, or try to conform them to Cooper's usage as I
could reconstruct it. I decided to try to imagine that I was
merely a more accurate and conscientious Fenimore Cooper and
to produce the edition that he would have produced had he
cared enough to do so.

Little did I realize what I had undertaken. I had first to determine what his basic rules of composition and style were, then
conform the text to those rules, and finally discover in his text
attractive chapter titles to leaven the lump of a series of merely
numbered "Letters." I still have the two-page style-sheet that I
compiled and the copy of the work in which I added and sub-
tracted commas, supplied or deleted periods or capital letters,
conformed the spelling—particularly of place names—and
added chapter titles. All went well. I was awarded a Guggenheim fellowship to follow Cooper's travel routes in Europe, to
work in the libraries where he worked, and to prepare texts of
the other four European travel books. I proceeded to complete
the second volume, this time on *England,* and set off with my
young family for a study year abroad. It was a great adventure,
and I thought my career well launched. A panel of scholars
obviously had approved my editorial techniques and wanted
more of the same.

Then came a letter about 1930 from my friend Oscar Cargill of
New York University asking me to take part in an anthology of
American literature for the Macmillan Company. My volume
was to cover the period from the beginnings to 1830 and thus
took me to seventeenth- and eighteenth-century texts—a field
much more complicated than that of Cooper's time with respect
to methods of printing and styles of writing. I was confronted

with the inherited Elizabethan eccentricities of Cotton Mather, the printings of Franklin's early press, and the flood of religious and political pamphlets that filled the bookshops of the colonial towns.

Naively, however, I made my selections mainly from previous late reprints and pasted up or photostated my text from readily available sources because they were the most readable and therefore best suited to the beginning student. But when the manuscript had actually reached the galley-proof stage, Cargill had a sudden attack of scholarly conscience and decided that all texts must be taken from first or at least contemporary editions of the original works. The decision seemed to me the right one even though a little belated and costly; but, after all, I did not have the problem of royalty fees, and we could afford it. So out went a third of the proofs and we started over.

The Library Company of Philadelphia was a godsend, for it had acquired on publication almost all the books since 1735 that I needed and still at that time had them on open shelves; but even so, our rule of choosing first or earliest available editions got us into some strange inconsistencies. For example, the only surviving copy of the 1791 first edition of *Charlotte, A Tale of Truth* (otherwise *Charlotte Temple*) by Susanna Rowson was not discovered until 1955; it was donated by Waller Barrett to the University of Virginia. I had to be content with a third, which was in the Library of Congress. This early novel was so popular that it had literally been read to death. Then there is the famous case of Franklin's *Autobiography*, which appeared first in a French translation, then in English in the bowdlerized version of his grandson Temple. My text was the first satisfactory one, edited by John Bigelow in 1889 and revised by A. H. Smyth. Today, it would of course be the Yale-APS *Papers*.

Jonathan Edwards also gave me as much trouble as he did his contemporaries. I had used the Sereno Dwight collected works of 1829 as more nearly complete than the earlier Austin one of 1808, but the Rev. Mr. Dwight had smoothed out the style of the old fire-eater to a point at which it flowed like a placid river, and much of the real Edwards was lost. Yet some of my selections were available only in this version unless I went up to

Yale and took my text from a new transcription of the original manuscripts. I compromised on the Dwight text for most selections but changed the youthful essay on the "Flying Spider" to a type-facsimile of the manuscript which had appeared in the *Andover Review* and seemed in its crudity to give force to the precocity of the eleven-year-old Edwards. In one case only I resorted to the parallel-text technique and printed both the corrected rough draft and the parchment copies of the Declaration of Independence from Carl Becker's monograph.

That anthology was so far ahead of all others in faithfulness to original sources that it held its place in the competition for almost forty years, but it is really a textual battlefield, a miscellany of styles and forms. It served, however, to make me aware of the ideal of a pure text, and the next thing I did was a photo-facsimile of Cooper's *Letter to Gen. Lafayette* of 1831 for The Facsimile Text Society. By now I was a firm believer in the theory that the only true modern reprint could be a photo-facsimile of the first edition; or at the worst, a type-facsimile which left in all the errors of spelling, missing or superfluous punctuation, and inconsistencies of style of the original.

In the meantime I had received a small grant to be used as a revolving publication fund for the last three volumes of Cooper's travels: *Switzerland, Italy,* and *The Rhine (Switzerland,* pt. II)— and I had edited texts according to my old formula for one or more of them. But Cargill's scholarly conscience had proved to be infectious and I was caught in a dilemma. I could not put out any more volumes according to a textual policy of which I no longer approved, and I could not change horses in midstream. As a result, I returned my grant to the donor (a fatal mistake), and only now is a uniform edition of all five travel books, including new editions of *France* and *England,* actually in progress. I have contracted for all the non-textual editing of the first part of *Sketches of Switzerland* only.

So much for my early education as a textual editor. At this stage I was a purist (-est) of the pure and I could take satisfaction only in photo-facsimiles like the volume of such photos of all drafts of the Declaration of Independence edited by Julian Boyd in 1945. Here was the beau ideal of a modern printing of an early and variant text, but it was unreadable by anybody but the scholar with a magnifying glass and an expertise in eighteenth-century handwriting.

If, on the other hand, I argued, you are going to modernize your text, why not go all the way as Tatlock and MacKaye did with Chaucer: "When the sweet showers of April have pierced to the root the dryness of March, and bathed every vein in moisture whose quickening brings forth the flowers; . . . then folk long to go on pilgrimage to renowned shrines in sundry distant lands." This is the obvious alternative, and between the two extremes lies a never-never land of confusion and anarchy—quaint-sounding texts that have been tampered with and are neither fish nor flesh.

But I was not to be left in this dismal quandary for long. Two groups of scholars had in the meantime been at work on the problem and had come up with different solutions. The one was the professional historians, led by Julian Boyd of Princeton with his Jefferson papers, and the other was the school of "Textual Criticism" or "Critical Bibliography" imported to this country by Fredson Bowers from the British studies of Pollard, McKerrow, and Greg. If we are going to keep on trying to find a reasonable middle way of reproducing old manuscripts and printed texts so that they are both "authentic" and readable, we must listen to both of these groups; for they have both found wide acceptance, have had generous support—both scholarly and financial—from the American Historical Association, the Modern Language Association, the National Endowment for the Humanities, and other societies and foundations, and have already produced enough reedited texts to fill a small library.

First, the historians, who in recent years have launched projects, usually through university presses, to edit and publish the total corpus of surviving writing, whether in manuscript or in print, of Jefferson, Hamilton, Franklin, Madison, and a dozen or more other founding fathers or later statesmen. Their basic rules of textual procedure were formulated by Oscar Handlin and others for the *Harvard Guide to American History* (1954) and are adopted with various modifications in most of these editions. Although these rules distinguish between the *Literal, Expanded,* and *Modernized* methods, there is one underlying rule to cover all cases: "that of consistency. State a method in the pre-

face or preliminary note, and stick to it!" (p. 95). I am taking as
my norm for this procedure the guidelines used by Labaree,
Bell, Willcox, and others in the Yale-APS edition of the *Papers of
Benjamin Franklin*, which was started in 1959 and is now (1976)
in its twentieth volume. *"The Papers of Benjamin Franklin,"*
declare the editors, "will follow a middle course between exact
reproduction of the eighteenth-century text and complete modernization. The purpose is to preserve as faithfully as possible
the form and spirit in which the authors composed their documents, and at the same time to reproduce their words in a manner intelligible to the present-day reader and within the normal
range of modern typographical equipment and techniques" (I,
xl). There follow slightly differing rules for printed and manuscript material. The result is a clear and readable text which preserves the essential flavor of the original, in sharp contrast to
the methods of the editors of the *Journals and Miscellaneous Notebooks of Ralph Waldo Emerson*, where an elaborate system of
printer's devices is set up to indicate on the page itself all eccentricities and variations in the manuscripts.

The guidelines by which the Franklin statement is applied in
practice are a nice compromise between literal precision and
common-sense flexibility:

(1) Although the choice of a source, especially when there are
several available (as a holograph manuscript and an authorized
first printing), is not specifically stated, one can safely infer that
the form finally approved by the author is the one used, without collation with other and variant forms.

(2) All items are made to conform to a single rule of presenta-
tion in routine respects. Italics are reduced to roman type
according to a stated rule of procedure, captions and addresses
of letters are printed in a uniform arrangement regardless of
how they appear in the original, abbreviations like an amper-
sand or obsolete usages like the long "s" are altered to their
modern forms, typographical errors are silently corrected,
punctuation and capitalization are reduced to the modern practice except where they are significant characteristics of the
author's style (such as Franklin's capitalization of all substan-
tives), corrections and cancellations made by the author in his

manuscript are printed in only their final form, and there are no "textual notes" to explain these liberties, except on rare occasions where meaning is involved—here footnotes do the work.

What emerges from this process is of course neither an original and authentic version of the author's work nor a complete modernization. Furthermore no attempt is made to conform the text to an ideal of the style of its day in the manner that I attempted futilely in Cooper's *Gleanings*. Probably in all but a very few and minor respects there has been no violation of the author's essential meaning, while mechanical obstacles like obsolete styles of spelling, punctuation, and typography have been removed and the modern reader's experience made more enjoyable and profitable.

Yes, say the literary textual scholars, that is all very well for the historian who is interested only in *what* the author said; but we literary historians and critics are interested primarily in *how* ideas are expressed—that is the art of the situation, and art is our specialty. We believe that form cannot be separated from meaning and, in altering the form in the slightest respect, the meaning is in jeopardy. We must ask of the textual editor the old three-pronged question, promulgated by Goethe and repeated by Croce and Spingarn (although challenged by Wimsatt and others): "What did the author set out to do? Was his plan reasonable and sensible? and, How far did he succeed in carrying it out?"

To confront these questions in any meaningful way, the reader must first discover from external evidence (that is, from what the author himself has said or implied by his actions), supported in every case by the internal evidence of the text itself: WHAT WAS THE AUTHOR'S INTENTION? This rule was succinctly formulated by James Thorpe in his *Principles of Textual Criticism* (1972): "The ideal of textual criticism is to present the text which the author intended" (p. 50). Easy enough!—but where can we find just what an author like Whitman or James or Dreiser intended when he changed his mind a number of times and kept revising his work up to the edge of senility? Whitman revised his poems in important ways with each of the many editions of *Leaves of Grass*. Some people prefer the first

edition of 1855; a good case has been made for the more
mature edition of 1860; and Whitman himself specified the
"deathbed" edition of 1892 as the only acceptable form and arrangement of his poems. Henry James revised all of his work in
later life, to the point of rewriting and even altering plot-
solutions, for the New York edition of 1907-09. And there is little similarity between Dreiser's *The Bulwark* in its first edition of
1945 and the earlier drafts of the story which date back as far as
1917. Which, if any, of these authors' intentions do you choose
for your "definitive" texts?

Again, when Emerson writes his brother in 1849, "I am just
reprinting my first little book of 'Nature' with various Orations,
lectures, &c. . . . and it gives me a chance to make many important corrections," (*Collected Works,* ed. R. E. Spiller and A. R.
Ferguson [Cambridge, Mass., 1971-], I, xxx), which "intention"
takes precedence—that of 1836 or that of 1849, or are they
equally valid?

The "copy-text" school of literary textual criticism also asks a
further question: Is there such a thing as an author's real intention—initial, mature, or final—in any work of art, or is the basis
of textual criticism a sort of neoplatonic construct, made up of
his intentions throughout his life and superior to any one
intention at any one time? Morse Peckham has expressed this
dilemma succinctly (if perhaps not altogether sympathetically)
in his essay "Reflections on the Foundations of Modern Textual
Editing" (*Proof* #1 [1971], p. 127):

> It is desirable to begin with a clear and simple statement about what
> a textual editor actually does. Given a group of manuscript discourses,
> or of printed discourses, or of manuscript and printed discourses,
> which he asserts to be sufficiently alike to be categorized as versions of
> the same postulated work, and which he judges to be unsatisfactory
> versions, on whatever grounds, he adds to the group another version,
> which he asserts to be more satisfactory, on whatever grounds, than
> any existing member of that group.

Actually, in practice, this new version is not quite so fortuitous
as Mr. Peckham whimsically implies. It is a synthesis of choices

made by the editor of variants he finds for the same passage in two or more versions. We could take this procedure of the new textual critics for what apparently it is or is designed to be: the exercise of a discriminating imagination in the construction of an instrument by means of which we can understand better the full significance of any work of art *in all its phases*, were it not for their assumption that the method is "scientific" and will produce a "definitive," "correct," "established," or at least "superior" text. In his textual introduction to the new edition of Emerson's *Collected Works*, my collaborator, Alfred R. Ferguson, is careful to say, "This edition provides for the first time *established* texts of Emerson's works which were originally published in his lifetime and under his immediate supervision. The text is critical and unmodernized," but the jacket blurb translates this statement as, "The edition will provide for the first time *definitive* texts of Emerson's writings, based on collation of all the editions published in his lifetime as well as the two major posthumous editions" (italics mine). Perhaps the establishing of a text makes it definitive, but it seems to me that the first statement makes slightly less claim to final authority than the second. The implication in both cases is that the editor has gained the right to have the final say on the grounds that he has used the exact methods of "science," eliminated errors, and restored "purity." To understand the basis for this claim, we should perhaps ask in more detail just what the assumptions and methods of the modern textual critic are, where the theory on which they are based originated, and how it achieved the authority that it now seems to command.

Textual criticism in the modern sense grew out of work in the bibliography of early English literature, particularly of Shakespeare's quartos and folios, by Pollard, McKerrow, and Greg between 1893 and 1942, as a means of solving bibliographical problems by comparative textual analysis. To take a simple and hypothetical example: if you wish to establish the chronological order of publication of two slightly variant printings of the same work and you find that one contains a few broken types on a page otherwise identical, it is safe to infer that the printing with broken type is later than that which is clean. Thus, textual collation has established bibliographical sequence.

In a series of monographs, these three British scholars demonstrated that much could be learned about the composition and history of the plays of Shakespeare (notably *Hamlet*) and his contemporaries by a close comparison, or collation, of the texts of the various quarto and folio editions.In those days of handpresses, open frames, and moveable type, of handmade watermarked paper and of little regulation of booksellers, compositors, pirates, and cut-throat competitive dramatic companies, the history of a text as determined from internal evidence could separate the role of the author from the roles of those who printed, acted in, or circulated his work, could remove a progressive accumulation of errors, and presumably could thus establish a pure text of the actual work of the author, merging all authoritative versions into one.

A paper by Greg on "The Rationale of Copy-Text" was read at the English Institute in New York in 1949 and, in the same year, Fredson Bowers established his *Studies in Bibliography* at the University of Virginia and published his own *Principles of Bibliographical Description*. Bowers and his followers soon carried the copy-text method over into the works of the seventeenth and eighteenth centuries and even made incursions into nineteenth-century and American as well as English literature. As printing had become more and more mechanized and book publishing and distribution a mass-production enterprise, with the rotary press, the stereotype plate, and machine-made paper, the factor of human error had become less and less significant and the old method of bibliographical description began to require more and more effort to prove facts of less and less importance. Gradually, from a procedure designed primarily to establish bibliographical sequences and to eliminate from a text errors that had crept in through its handling by others than the author in successive editions, it had become a method for constructing a synthetic or composite text in which the editor might try to reproduce, not only the author's original intention, but the whole of the creative process, from inception to final revision. In short, what had happened was that a technique for establishing the bibliography of successive versions of a work of art by an analytical collation of variant texts had been put to the reverse use of establishing a synthetic and eclectic text of the work of art by a comparative study of the bibliography of surviving versions. Thus "Critical Bibliography" had become "Textual Criticism," a form of scholarship which is neither bibliography nor criticism, but a creative act performed by a kind of surrogate author who knows more about the real author's total intention than the author did himself.

This concept raises all sorts of philosophical questions about the nature of art and the relationship of the work of art to its creator and to its audience. I will not try to discuss these questions here except to ask whether creative efforts of a single author directed at a single work but taken from different periods of his career can ever be finally woven together into a single text which then becomes *the* work of art. The second question follows: even if the course of reasoning followed by the editor in making his choices is fully exposed in textual introduction and page-and-line notes showing all the variant readings from which the choices were made, is the final result a "definitive" text of the author, or is it a synthetic text revealing mainly the judgment of the editor? And if it is mainly the latter, what becomes of the "New" critic's main assumption that the work of art exists apart from the author's presumed intention and can be analyzed as an objective entity? In discussing "the two convenient detours around the acknowledged and usually feared obstacles to objective criticism," Wimsatt and Beardsley define the Intentional Fallacy as "a confusion between the poem and its origins," and the Affective Fallacy as "a confusion between the poem and its *results*" (*The Verbal Icon* [1954], p. 21). Surely a synthetic text created by the subjective choices of an editor is a by-product of both fallacies and cannot provide an aesthetic entity for objective analysis by the critic, even though it can serve as a useful instrument for critical examination of the evolution of an author's entire corpus of work.

Whether we agree with this conclusion or not, there are many scholars who have accepted this concept of the work of art as a synthesis of all phases of the author's intention and have undertaken to produce "established" editions of the writings of our major authors according to strict guidelines based on this theory. The group I refer to is of course the Center for Editions of American Authors, until recently sponsored by the Modern Language Association and subsidized by the National Endowment for the Humanities. After a decade and more of successfully supporting and setting their seal of approval on many volumes, the CEAA, however, began to lose credibility by the accumulation of misunderstandings and costly mistakes which are inevitable in a bureaucracy. With an NEH change in personnel and policy which withdrew its financial support from the project as a whole, preferring to deal individually with each author-edition, support for CEAA was terminated in 1976, and a new Center for Scholarly Editions (not limited to American) was substituted by the Modern Language Association to assist in textual scholarship and to award the seal of excellence without subsidizing individual editors or projects.

It is too soon to know how a far more open and consultative procedure, coupled with a somewhat more conservative philosophy of emendations, will work, but two planks in the announced platform of the CSE are encouraging. They are: "1. What is the rationale for emendation (of this volume or edition)? Is it consistent and convincing? and 2. Are recorded emendations consistent with the stated policy of emendations?"

I was committed to the CEAA project from the start when I suggested to then President Barnaby Keeney of Brown University that the new National Endowment for the Humanities, of which he had just become Chairman, subsidize the CEAA as an initial project. But because of my basically relativistic position in all textual matters I have not personally become involved in the recent efforts to regularize textual procedures and to apply standards and methods derived from the Greg-Bowers or other schools of thought. As a result, I have been associated as co-editor with Alfred R. Ferguson, one of the more extreme of the eclectic-critical text group, in the first volume of the CEAA-approved *Collected Works of Ralph Waldo Emerson,* and I have supplied the historical introduction and notes for the first volume of Fenimore Cooper's travels without doing more than express my opinion on textual questions as they have arisen. I will therefore conclude these remarks by explaining how this process seems to work, even though it has been explained and discussed many times before. To me it is just one of a number of reasonable alternatives open to the textual editor of a literary work.

First, the textual editor collects or locates multiple copies of all editions of the work which could have involved the action or the approval of the author (including in some cases even posthumous editions on the chance that they have used the author's notes or corrections). This has been an ex post facto operation in many of these editions and has caused all kinds of delays and complications; the projected Cooper edition has profited by the failure of CEAA to recognize the logic of its inclusion in their plans by developing at the American Antiquarian Society in Worcester probably the best collection of multiple copies of all editions of an American author now in existence.

The textual editor then selects his "copy-text." Originally the copy-text could be any one of these editions, but preference inclined to adopt the "best," which was usually the latest version of the original composition as finally approved by the author; gradually the realization that chance errors as well as the author's revisions could creep into such a text has led to a reversal of the rule of choice in favor of the earliest available version approved by the author. The principle of establishing an historical order of texts goes all the way back to McKerrow and the Shakespeareans, and it was logical that the American scholars should thus rely on a chart of textual ancestry in a sequence of texts that could be collated in chronological order. An attempt could then be made to correct the copy-text in ways that reflected changes in the author's intention, while at the same time disregarding changes that seemed to be the result of mechanical or human error. The CEAA has generally adopted the rule that when one or more manuscripts exist, the copy-text should be the pre-publication finished version of the author, if that can be determined, and that when all manuscripts have been destroyed or have otherwise disappeared, the earliest printed text that could be said to have been seen by the author should be the copy-text.

The first step in the actual editing comes when multiple copies of the copy-text are compared, usually by a Hinman or other collator, to eliminate "accidentals" which might have crept in through various printings or issues of the same edition. When this has been done, the resulting text is then collated several times without mechanical means against all later revisions that were made under the presumed supervision of the author. By this process, all "substantive" changes are detected and recorded, as well as "accidental" changes created by other than mechanical causes. At this point the editor has a table of variants, both substantive and accidental, which presumably reflect both changes in the author's intention and intrusion of the editor's or publisher's influence on one edition or another. Now the editor must begin to compose his "definitive" text, accepting or rejecting variants as his judgment dictates and relegating to the textual notes all variants which are not retained in his final text.

It is at this point that the CEAA admitted different rules to govern its procedure in different cases. The Bradley-Blodgett variorum edition of *Leaves of Grass* uses the final or "deathbed" edition as copy-text for all poems except those eliminated by Whitman in his final editing of his work. These poems are restored or printed for the first time from the latest revision extant. The copy-text approved by Whitman is then printed verbatim and all variants in earlier editions are recorded in copious textual notes. The editors are thus relieved of all subjective choice except in the case of manuscript variants which at first were regarded as too many and too inconsequential to be completely recorded. This decision was later reversed and the rule that all variants in both manuscript and print should be included in the textual notes was adopted, with resulting indefinite delay.

At the other extreme is Emerson's essay on "The Young American," which is included in the volume in which I was involved. Emerson printed this lecture in pamphlet form after its first delivery to the Mercantile Library Association on February 7, 1844. The time was the era of "Manifest Destiny" and the audience was a group of young men engaged in trade and manufacture. The tone of the essay, as well as its ideas, is very much out of key with other things that Emerson was writing at that time; it is a paean of praise for the materialistic progress of the United States and its promise of future opportunity. When the revision came in 1849, the mood of the times had changed; the optimistic enthusiasm of the earlier version obviously was not retained in the author's later thoughts. As a result, a number of long paragraphs was omitted in the finally approved version and others toned down. What then was the author's intention? There were obviously two intentions, dating five years apart, both of which should, if possible, be preserved in some form. At this point my textual editor decided on a synthetic text which would preserve both intentions by restoring the excised passages as well as including any new material introduced into the second edition. In this way we could have the best of both worlds. The combined texts produced a far richer sense of Emerson's whole creative process and the important part that his audiences played in his thinking than either version could do alone, but I must confess to some uneasiness at the degree to which Ferguson had exercised his agreed prerogatives as an eclectic critical editor.

Nevertheless the CEAA seal was immediately bestowed upon the edition, and Ferguson set to work on the text of the second volume, following the same guidelines. With his death in May 1974, however, the reorganized editorial board had some second thoughts and adopted a stricter check on editorial procedure by withdrawing the editor's right to restore passages which the author had deleted in his revision or to reject on subjective grounds any other presumed authorial revisions. The new statement reads, "Because the textual problems of subsequent volumes differ, all revisions identifiable as Emerson's will ordinarily be accepted." By drawing the reins a bit tighter we approach more nearly objective editorial standards, but the basic principle is still relative: set the rules and then live up to them in practice.

The only remaining question is whether or not the "copy-text" theory has developed a set of rules which are definitive or scientific in any special way. My contention is that, even in its strictest forms, it has developed only a consistent and flexible way of producing a valuable form of synthetic text, but that it is still critical and subjective rather than definitive. It is only one of a number of methods of probing an author's full creative process. I do not deny that it has forced scholars to think carefully about problems which they previously tended to avoid, but at a tremendous cost of detailed and essentially clerical work of little significance. My own preference, if any strict editorial procedure is to be chosen over others, would be the old-fashioned unedited variorum text of either the first or an early revised edition which was published in the author's lifetime, with a table of textual variants of all sorts from other editions approved by the author.

I have experimented with many other kinds of texts over the years, and I am more than ever convinced that the idea of a definitive text is an impossible dream, a tilting at windmills. I now accept, with varying degrees of enthusiasm, the reconstructed text of my early editions of Cooper's *Gleanings*, the photo-facsimile of *Letter to Gen. Lafayette*, and the eclectic-critical text of the first volume of Emerson's *Collected Works*. And I haven't had time to explore here some of my other experiments as thoroughly as I have these three. Perhaps my favorite job is the first printing of the previously unpublished *Early Lectures* of Emerson from the manuscripts in the Houghton Library, where we used a method of clear-text transcription similar to but not as extreme as that of the historians, but with full textual notes which the historians usually do not supply. I have referred also to minor textual jobs in my anthology which were done by type-facsimile and parallel passages. Finally, my most radical experiment was with *The Van Wyck Brooks - Lewis Mumford Letters* (1970) where, by selecting for balance and emphasis, silently cutting irrelevancies, and conforming careless accidentals, I attempted to present a continuously interesting life-long dialogue between two speculative thinkers in a form that tells a story and is free of distracting material, both substantive and accidental.

And so I come back to the position with which I began these remarks: there are many kinds of texts that serve many different uses, and the editor alone has the right to choose the kind that he will produce, just so he announces his procedure in a preface and then sticks with thorough scholarly integrity to his own rules.

II • AMERICAN LITERATURE AND CULTURE: HISTORY AND THEORY

With foundations laid on the broad base of liberal studies and with the two tools of bibliography and textual criticism at least examined if not wholly mastered, I was ready to move into the newly evolving discipline of American literary history. It slowly became apparent that I was not to spend my scholarly career as a textual editor, a bibliographer, or even a biographer. The concentration on the work of one author seemed increasingly restrictive. I found myself drawn more deeply into the philosophy of literary history in general and specifically into what seemed to me the as-yet unwritten literary history of the United States. My first moves in this direction were contemporaneous with my work on Fenimore Cooper. I joined the small group of scholars who were beginning to define American literature as a field for specialized scholarship distinct from that of English literature and to form an American Literature Group in the Modern Language Association of America. That story is told in the reminiscent talk, "Those Early Days," in chapter 12 of this volume, and it is further documented by essays and addresses in my other collections. Still mainly an undergraduate teacher of English literature at a small college, I was gradually becoming one of the leaders in the emerging scholarly field of American literary history. The break finally came when I returned to the University of Pennsylvania in 1945 to join the group that was developing a new department of American civilization. And so the egg laid by my dissertation finally hatched!

That is the surface story. Underneath there had been slowly developing, out of my basic concern for the meaning of humanistic scholarship, a deepening and broadening involvement in the theory of American literary history. That theory is probably best summarized in Chapter 10 in the Bicentennial address, "The Cycle and the Roots," which is the central and definitive essay of this and my other three volumes. The horizontal movement of successive waves of Western European—especially English—culture across the American continent and the vertical rooting of an indigenous American culture in the new soil both follow the cyclic processes of all history and of life itself. Around these two symbols the story of the evolution of American literature gradually shaped itself in my mind and in all my writing after 1945.

The ancestry of this theory could very easily be traced back to Vico, Herder, Hegel, Darwin, Marx, Taine, and perhaps Freud, but it came to me through Franklin's pragmatism, Emerson's transcendental theory of values, and the theory of Henry Adams that "man as a force must be measured by motion from a fixed point." Adams adopted the Virgin of Chartres as his fixed point of Unity and the Dynamo as his fixed point of Multiplicity. With these two symbols he "hoped to project his lines forward and backward indefinitely, subject to correction from anyone who should know better." My method is similarly pragmatic and symbolic. Henry Adams taught me that history is a process in which I could be a creative part; in short, an art.

4 | THE AMERICAN LITERARY DECLARATION OF INDEPENDENCE

It was not until 1967 that I took up the challenge of my dissertation and explored more thoroughly the emergence of an American sense of identity in the early conflict between loyalty to the English tradition and the demand for a totally new literature, the product of an indigenous culture. The result was a collection of statements on both sides of this debate, up to Emerson's "American Scholar." The American Literary Revolution, 1783-1837 (1967) *was published simultaneously in hard covers by the New York University Press and in paperback by Doubleday and Co., Inc., in their "Documents in American Civilization Series," edited by Hennig Cohen and John William Ward.*

The essay that follows was based on the editorial comment in that volume and, in 1969, was contributed to Literatur und Sprache der Vereinigten Staaten, *a festschrift in honor of Professor Hans Galinsky of the University of Mainz, edited by Hans Helmcke, Klaus Lubbers, and Renate Schmidt-v.Bardeleben.*

Galinsky was one of the pioneers in American studies in Germany, the founder of an institute on the subject at his university and the first president of the Deutsche Gesellschaft für Amerikastudien. He has traveled and taught in this country many times, and I visited his institute in Mainz when I was lecturing up and down the Rhine in 1958. Hans Helmcke, his assistant, visited us at Pennsylvania and has now returned from a professorship at Heidelberg to Mainz on Professor Galinsky's retirement in 1977.

I

When Emerson concluded in Phi Beta Kappa address on that hot August day in 1837 with the charge that "The mind of this country, taught to aim at low objects, eats upon itself" and called upon the American Scholar to "plant himself indomitably on his instincts, and there abide," his audience by all accounts was startled. Here was a new young voice issuing a declaration of intellectual and spiritual independence; but, as Emerson wrote to Whitman upon first reading the *Leaves of Grass* many years later, such a challenge "must have had a long foreground somewhere, for such a start."

The fact was that the American Scholar address was the end and not the beginning of a slow development into American literary independence which began almost with the signing of the peace treaty of 1783. It was at once an affirmation that such independence was needed and, as a great work of American literature in itself, that it had been achieved. The slow growth of an American literature from the naive and abortive efforts of the post-Revolutionary era to its full flowering in the writings of the 1840s and 1850s is a historical process that can be studied and understood. The documents for each step of the progress need only to be assembled from contemporary magazines and pamphlets in order to follow the story through, chapter by chapter.

II

In the period between the Treaty of Paris (Sept. 3, 1783), which settled the independence of the new nation, and the Treaty of Ghent (Dec. 24, 1814), which seems to have confirmed independence as an accepted psychological reality on all sides, Americans in general were intellectually and culturally on the defensive. The argument that political independence should automatically bring with it autonomy of the mind and spirit, resulting in the rapid appearance of an indigenous culture, was enthusiastically seized upon, particularly by young intellectuals, but was immediately met by arguments that (1) a common language and a common cultural tradition made dependence on England for many years inevitable and even desirable, (2) the raw state of civilization in so unexplored and unexploited a land postponed indefinitely any hope for the amenities and cultivation of the Old World, and (3) the longstanding thesis, which had been advanced by Buffon and was early challenged by Jefferson, that the human race inevitably deteriorates in the Western Hemisphere. British and European travelers in the United States, eager to discourage emigration from their own countries and unhappy with the accommodations and habits of the Americans, as well as British critics of American writings in the revered London and Edinburgh reviews and quarterlies, did little to reassure American hopes and self-confidence.

Nevertheless, the Americans set to work to develop the instruments of literary culture (colleges, printing presses, bookshops, libraries, postal and other means of communication, protective copyright legislation, theaters, etc.) and to write, produce, and publish their own poems, plays, novels, and both familiar and formal essays on all aspects of the American experience and American ideas. Some thought of "literature" merely as serious writing on any or all subjects of human concern (theology, law, medicine, morality, art, the physical and mechanical sciences, and belles lettres (in the accepted eighteenth-century sense of the term); others limited their definition to the poetry, plays, novels, and lighter essays which were considered the evidence of a more cultivated and perhaps higher stage of civilization. But the majority of Americans during these years were fired with the desire for cultural accomplishment, aware of their handicaps and obstacles, and by 1800 pretty generally discouraged. The period of ten years just before the War of 1812 was psychologically a low point for American literary nationalism, a state of mind which the appearance of Barlow's epic *Columbiad* and Irving's whimsical *Salmagundi* did little to alleviate.

It is fitting, therefore, that this discussion about the prospects for an American literature should open with the remark, "There are few writers of books in this new world, and amongst these very few that deal in works of the imagination." The supposed writer is one Mr. Robert Slender who, in the eighteenth-century fashion, was a recently expired and lamented *alter ego* of the poet and political satirist, Philip Freneau.

Mr. Slender, it would seem, was a stocking and tape weaver by trade who left behind him at his untimely demise nothing but a strong box in which was discovered "a bundle of manuscripts, penned in a very antiquated and perplexing hand," from which his supposed editor extracted a brief essay entitled, "Advice to Authors." "In a country which two hundred years ago was peopled only by savages," says Mr. Slender, "and where the government has ever, in effect, since the first establishment of the white man in these parts, been no other than republican, it is really wonderful that there should be any polite original authors at all in any line;" and he advises such as there are "to graft your authorship upon some other calling, or support drooping genius by the assistance of some mechanical employment, in the same manner as the helpless ivy takes hold of the vigorous oak and cleaves to it for support."

Note at once certain assumptions in this tongue-in-cheek advice which neither Freneau nor the best of his contemporaries followed, to their cost. Literature, it would seem, must be 'polite,' or in other words the product of the sophisticated upper class which quite logically could never exist in a republic. The importation of such works from the Old World must therefore continue—probably indefinitely—and a home-grown product could be nurtured only by grafting it on the more immediate and practical requirements of life in the New. The pros and cons of this grim point of view underlie much of the more serious debate which was to follow in the years to come.

But, even so, a generation of ambitious and patriotic young writers immediately sprang into action and began writing, in their spare time, poems, plays, novels and essays based on *American* experience. This was difficult because both writer and reader were familiar only with British models (or occasionally European), and the rigid literary conventions of the time made the adaptation of the new content to the old forms and traditions difficult to the point of impossibility. Nevertheless these small groups of young writers, mainly in the Atlantic seacoast towns, set about their task of experimentation with enthusiasm, and the first quarter century of independence produced at least a sprinkling of poems and essays descriptive of American scenery, plays and novels about American society and character, and familiar as well as formal essays on American problems and practices. As the book-lists of the time will show, the total of such experiments was slight in proportion to the great numbers of religious, political, and practical works which began to come from the American presses and to the competition of imported belles lettres; and most of these young men had lost courage and given up the battle by 1800; but a glance at a few of their Prologues and Prefaces will at least set the terms of the problem if not its solution.

Perhaps the best spokesman for the poets was Joel Barlow, one of the so-called "Connecticut Wits," a graduate of Yale, and a political sympathizer and friend of Tom Paine. Of American authors of the day, with the possible exceptions of Freneau and Charles Brockden Brown, he was the most persistent in his determination to help create an American literature. A national literature, he argued, should have an epic celebrating its history and its heroes, and the obvious place to begin was at the beginning with Columbus. But Columbus was a Genoese sailor in the employ of Spain and could not therefore symbolize a glorious American past. Barlow's solution to the problem was to substitute a dream of future glories for a history of past achievements, in which technique he had the support of Virgil and Milton. This rejection of the past was to become a dominant trait of the national character, reflected with more philosophical depth in Emerson and persistent even today.

The writers of fiction were not so ambitious. Charles Brockden Brown who came nearest of them to succeeding as the first professional American novelist, soon lost heart and turned to magazine editing for a livelihood. As he correctly points out, however, in his Preface to *Edgar Huntly* in 1799, he not only substitutes for the "puerile superstition" and "Gothic Castles" of the British romances, the incidents and perils of the western wilderness, but he recognizes that "new springs of action" and other daily American experiences must be essentially different from those of Europe and "peculiar to ourselves." Even though he makes very little of the issue of nationalism as such and explores such subjective regions as morbid psychology and pseudoscience, he implicitly makes the distinction that Poe later developed between superficial nationalism and genuine originality and thus helped to prepare the way for the "black" romance, which has only recently been recognized by Richard Chase, Harry Levin, and others as a characteristic American literary genre.

The native drama was even slower to develop. When *The Contrast* was produced by Thomas Wignell, the English actor, at the John Street Theatre in New York City on April 16, 1787, it made dramatic and literary history, as well as the reputation of its author, because it was the first American play on an American theme to be professionally produced in the United States. Tyler accurately copies the spirit and style of the English comedies of Sheridan and Goldsmith, then so popular on the English and American stages, and adds to them the theme of the simple honesty of the democratic native American, a theme which goes back as far as Jefferson. This is perhaps the most successful attempt up to this time to use a popular British literary form almost without change to give expression to a distinctively American patriotic idea.

In publishing his play, however, Tyler shows that he was fully aware of the significance of his experiment. "In justice to the Author," so reads the advertisement, "it may be proper to observe that this Comedy has many claims to the public indulgence, independent of its intrinsic merits: It is the first essay of American genius in a difficult species of composition; it was written by one who never critically studied the rules of the drama and, indeed, has seen but few of the exhibitions of the stage; it was undertaken and finished in the course of three weeks; and the profits of one night's performance were appropriated to the benefit of the suffers by the fire at *Boston.*

"These considerations will therefore, it is hoped, supply in the closet the advantages that are derived from representation, and dispose the reader to join in the applause which has been bestowed on this Comedy by numerous and judicious audiences in the Theatres of Philadelphia, New-York and Maryland."

But such outbursts of patriotic productivity were few and

were already dwindling by 1800. Some of the reasons why this thin stream of native literary production became a trickle and all but dried up thereafter may be found in an apologetic Preface by Charles Brockden Brown to the first bound volume of his quarterly review for 1801. Two years of publishing a magazine had taught him that the hope of contributions from his fellow members of the Friendly Club, which had brought him to New York, was vain; and the effort to fill the pages himself could not be sustained forever. The decision to publish only quarterly and to use more informational and borrowed material had likewise failed to solve the problem. There was as yet an insufficient public to support a genuinely literary journal; and the reasons Brown gives are the usual ones: Americans are too busy with practical matters to give attention to original and creative work in either science or literature, and London is too near to permit competition from an American center of the arts. The first period of national literary effort was drawing to a disappointing close.

In addition to the practicality of the American mind and the nearness of London, other reasons commonly given for the failure were the lack of an American language and the absence of the means of production and circulation of books and magazines (publishers, bookstores, libraries, adequate copyright protection, etc.)."As an independent nation," wrote the lexicographer Noah Webster in 1789, "our honor requires us to have a system of our own in language as well as government." "It must be our care therefore to be receptive to new words and idioms that are created by local causes but to be cautious both about following the English usage and about too much undisciplined diversity in the American." And Samuel Miller, prominent Presbyterian clergyman of New York City, writing in the first year of the new century, attributed the slow development of a native literature to: "(1) defective plans and means of instruction in our seminaries of learning, . . . (2) Want of leisure, . . . (3) Want of encouragement to learning, . . . (4) Want of books."

Finally, among the commentators who sought the causes of failure in other than superficial factors was Fisher Ames, famous in his day for his passionate rhetoric and staunch Hamiltonian Federalism. As an amateur classical scholar, Ames was concerned with the cultural life of his place and time and, in an essay on "National Literature," he draws some ominous parallels and predictions by contrasting the civilizations of Greece and Rome with those of modern nations, particularly the American. The argument that equalitarianism and commercialism, as basic elements in the structure of American life, are in themselves destructive of the human spirit and that therefore Americans cannot hope to develop a life of the mind and the arts will be heard again many times but perhaps not again with the same passionate eloquence and gloomy despair. "Excepting the writers of two able works on our politicks," he laments, "we have no authors. . . . Shall we match Joel Barlow against Homer or Hesiod? Can Tom Paine contend against Plato? . . . Has our country produced one great original work of genius?" To an obvious negative to all of these questions he brings the charge that "the single passion that engrosses us, the only avenue to consideration and importance in our society, is the accumulation of property; our inclinations cling to gold, and we are bedded in it as deeply as that precious ore in the mine." And the Virginian George Tucker confirms a few years later that "The inferiority of the United States to most of the countries of Europe in literary productions is a fact too manifest to be disputed." But, he asks, "is this difference owing to the inferiority of our natural genius, as some have alleged, or to causes that are temporary and accidental?" In denying inferiority as a cause, he, like others of the early commentators, leaves the problem clearly stated but unsolved. More searching examinations of the causes were yet to come.

III

Historians seem to agree that there was a sharp rise in the spirit of nationalism in the United States after the second war with Great Britain in 1812-14. Even though the actual terms of the peace treaty "left everything much as it had been before the war began," says George Dangerfield, it actually "meant that in the future Britain would cease to regard the United States as a colony which paid its own expenses, and that she would look upon American expansion with a favorable eye, so long as it provided an enlargement of British industrial opportunity." In an even larger sense, it means the end of the Napoleonic era, during which the American continent had been one of Europe's outlying battlefields, and the beginning of an era in which the United States was to realize its "manifest destiny" as a wholly independent power in control of a separate continent.

The founding of the *North American Review* in 1815, the first wholly original in content and the longest lived of American literary journals, may or may not have had something to do with this development. Certainly the early issues, which carried the subtitle "Miscellaneous Journal" and appeared bimonthly, reveal no sharp break with its predecessors; but its first editor, William Tudor, succeeded where Brockden Brown had failed, in rallying to his aid a strong group of cooperating contributors in the former members of the Anthology Club, the sponsors of The *Monthly Anthology* (1803—1811). Although there were many vigorous if usually short-lived literary magazines in Boston, Philadelphia, New York, Baltimore, Richmond, and other towns to the North and the South during this period, the discussion of the problem of literary and cultural nationalism in their pages, where it occurred, did not probe much beneath the level of the earlier debates. The *North American* group had, however, developed among themselves a far deeper and more searching understanding of the issues involved, and for five years they conducted a debate in its pages which can only be appreciated by bringing the best of their essays together. As Harry Hayden Clark has pointed out, the reputation for political and literary reaction which the *Review* earned and ultimately deserved does not apply to these years when Tudor, the three Channings, Phillips, Palfrey, and Edward Everett were championing the new romantic poetry and novel and were vigorously arguing for a national literature.

The secret of the unanimity and firmness of the intellectual and aesthetic grounds upon which this group of critics based their opinions, and even their differences, lay in their familiarity with the best current Scottish, English and even, indirectly, German critical thought. Robert E. Streeter has identified the

Scottish rationalist, Archibald Alison, author of *Essays on the Nature and Principles of Taste* (1790), and the Association psychology upon which his critical principles are based, as the primary influence in the critical thinking of the American group (*AL*, Nov. 1945, 243–254). It was too soon for the impact of Coleridge and the German philosophers who had so much to do with the shaping of Transcendental literary thought a few years later, but Association psychology supplied a rationale for the relationship between author, material, and reader which gave the elements of an organic process to literary creation and provided the substance that the debate on nationalism had previously lacked.

It would be easy to put too much emphasis on the doctrinaire aspects of this influence, for the American critics did not always understand the philosophical concepts with which they were working, but the essential principle of Associationism, that thought is composed of elements drawn from immediate experience, provided a new justification for denying the neoclassical emphasis on forms, standards, and imitation and substituting an immediate emphasis on experience and on the active process of shaping it into artistic expression. The arguments, therefore, that Americans should stop imitating British and European literary models, should seek to understand their own scenery, history, and social life, and should put into writing what they actually saw, heard, and felt now had something more than a patriotic justification, a line of reasoning that would apply to any literature, past or present. On these principles, this first group of *North American* reviewers were in substantial agreement, and the argument from patriotism no longer was necessary. Where they were likely to disagree was in the timing of the process: some condemned previous American writers as incompetents and laggards and urged the immediate realization of the potentials of a national literature; others preached patience and a constant discrimination between what was really good or bad in the American literary product while continuing to read and enjoy foreign current writing and foreign classics.

The opening shot in the new battle of wits was fired by Walter Channing, physician brother of William Ellery Channing and Edward Tyrell Channing (both of whom were soon to make important contributions to the unfolding debate) and father of Emerson's poet-friend, William Ellery Channing the younger. In his "Reflections on the Literary Delinquency of America" in the November 1815 issue, this physician-Channing issues a vigorous call to cultural nationalism, but he also deplores the "melancholy record" of American literary effort to date and supplies the elements of a philosophical approach to the problem in the proposition that literature is the expression of experience in language which that experience itself creates. About the future possibilities of achievement in literature and science he has no doubt if once Americans can be awakened to appreciation of the unique and distinctive nature of life on the new continent. Other writers in the *North American* developed the argument from his premises.

Among these other writers was Channing's younger brother Edward, who was the only one of the three whose primary concern was with literature as such. As Boyleston Professor of Rhetoric and Oratory at Harvard from 1819 to 1850, he was undoubtedly a major influence in shaping the minds and writings of Emerson and Thoreau, as well as of many of their contemporaries. His emphasis, therefore, in his remarkable essay, "On Models in Literature," which appeared in July 1816, upon the sanctity of original genius, the possible tyranny of too much study of the classics, and the need for a national literature which is the direct expression of experience may explain much that came later.

"When I lay down the reviews or go home from a party of critics," he writes, "I pity the whole race of authors. . . . A heavy burden it will be for poetry when society is made the school of genius instead of solitude. . . . The imitator, the man who gets his stock of thought and sentiment of beauty from books, is cautious, constrained, and modelled throughout. . . . What we contend is that the literature of a country is just as domestick and individual as its character or political institutions. Its charm is its nativeness. . . . So long then as a country is proud of itself, it will repel every encroachment upon its native literature." Not once in his entire essay does he mention an American literature as such, but his argument provides the philosophical grounds on which his patriotic reader may erect his own structure, complete with flags and drums. The debate was getting its roots down into the real soil of its problem, and the inventories of American literary accomplishment by Bryant and the elder Dana in the next few years showed the result of this more careful thinking in their balanced and judicial appraisals both of individual works and authors, and of the problem in itself.

Most of Bryant's opinions, in his review of Solyman Brown's versified *Essay on Poetry*, with perhaps the exception of those on Freneau and Clifton, have stood the test of time. A youth spent in study and contemplation had made him already familiar with poetry itself as well as with the poetic theory of his English and Scottish contemporaries, and he spoke from a knowledge of both eighteenth century neoclassical theory and practice and from the early romantic view of poetry as a "suggestive" art. His debt to Alison and Burke for the theory of Association was almost as great as that to Wordsworth and the earlier poets of nature. His *Lectures on Poetry*, delivered in New York in 1825, are the first attempt by an American to develop a systematic poetic theory.

And Dana, picking up the inventory of American literary achievement where Bryant had left it, used the appearance of Irving's *Sketch Book* as an opportunity, not only for a critical and appreciative critical review of all of Irving's work to date but also for some general remarks on the state of American literature and of its prospects. Although he accepted the basic literary philosophy of his Channing cousins, his temperament was more restrained and his mind more critical than theirs. In spite of his recognition of Irving as the first American man of letters who could have any pretensions to the claim of genius, he discusses carefully what he finds of good and bad in his style, and he warns that American literary nationalism can only be self-defeating if it loses sight of literary values in the national cause. The argument from Association could be worked either way.

IV

No major historical events seem to mark off the decade of the twenties unless the Missouri Compromise of 1820 be taken as a measure of expansion to the West and the election of Andrew Jackson be taken as a sign of deep political and social change, both as portents of trouble to come. In American literature, however, it was the period of coming-of-age. 1819—20 saw the publication of *The Sketch Book*, 1821 the first collection of the poems of William Cullen Bryant and of the first American novel by James Fenimore Cooper, *The Spy, a Tale of the Neutral Ground*, and 1827 Poe's *Tamerlane and Other Poems*. Catherine Sedgwick and Fitz-Greene Halleck, as well as James Kirke Paulding, established themselves as professional writers, and Timothy Flint was writing of the land beyond the Alleghenies while Nathaniel Parker Willis was reporting gossip from the literary and social circles of Europe to which his letters of introduction had given him a welcome. James Nelson Barker, John Howard Payne, and William Dunlap were among those whose plays on American and other subjects had been produced, and Daniel Webster and Edward Everett were making oratory a literary genre. The *North American* maintained its ascendency with a succession of distinguished editors, but, with a growing conservatism, lost some of its national influence as other journals were established in Philadelphia, New York, Baltimore, and the South and West. Meanwhile the debate on a national literature became more widespread and took a subtle turn of emphasis. With growing political and social maturity, the question of *national character* inevitably was raised as literary influences from overseas gradually shifted from those of the Scottish rationalists to the English and German romantics. Wordsworth and Scott became widely read and Coleridge and Carlyle made their early appearance in the English and Scottish reviews which were followed closely by intellectual Americans. A more rounded and organic view of the national character and of the role of the literary "genius" called out the three principal statements on literary nationalism of the decade: those of Ingersoll, Everett, and W. E. Channing, and was reflected less dramatically in other reviewers and critics. The completion of the first edition of Webster's American Dictionary added perhaps the final touch to literary maturity.

A Philadelphia lawyer, Charles Jared Ingersoll offered the first major consideration of the problem in *A Discourse Concerning the Influence of America on the Mind* in 1823 as the annual oration of the American Philosophical Society. Accepting the basic assumption of the *North American* group that literature should be the expression of experience, but broadening it to include any written expression of intellectual achievement, he attempts a defense of the national character in a review of the entire spectrum of national achievement. His tone is temperate, but there is a running comparison with British parallels which makes his position strongly patriotic as well as thoroughly informed and judicious. Later writers on literary nationalism adopted his concern for national character but differed with his conclusion that the American mind is essentially practical and pragmatic.

In April of 1824, Emerson wrote in his Journal, "I am beginning my professional studies. In a month I shall be legally a man. . . . " That summer he had the opportunity of hearing his former Professor of Greek, Edward Everett, deliver the Phi Beta Kappa Oration to the same point at Cambridge in the presence of Lafayette, who was then on his triumphal return tour of his adopted country. The theme of literary nationalism was not new to the orator of the day; as Phi Beta Kappa poet in 1812 he had versified the basic problem of putting America into poetry with such unpoetic place-names as Mas-sa-chu-setts, Bunker, Memphremagog, and Connecticut:

> Would he one verse of easy movement frame,
> The map will meet him with a hopeless name;

but in this first of his major orations (of which there were to be many) he looked upon the problem in a larger perspective. Accepting Ingersoll's premise that the problem was basically one of national character, this former editor of the *North American* defined, against the background of Greek literature which he knew as a specialist, "the peculiar motives to intellectual exertion in America" as, with Ingersoll, the principles of self-government and individual sovereignty of the people, the extent and uniformity of a common language, and the rapid increase of population with the corresponding development of civilization. These were new and vital ideas which might have been expressed in fewer pages, but their influence in their day and upon the young Emerson was not altogether because of the oratorical powers of their speaker.

With the third of the Channing brothers entering the lists in 1830 in a belated review of Ingersoll's *Discourse*, the controversy achieved its most fully developed theoretical base. Thus Channing reemphasized the idea that great literature is the expression of great minds and that therefore a national literature, to be great, must be the expression of a lofty and distinctive national mind, but he differed sharply with his opponents on the relative value of practical and professional vs. religious and moral qualities of mind. He also differed from Ingersoll and took one further step nearer to Emerson in the value which he put on the spiritual qualities of the individual and in the finally religious rather than worldly tests of character, whether individual or national.

"We begin," he writes, "by stating what we mean by national literature. We mean the expression of a nation's mind in writing. We mean the production among a people of important works in philosophy and in the departments of imagination and taste. . . . We mean the thoughts of profound and original minds, elaborated by the toil of composition and fixed and made immortal in books." By these standards he feels that his countrymen have, to date, fallen far short of his ideal goal, but that the error can be corrected only by recognizing superficial knowledge for what it is and directing the national mind to a "resolute devotion to a higher intellectual culture." Only thus can we move from our concern for "useful knowledge" to a richer utility, "the idea that beauty is an indestructible principle of our nature," and thus develop a national literature worthy of its classical and foreign competitors. Here is ground surely for an American literature which could be both national and universal.

V

While all this debate was going on a native American literature was, more or less of itself, coming into being. The early years of the new century saw the further expansion of popular and higher education and the development of the instruments of culture. Bookstores and libraries were set up in most of the larger communities, theaters became more numerous, and books and magazines, both domestic and imported, became more available. The times were getting ready for the professional American writer and his readers.

One does not normally look to professional novelists, dramatists, or even essayists or poets unless they are also literary critics, for well-formed aesthetic philosophies, but many authors discuss at length their own aims, methods, and accomplishments as well as the difficulties they encounter in their careers. The earliest successful American men of letters were no exceptions to this rule. Although, as we have seen, the theory of a national literature was slowly taking shape, for most of the writers themselves the primary question was still how they could express their own experience (which of course was mainly an American one) in linguistic and literary forms and modes which had been developed in a borrowed and alien rather than a native tradition. In some like Irving, Paulding, Cooper, and Longfellow, the problem was little more than a practical one, motivated by varying degrees of patriotic enthusiasm; in others, like Bryant, Poe, and Emerson, who were all literary critics as well as creative writers, the theoretical aspects of the problem came in for varying degrees of ethical and aesthetic consideration. On the other hand, the existence and development of a broadly based and generally accepted concern for literature as a major aspect of general culture provided the motivation, the underlying theory of aesthetic expression, the instruments of production and communication, and the receptivity of a sufficiently large reading public to make the situation of the aspiring writer of 1820 very different from that of his opposite number in 1800. Without the running debate on literary nationalism which we have now reviewed, the emergence of the Romantic Movement as an indigenous phase of our American literary history would probably not have occurred.

The earliest of the successful professional American men of letters, Washington Irving, probably did more and said less about American literary nationalism than any other author of his day. Except for some sly remarks on the English attitude toward America and an essay or two which were mild enough to offend no one, he sought refuge in conformity to the English literary fashion of his day and then wrote about what he pleased. That fashion was dictated by the publisher John Murray and by Samuel Rogers and the St. James Square group rather than by radicals like Keats and Leigh Hunt out in Hampstead. His first two ventures into literature, the *Salmagundi* papers, which he did with his Knickerbocker friends, and the *Knickerbocker's History of New York*, which caused Sir Walter Scott to laugh, were tinged with an American freshness which his compatriots missed in his later work. The "Author's Account of Himself" describes his literary personality, Geoffrey Crayon, Gent., the supposed author of *The Sketch Book*. It conforms to and echoes every English essayist from Addison to Goldsmith without losing its own integrity. Irving was the first American to conquer both the American and the British reading publics; this was an accomplishment. And, by a careful attention to the copyright laws of both countries, he managed to be, with intervals of statesmanship and historical writing, the first professional American man of letters.

But it was James Fenimore Cooper who knew most about the total situation confronting the American author, its incentives, its possibilities, its materials, its means, and its obstacles. By 1828 he had experimented with novels of English domestic life, the American Revolution, the frontier settlement, the sea, and the wilderness life of the Indian, he was widely read and greeted with mixed criticism both at home and abroad, he was already under attack for his political and social ideas, and he had gone to Europe to broaden the education of his children and to try to arrange for profitable foreign publication and translation of his writings. His *Notions of the Americans, Picked up by a Travelling Bachelor* of that year was a thinly disguised defense of American ideas and institutions against the attacks of British travellers and critics. His fictional device was an international club of travelling gentlemen of whom the author was presumably English, Cooper himself his American host in the person of John Cadwallader of up-state New York, and the ad-

dressee of the two letters on language and literature the Abbate
Giromachi of Florence, Italy. He speaks here with the authority
of the practitioner rather than the theorist, and his initial
enthusiasm for the literary life was still running high although,
as the first American to make a professional career of the novel
of American life, he already recognized the difficulties and
problems that lay in his path.

Two principal obstacles, Cooper thought, were delaying the
realization of a native literature: competition with the literature
of England and the poverty of native materials. "There is
scarcely an ore which contributes to the wealth of an author
that is found here in veins as rich as in Europe. There are no
annals for the historian; no follies (beyond the most vulgar and
commonplace) for the satirist; no manners for the dramatist; no
obscure fictions for the writer of romance; no gross and hardy
offences against decorum for the moralist; nor any of the rich
artificial auxiliaries of poetry." There is little doubt that Cooper
was here describing, in the person of his traveller, the obstacles
with which he had contended, but Cooper the writer did not
share his traveller's pessimism, as his experiments and relative
success in most of these departments of literature will testify.
That success, I feel, was due in part at least to the shift of American critical concern from literary patriotism to literary nationalism. The final step, to a literary nationalism which was also
universal, was yet to come.

By 1836 this movement was in full tide and the debate on literary nationalism began to dissolve into literary achievement.
Edgar Allan Poe entered the debate that year with his review in
the *Southern Literary Messenger* of the collected poems of Joseph
Rodman Drake and Fitz-Greene Halleck. Basing his definition
of *good* poetry squarely on his understanding of Coleridge's distinction between Imagination and Fancy, he calls to account
those American critics who welcome the work of an American
poet merely because it is American in setting and feeling and
reveals what Poe considers to be an inferior brand of the "poetic
sentiment." His distinction between poetry which is based on
mere comparison with nature and poetry which reveals a
higher moral or poetic truth takes little account of the Associa-

tionist emphasis on the value of immediate experience. Drake's "Culprit Fay" bears the brunt of his attack.

"We are bidden," he says, "to imagine a race of Fairies in the vicinity of West Point. . . . We are informed that an Ouphe of about an inch in height has committed a deadly sin in falling in love with a mortal maiden, who may, very possibly, be six feet in her stockings. . . . And he is therefore sentenced to what? To catch a spark from the tail of a falling star, and a drop of water from the belly of a sturgeon. What are his equipments for the first adventure? An acorn helmet, a thistle-down plume, a butterfly cloak, a lady-bug shield, cockle-seed spurs, and a fire-fly horse. . . . Such are the puerilities we daily find ourselves called upon to admire as among the loftiest efforts of the human mind, and which not to assign a rank with the matured and vigorous genius of England, is to prove ourselves at once a fool, a maligner, and no patriot."

Poe's own contribution to the national literature, he hoped, would be poetic in a different and more universal sense.

When Emerson, therefore, was invited the next year to deliver in his turn the annual Phi Beta Kappa oration at Cambridge, American critical theory and practice had at last merged, and he could plant his feet firmly on the foundations of an emerging American literary tradition. Building on the work of his predecessors, he carried the argument for a national literature to its extremest point: the freedom and integrity of the individual soul. Patriotism; Associationism; Idealism. "We have listened too long to the courtly muses of Europe," he told his listeners. "The spirit of the American freeman is already suspected to be timid, imitative, tame." But he also admonishes them that "the world is nothing, the man is all; . . . it is for you to dare all," so that "a nation of men will for the first time exist, because each believes himself inspired by the Divine Soul which also inspires all men." The argument for literary nationalism had run full circle and had finally substituted the achievement of a genuine native literature for the problem of how to bring such a literature into being. The way was now open for Hawthorne and Melville, Thoreau and Whitman, and their inheritors to our day.

5 | THE ROOTS OF NATIONAL CULTURE TO 1830: THE FIRST FRONTIER

However long it took me to confront fully the problem of American cultural identity for itself, I found myself immediately committed to a career of defining and writing the new American literary history. The opportunity to "begin at the beginning" was, like so many crucial turns in my course, an accident of chance. Although not a specialist in the Colonial period, I was invited to contribute the first volume of American Literature: A Period Anthology, *edited by Oscar Cargill (4 volumes, New York: The Macmillan Company, 1933). I began with the writings of the early colonists, moved on to the makers of the new nation, and concluded in 1830 with Irving and Cooper. The songs and tales of the Indians formed an appendix, the first time that the voice of the aborigines was heard as the earliest American literature.*

This was my first use of the organic image of cyclic growth in the study of literary history. It was also my first attempt to deal with literature as the expression of a people in a time and place. The four stages I found in the growth of the literature of the Atlantic seaboard colonies seemed reflected in the stages of natural growth: the root, the sprout, the trunk and branches, and the leaves and flowers.

By about 1760, the frontier had pretty much completed the settlement of the eastern seaboard and had begun to move west. There had been the first stage of confronting the native inhabitants and reporting in "letters home" the conditions of the new civilization; the second stage of political and religious controversy had followed with the issues of Puritanism and Rationalism and the establishment of Church and State in various forms in the individual colonies. The third stage of developing an imitative literature had appeared only sporadically by the time of the Revolution; a fully mature native literature was still to come.

American literature was as cosmopolitan in its origins as it has been in its mature developments. Most of its distinguishing characteristics may be traced by one channel or another to European tradition. Our national culture, with the exception of the Indian, Negro, and Mongol strains in it, is a product of the migrations of the Western European peoples. The substratum of folksong, legend, and dance, which is present in all literatures, occurs in that of the United States chiefly among the Indians and, in a transplanted form, among the Negroes and the pioneers. Our literature of conscious art is largely derivative, or is a product of the impact of older cultures on a new environment.

The importance of the frontier movement in the later periods of American literature has received deserved emphasis, but the larger meaning of that movement as a phase in the westward progress of European civilization does not always receive the attention it deserves. In this larger view, the settlement of the eastern seaboard is the first chapter in the history of the American frontier, the explorers are the earliest pioneers, and the explorations of the interior by the French and Spanish are footnotes to that chapter. The first mature literary culture in America, the romantic movement which culminated in the writings of Emerson and his contemporaries, grew in the soil of the thirteen original colonies. There is some doubt as to whether the literature of the continental nation, as it was heralded by Walt Whitman, has even yet reached its maturity.

The first stage of literary culture in any primitive environment is the initial impact of the old upon the new. The pioneer blazes his trail and the settler follows with his ax. If these men write, their eyes look westward and they record first impressions and primitive emotional responses. They write narratives of discovery and settlement, and songs and ballads of the trail and camp.

The second stage of literary growth on the frontier results from the effort of men to make homes for themselves in the new environment. With group settlements of a more or less permanent nature, men begin to exchange their ideas and impressions among themselves. They discuss political, social, and religious problems. The local news sheet prints stories and verse copied from journals the pioneer has brought with him from his former home, and each community soon produces its own story-tellers and its own bards. Eyes have already begun to look back to the land of origin, and there is a curious and crude mingling of the old with the new. The back-trail movement is already suggested, and with it, conscious literary production begins. The crude materials of the new environment are rough-hewn into the traditional forms.

The third stage in the progress toward culture is a sudden revulsion from the crudities of the new environment. The settler has become homesick for his racial past, and he goes back to the eastern sources of wisdom and beauty in order to improve his condition. Physically he remains the man of the frontier; mentally he has become the complete back-trailer. Whether he be Brockden Brown with his eyes on England, or William Dean Howells with his eyes on Boston, his mind and heart are those of the back-trailer.

The final stage is that in which civilization strikes root in new soil and sends out its own branches. The materials of the new environment are no longer rough-hewn into old forms. Life has matured and its expression is complete— both old and new at once, and in harmony. The new environment is understood for itself and finds its own expression in accord with tradition.

If we apply this process to American literary history, we find all four stages represented in the period which we are studying here. The explorers and settlers of the eastern seaboard mark the first stage with their narratives of adventure. The process of settlement continued in these terms until the wall of the Appalachian Mountains and the resentful Indians together arrested the pioneer and brought about a permanent settlement along the coast from Boston to Charleston. Without too arbitrary an insistence upon dates, we may fix this period as extending from 1492 to about 1700. The second stage extends from 1700 to about 1760. During this time the settlers were developing their communities, establishing their first schools, printing their first newspapers, magazines, and books, debating their political, social, and religious ideals, collecting their libraries by importation from Europe, and in general adjusting their desire for a civilized life to an environment which was not yet ready to supply all the amenities of civilization. The third stage extends from 1760 to the close of the century and beyond. The Revolutionary War was the result and not the cause of adolescent pride in awakening powers and knowledge. The desire for independence is the first sign of manhood. In literary history, the characteristic production of this period is not so much the controversial writing of patriots and Tories as a sudden torrent of novels, verse, plays, and essays in imitation of English and continental classics and best-sellers. The back-trailer movement was the determining factor in spite of a strong and growing spirit of nationalism. In the terms of literary criticism, this was predominantly a period of convention because even romantic writings were imitative and therefore in the spirit of convention. The final stage is marked by the beginning of an American romantic movement in the work of Channing, Bryant, Cooper, Irving, and their contemporaries. These men were divided in their cultural loyalties between a growing comprehension of the meaning of the American environment and a romantic interest in European culture. Put Cooper's *The Pioneers* beside his *The Bravo*, and the conflict in their minds is vividly illustrated. The essay in exhortation for a national literature was invariably written by a man who respected and feared Europe while he loved and overrated America.

American literature reached its first maturity in the Concord and Cambridge groups and in the work of Poe, Melville, Whittier, Boker, and Simms, between 1820 and 1850. The evolutionary development was thus allowed to complete its cycle on the Atlantic seaboard at the same time that the process was being repeated in the first of its four stages, but this time against the

background of the whole nation, with pioneers like Daniel
Boone and Davy Crockett.

The only native literature with which the white settlers came
into direct contact was that of the Indians. These races, originally nomadic, had developed a settled habit of life by the end
of the fifteenth century when the mistake of calling them Indians was first made by the searchers for a Western trade route to
the source of spices. In the Southwest and in Mexico they had
built up a civilization which was comparable in its level of culture to many of those of Europe and Asia. The tribes of the
Atlantic seacoast had developed a less complex civilization, but
they had nevertheless a sense of tribal unity, of political, economic, and social organization and at least an oral literature of
their own. Indians figure in the works of Freneau, Paulding,
Cooper, and even Longfellow, not so much for what they were
as for what the white man believed them to be. Only recently
has their culture been at all understood for itself and absorbed
into our literary tradition.

The Indian provides the first element in the cosmopolitan
origins of our literature; the explorers and early settlers, the
second. America was discovered and settled first by Spaniards;
the French were as active as the English during the seventeenth
century; and the Dutch, the Swedes, and almost all the other
races of Europe made their contributions to the westward
migration which established the white man on our shores. Even
today a cursory study of the Atlantic seaboard will reveal cultural survivals of the Spaniards in Florida, of the Dutch in New
York, of the Germans in Pennsylvania, and of the French in
southeastern Canada. The Mississippi Valley has not entirely
forgotten its French origins; and the Southwest and far West are
still proud of their Spanish traditions. To forget Columbus,
Coronado, Champlain, and their fellows is to ignore vital factors in the story of America's cultural origins. But like that of
the Indians, the part which these early adventurers contributed
to the ground work of our literary history has only recently
been recognized as our heritage in the writings of Willa Cather,
Archibald MacLeish, and Mary Austin and of the historians,
archaeologists, and anthropologists.

Our principal attention must therefore still be directed to the small band of English settlers on the Atlantic seaboard. The dogged perseverance of the Puritans and the serene confidence of the Quakers in the face of appalling obstacles leaves the modern mind aghast. Less unifed perhaps, but none the less enduring were the motives for settlement in the South. The Catholic cavaliers of Maryland and the Virginia gentlemen shaped the destinies of these colonies in the early days, but the middle-class pioneer and small farmer did the actual work of clearing the forests and of laying the foundations for an agricultural society in the South as they did in the North. The progress of these English tradesmen and farmers from the bare conquest of a wilderness to a state stable enough for the luxuries of culture was slow. The Spaniards, the French, and the Elizabethan seamen gayly transplanted their cultures and went home again, leaving them to decay and to survive only in memory and in written record. The English middle class were less concerned with the amenities; they laid the foundations of a new state in religious, economic, and social adjustment to a primitive environment, and, with their German and Scots-Irish neighbors, left the development of culture to their descendants of later generations.

With such origins, the Colonial mind could hardly be unified. Its predominant characteristic is diversity rather than unanimity of opinion on questions of first importance to man on this earth. No men could be more at odds in their readings of life than were John Smith and John Winthrop, Cotton Mather and William Byrd. Puritanism was only one, even though probably the most enduring, of many elements in seventeenth- and eighteenth-century thought in America. Even within Puritanism itself the strict Calvinism of the Massachusetts Bay Colony is offset by a liberalism among the Plymouth colonists, which historians have traced back to John Wyclif and his Lollard priests of Chaucerian England. Except for the Quaker influence in Pennsylvania, the dominant trait of the middle and southern colonists was a practical interest in the problems of this world, which led them to science, agriculture, the law, society, and politics. It was the blending of this secular practicality and rationality with the disciplined idealism of New England that laid the philosophical foundations for the political thinking of the revolutionary period.

The four colonies which did most to determine colonial thought were Massachusetts, Virginia, Pennsylvania, and New York. The other nine were either offshoots from these four or strongly influenced by them. New York and Virginia were basically cavalier and aristocratic; Pennsylvania and Massachusetts, middle class and democratic. The Church of England had its greatest following in the first pair; the dissenting sects in the second. New York was distinguished from Virginia in that its social organization was created by the dutch patroons, whereas that in the South was modeled on an English pattern. Pennsylvania's differences from Massachusetts were not social. Penn, himself a landed proprietor at home, attracted to his following the same classes of tradesmen and farmers that came over in the *Mayflower* and the *Arbella*. Difference in religious beliefs, however, shaped their social attitudes and made the resultant colonies very different in character.

Virginia and Massachusetts have retained their distinctive characters even to the present; and at least one cause of the Civil War seems to have been the clash between their sectional interests and ideals. Paulding recognized this situation as early as 1812 when he likened the "Southland" to the ticklish toes, and the "Down East" to the ticklish nose, of the nation. But by his time the New York proprietors had lost their influence because of their Tory sympathies, and the "Middlelands" could be characterized as "steady, sober-minded farmers." The "Far West" was to him a vague region of little character at all. The colonial writers of Massachusetts and of Virginia each strongly reflect their respective backgrounds of religious, social, and economic ideals. New York and Pennsylvania writers reveal backgrounds almost as narrowly determined in the early days, but by the end of the eighteenth century the sharper lines in their thought had been softened; and it was they who first attempted an orderly expression of their lives in literary and other art forms. The so-called "Philadelphia" and "Knickerbocker" groups were the first to take literature seriously and for its own sake.

The story of the New England church-state is told in the rise
and fall of the Mather dynasty through four generations. The
dogmatism of Richard Mather and John Cotton, the founders of
the family, is mild when compared to that of their grandson and
namesake, Cotton Mather. They and their contemporaries,
however, accepted fully the doctrine that the Puritans were a
second chosen people and that Massachusetts was a new
Canaan. Life in this world was shaped in terms of rewards and
punishments in the next, meted out by a God who was just in
the old Judaic sense and whose praise was sung by poets from
Michael Wigglesworth to Robert Frost. From the Mayflower
Compact to the Half-Way Covenant of 1662, the progress of
American Puritanism is marked by an increasing determination
on the part of a few strong-willed leaders to establish a Holy
Commonwealth in fact as well as in theory. The wars with the
Indians without and Satan within were holy wars which culminated in the witchcraft trials at the end of the century, an example of religious fanaticism that can only be explained by a zeal
born of desperation and fear. The greatest of the Captains of the
Lord was Increase Mather, of the second generation. His was a
war with heresy which had become organized in the defiance
of the Brattle Street Group and the Stoddardeans during the
final decade of the century; but with the revocation of the Massachusetts charter in 1692 the temporal authority of the church
came to an end. The zeal of its leaders was vainly intensified in
Cotton Mather, of the third generation, who lived his best years
during this period of loss of power. His history and defense of
the movement, the *Magnalia*, has aptly been termed by Schnei-
der to have been, "even at the time of its publication in 1702, little more than a ponderous monument erected over a dead
cause." Increase Mather died in 1723, Cotton in 1728. Samuel
Mather, of the fourth generation, carried on the war with his
Apology for the Liberties of the Churches in New England (1738), but
temporal power was gone.

The fall of the church-state in New England may be interpreted, in political terms, as the failure of an oligarchic dictatorship
to master a people of independent spirit. But the deeper causes
of its failure lie buried in the creed upon which it was founded.

The desire for liberty of conscience which brought the Pilgrims to America was the seed of that critical independence of mind which flowered in the rationalism of Franklin and Paine, and not in the determinism of the Mathers. The Puritans were better organized in the early days than were their antagonists, but the latter were nonetheless vocal and persistent, and the end of the Colonial period is marked by their complete triumph.

The first step in the destruction of Puritan authority came from within the Massachusetts Bay Colony itself in the Arminian and Antinomian heresies, in the persons of the early radicals, and in the political liberalism which grew out of the attacks on church government. Thomas Hooker was a mild liberal, but Roger Williams, the most influential of these early radicals, attacked both the dogma and the organization of the church-state. In the "Bloudy Tenent" controversy with John Cotton, he assailed the root of that dogma, the doctrine of "persecution for cause of conscience." But Williams was primarily a political and social rather than a religious thinker. The enduring significance of his revolt lies rather in his substitution of the social compact for the divine right theory of the state, whereby he laid the foundations for Jeffersonian democracy. Like Williams, John Wise began his revolt on theological grounds, but his real interest was in the institutional rather than the doctrinal problems of the church, and his thought led to similar conclusions. In the revolt of these two men, and in the broad tolerance of William Penn, may readily be discovered the roots of the political idealism which brought about the Revolutionary War and determined the character of our government.

A more philosophical form of reasoning, the analytical study of science and natural phenomena, disturbed the Calvinistic integrity of the two ablest defenders of the faith, Cotton Mather and Jonathan Edwards, the former in his age and the latter in his youth. More serious, however, was the call to reason as opposed to authoritarian dogma which was early heard outside the fold of the elect. Robert Calef made a direct attack upon the witchcraft fanaticism of the Mathers, but his mind was not sufficiently orderly to produce a positive philosophy as a substitute for that which he scorned. It was Benjamin Franklin and his friends in the Middle and Southern colonies who first accomplished a satisfactory transition from dogma to reason. Although the term "philosopher" was perhaps applied more frequently to Franklin, both at home and abroad, than to any other American of his day, he was not a metaphysician in the strict sense. His was a natural philosophy, the product of an objective curiosity about nature and a belief in man. Although his earlier essays contain a clear statement of a deistic creed, he was more utilitarian than contemplative in his habit of mind. He was a pragmatist a century before the term was invented, and he formulated a creed and a philosophy in order to use rather than to enjoy them. Having established an objective nature, he proceeded to devote his attention to its scientific analysis, an impulse which Mather and Edwards had felt before him, but without the same philosophical justification. After convincing himself of the free will of man by arguing its contrary, he turned the moral zeal of his ancestors toward teaching him how to live happily and profitably in this world rather than to prepare for the next. His belief in a benevolent God of limited powers allowed him to take that personage for granted in his interesting and active daily life; while his spirit of inquiry stimulated an intense activity in the sciences of botany, medicine, and electricity, particularly in Philadelphia in the work of men like John Bartram and Benjamin Rush, during the years immediately before and after the war.

The deism of Tom Paine, in his *Age of Reason* 1793-95), was of a more methaphysical nature than was that of Franklin. During his sojourn in America, Paine thought more about politics than religion or philosophy, but his *Age of Reason* is so logical a climax to his earlier radicalism that it must be claimed for American literature if the political pamphlets on the Revolutionary War are included. Entirely unoriginal as it was, this tract carried the thought of French and English rationalists to the banks of the Ohio and the mountains of Kentucky.

Similar in its inquiring spirit and its emphasis on common sense was the philosophy which found congenial soil at Princeton after the advent of President Witherspoon in 1768. It must be remembered that Brackenridge, Freneau, and Madison were among the students who came under this influence, just as Godfrey and Hopkinson came under a similar influence at the infant University of Pennsylvania; and the seething political activity of these undergraduates bears testimony to the absence of other-worldliness in their intellectual life. Calvinism had little power in the states of Pennsylvania and New Jersey when the minds of Franklin, Mason, Jefferson, Adams, Hamilton, and their fellows were transmuting these "common sense" philosophies into the system of government and the social organization which gave first form to the national character.

The philosophical idealism which early developed, both within and without the fold of Calvinism, has even more place in American literary history than have these more materialistic schools of thought because, in its late development in the minds of Emerson and the Concord transcendentalists, it became one of the most vital factors in the romantic movement in this country. Its influence had already been clearly felt in New England before Bishop Berkeley came to Newport, Rhode Island, in 1729 and discussed with his American friends the theory that matter does not exist. His threat to the dogmatic and authoritarian position of the New England Calvinists lay rather in the incentive he gave to free and speculative thought than in any fundamental heresy in his system. But there was no holy war; the danger was too far-reaching to be immediately alarming. Berkeley made few American friends or disciples except Samuel Johnson, tutor at Yale and later president of King's College (Columbia). Franklin revealed his sympathy with the movement by assuming the expense of printing the latter's *Elementa Philosophica*, which was used as a text at both Columbia and the College in Philadelphia.

As an undergraduate at Yale, Jonathan Edwards expressed, in his paper *Of Being*, an idealism almost identical with that of Berkeley, but investigation has failed to prove that there was any direct influence of the English philosopher upon him. Rather, we may attribute the early liberalism, which later hardened into a dogmatic Calvinism, to his reading of Locke and other rationalist philosophers in college. His youthful experiences during a personal religious awakening led him to a mysticism not unlike that of Woolman and the Quakers. The "sense of divine things" of which he writes in his personal narrative brought to him a humility that was intense and immediate. There was no intermediary authority, either of Bible or minister, between his own soul and the spirit of beauty which was his God. The Judaism of the Mathers broke down before the intensity of this personal experience, and the last of the great Puritan divines prostrated his spirit before the "fresh Visitations of Heavenly Love," of which the Quaker Woolman wrote with such singleness of heart. That early evangelical revival at Northampton, which has been termed the "Great Awakening," was the result, when Edwards himself became the authority that administered justice and the spirit of the Mathers returned. But his mysticism never entirely left him, and it prepared the way, a century later, for the intensely personal religion of William Ellery Channing and the Unitarians, and later for the revolt of Emerson, an arch-rebel among rebels, who finally declared that self-reliance rather than reliance upon book and dogma was the only key to salvation.

During the century between Edwards and Channing there was little development of idealism as a metaphysical system. The issues which led up to the Revolutionary War, and the problems of reconstruction, turned men's minds from abstractions to more materialistic habits of thought. There was, however, one counter-movement, in spirit akin to Edwards' most extreme mysticism. Between 1738 and 1769, George Whitefield, one of the most enthusiastic and compelling followers of Wesley, made seven trips to America in order to preach the Evangelical revival. An enemy to common sense and dogma alike, Whitefield made many converts to the faith which comes from emotional conviction. The movement took firmest root in the South, but its influence was felt throughout the colonies, and at least a slight connection may be traced between it and the more intellectual liberalism of Channing.

Channing's attack on Calvinism was direct and vigorous. Slight in body, but silver-tongued, his persuasive eloquence carried the younger elements in New England with him when,

in his Baltimore sermon of 1819, he gave the Unitarian revolt its
first clear definition. Abroad, his name was linked with those of
Irving and Cooper in the first group of writers in that national
literature for which he pleaded so earnestly. As a literary critic,
his work was limited to a few reviews in the *Christian Examiner*,
and it all was colored by his religious convictions. But his
thought gave courage to the fearful and provided a metaphysical reason for independence, a valuable supplement to the
political independence derived from the common sense rationalism of Franklin.

The political events that caused the Revolutionary War
focused all of Colonial thought on an immediate and practical
issue. It was not difficult to lead the various types of individualism developed by Roger Williams, Jonathan Edwards, and Benjamin Franklin up to Tom Paine's succinct conclusion: "'Tis
repugnant to reason, to the universal order of things; to all
examples from former ages, to suppose, that this continent can
long remain subject to any external power." He cut the issue
clearly: "Should the colonies remain a part of the British
Empire, or should they not?" His answer was that they should
not, and this he called common sense; but not all his intelligent
compatriots saw the problem in so white a light. John Dickinson, temperamentally a conservative, was whipped into the
rebel position by what he believed to be unjust taxation. Franklin made up his mind slowly and gave his love of conciliation
full play. Jefferson, the wisest political philosopher in the rebel
camp, reasoned himself to a firm conviction in democracy and
wrote arguments similar to Paine's into the Declaration of Independence. Samuel Adams and Patrick Henry were born agita-
tors, and rebellion came easily to them. But lawyers and
statesmen like Alexander Hamilton, John Adams, and James
Wilson reached a similar point of view less hastily; for not all
political radicals favored a break with England, not all conser-
vatives were Tories. The revolutionary issue was less one of reasoned political philosophy than an indignation against tyranny
in a specific case. Rebels were not all Democrats, nor were all
Tories Federalists, when the later issue, the best form for the
new government to take, shaped itself into a clash between liberal and conservative thinkers.

The Loyalists fell into such extreme disfavor after the break with England that their writings have received less emphasis than they deserve. Samuel Seabury, the first American bishop of the Protestant Episcopal Church, was a man of cultivated mind and the author of a number of vigorous sermons and political tracts. William Smith, the first Provost of the College in Philadelphia, was a thorough liberal in his thought on religion, education, and politics, but his oath of personal allegiance to the King made it impossible for him, as it was for Seabury, to indorse absolute separation. Jonathan Boucher, also an Anglican clergyman, gave perhaps the most vigorous expression to toryism in sober prose, as did Jonathan Odell in satire and Joseph Galloway in pamphlets almost as vigorous as Paine's. Nor were the Loyalists without their verse apologists, as the ballads of the Revolutionary War will bear witness.

The poetry of the so-called "Hartford Wits" reveals clearly the distinction which must be made between the revolutionary and the national issues. Conservative as Dwight was in theology, he joined with Trumbull, Barlow, and their lesser associates in patriotic zeal and the spirit of rebellion. But Barlow alone of the group was a Democrat in the post-revolutionary days. His later poems and pamphlets are as radical as his earlier, and his visit to France made him follow Paine's thought in most matters of importance to government and religion.

The literary groups of New Jersey and Pennsylvania were similarly divided upon the two issues. Francis Hopkinson was a Loyalist up to the eve of the war, devoted his poetry to the cause of revolution, and served the Federalists with his prose satire after the peace. Philip Freneau was, however, a rebel and later a Jeffersonian Democrat, as was his college mate, Brackenridge.

Although there were many shades of opinion on the national issue between Democracy and Federalism, the extreme spokesmen of the two groups were respectively Thomas Jefferson and Alexander Hamilton. John Adams was a Federalist of milder stamp than Hamilton, and James Madison joined with the latter in the series of papers which took its name from that of the party in whose support it was published.

Jeffersonian Democracy in its purest form rests upon faith in the integrity, idealism, and capacity for self-government of the average man. It was suggested in the thought of Williams, Wise, Penn, and other early radicals, but it came to America, in 1775, in an almost unpolluted stream from the French encyclopaedists. The political philosophy in its application to the immediate situation in America found perhaps its briefest statement in the Declaration of Independence. Hamilton's *The Federalist* served a similar purpose for the opposing belief that man is selfish and ignorant and that he requires a strong and arbitrary government to regulate his actions. The war between these two political philosophies shaped the early and influenced all the later years of our national life. Their effect upon our literature was indirect, as most of our early literary men were not active in politics after the turn of the century, but Cooper, Irving, Bryant, and many others were strongly influenced by their political sympathies.

By the middle of the eighteenth century, therefore, the men of our first frontier had marked out the geographical and mental boundaries of a new civilization and had laid foundations in political, social, economic, religious, and philosophical thought upon which we as a nation have been building ever since. The time was ripe for the later generations to turn to the amenities of a more settled and cultured life.

6 | THE AWAKENING OF LITERARY CONSCIOUSNESS, 1760-1830

This is the second half of the introduction to The Roots of National Culture *(1931), and with it my theory of the development of a new literature on the western frontier of Europe began to take shape. Although there had been sporadic attempts at what was then known as "polite literature" or "belles lettres" (i.e., writing with aesthetic purposes and forms in mind) all through the Colonial period, the sudden burst of energy immediately after the Revolution in all the young cities of the eastern seaboard can only be explained by the enthusiasm of a discovered national identity. "Now that we are free and independent in the great world of nations, we should have a literature at least as great as the others!"*

The sad part of the story is that originality cannot be produced overnight. What resulted was of course a great flood of imitative novels, plays, epics, and Addisonian essays that echoed the neoclassic-romantic battles of Britain and the Continent with only the insistence on native themes and ideas to make them American. The third stage of development — imitative "belles lettres" — lasted from the morning after the Revolution until about 1830-35, when suddenly such writers as Irving, Cooper, Bryant, and Poe appeared. The new nation had by then at least the beginnings of a great literature of its own.

The novelty of this approach to our literary history was not fully appreciated at the time The Roots *appeared, but unconscious agreement is the surest form of flattery; and if what I have just explained seems now quite obvious, it was not so in 1930, a century after literary autonomy had been achieved.*

The development of a conscious literary culture is the natural consequence of the action of civilization upon frontier conditions. The colonies were slow in reaching this stage in evolution, but by 1760 there were sufficient schools, colleges, literary societies, libraries, printing presses, and theatres to create a public taste for literature and a source of income for literary men. George Sandys, English treasurer of the Jamestown colony, published in 1626 a translation of Ovid's *Metamorphoses,* a part of which he had made during his short residence in Virginia, Benjamin Tompson deliberately elected the life of a poet and suffered the natural consequences in the uncongenial New England cultural climate, and the mystical lyrics of Edward Taylor remained unpublished until more than two centuries after his death in 1729. Even Benjamin Franklin, who perhaps did more than anyone else to prepare the way for an American literature, both in his own work and in his reprints of English novels, was himself primarily a man of affairs and not of books. Charles Brockden Brown was the first American seriously to attempt the profession of literature. The six novels, the dialogue, and the monthly magazine which he produced between 1798 and 1804 were offered to a reasonably large public which had been educated in American schools and nurtured on American reprints of English literary works. The foundations of a national literature were firm enough to make the erection of a superstructure seem practicable. The architecture of that building was English.

By 1764, there were already six colleges in the colonies. First, Harvard, which was authorized by the general court of Massachusetts in 1636 and graduated its first class in 1642, and William and Mary, established in Virginia in 1693, are the only colleges which date from the seventeenth century. In 1700, however, the more liberal Calvinists withdrew from Harvard and made their contribution to the decline of Puritan authority by the founding of Yale the following year. The University of Pennsylvania (1740), Princeton (1746), and Columbia (1754) complete the list. The University of Pennsylvania was the only one of them which was nonsectarian, and religious training was almost as large a part of their early curricula as was education in the seven liberal arts. Latin, Greek, philosophy, and mathematics provided the secular training which had long been the rule in English secondary schools, and the standards of attainment were approximately those of Eton, Harrow, or Westminster. There was little study of English or other modern literatures, almost none of history or geography, and comparatively little of natural science. Nevertheless, these eighteenth-century colleges provided the Hellenic attitude toward culture which was necessary before other than theological and practical ideals for the mental life could be openly accepted.

The founding of literary societies and circulating libraries had an even more immediate effect than the colleges in arousing colonial interest in cultural ideals and problems. The plantation aristocrats of the South like William Byrd of Westover and Massachusetts theologians like Cotton Mather, who confesses to "a mighty Thirst after the Sight of Books," had large private collections which contained works of "belles lettres" as well as of philosophy and history, but their influence did not extend far beyond their owners. Boston had a short-lived public library in 1656, but Franklin seems to have been the first to have developed the plan of collecting books for even a limited public circulation. Between 1730 and 1760 his Junto society for the discussion of science, literature, morals, and religion led to the establishment of the Library Company of Philadelphia (1731), the Redwood Library of Newport (1747), the Library Society of Charleston (1748), and that of New York (1754). The libraries of Harvard and Yale were large enough by the middle of the century to issue catalogues, and that of the New York Society Library (1793) listed five thousand titles. Boston, Salem, and other cities had literary clubs or libraries early in the century, one result of which was the incorporation of the Boston Athenaeum in 1807. The national government had a library as early as 1800, but it was not until after its destruction by fire in 1814 and the subsequent purchase of Jefferson's books that the Library of Congress was more than a reference collection for the use of members. By 1829 it ranked fourth in the country.

The groups which founded these libraries were invariably composed of the moneyed classes, who seem suddenly to have awakened to the intellectual and cultural poverty of the

country. Their interests were chiefly theological, political, and
scientific, but volumes of Shakespeare, Milton, Richardson,
Goldsmith, Johnson, and other English authors, both classic and
contemporary, frequently found their places on shelves
weighted down by collections of travels, ancient history, and
moral philosophy. The shelves grew lighter with works of contemporary novelists and poets as the century advanced, but
such strictly literary clubs as Brockden Brown's Belles Lettres
Club, the Anthology Club of Boston, and the Authors' Club of
New York, which was founded in 1837 with Irving as president,
did not appear in great numbers until well after 1800. Nor must
we forget the traditional lure of light fiction for the weaker sex,
which, late in the century, broke the bonds of the stern colonial
ideals of womanhood and flooded the country with imported
and reprinted novels and fireside journals. It was Cooper's habit
of reading such books to his wife and daughters that suggested
the career of a novelist to him.

In spite of strict censorship and discouraging economic conditions, printing was among the first of the arts to be practiced
by the colonists. Stephen Day set up a press at Cambridge in
1638 and printed, among other things, *The Bay Psalm Book* and a
translation of the Bible into the language of the Indians. In the
century which followed, presses were set up in Boston, New
York, New London, Philadelphia, and Ephrata, Pennsylvania.
When Franklin first arrived in Philadelphia in 1723, he had a
choice of at least two established printers to whom he might
apply for employment.

Perhaps the most serious handicap that our early writers had
to contend with was the lack of regular publishers. Colonial
books by Americans were at first regularly printed in London,
as were the poems of Anne Bradstreet in 1650, but Franklin was
printing books by 1740. Other printers did the same, but they
seem to have shown little interest in those by American writers,
preferring the sure sales of the classics and of English novels
and poetry. Pirated editions of English books steadily increased,
and the first American copyright law in 1790 failed of its intention of helping American authors because it merely made their
work more costly than that of others. Usually an author had to

pay for the publication of his own work and stand the risk of sales. He might contract with a printer like John Wiley or Mathew Carey to do it or he might turn to a bookseller like William Caritat of New York. The bookseller might run an advertisement in the local press for a few days and arrange with agents in a few other cities to do the same, but the book-trade had little organization. Freneau's advice to authors to graft their authorship upon some other calling has the bitter ring of personal experience. It was a usual practice before 1800 and often led to the abandonment of authorship entirely. There were practical reasons why the promising start that was made in the last decade of the century petered out. There were insufficient readers of books to make the profession of letters pay, and there were inadequate means of reaching those that there were.

The product of the colonial presses consisted chiefly of broadsides and pamphlets. An attempt to print a newspaper in Boston in 1690 was suppressed, and it was not until 1704 that the first successful paper, the *Boston News-Letter*, appeared. Seven other newspapers had at least survived their infancy when Franklin established the *Pennsylvania Gazette* in 1729, and there were successful ventures of the kind in Boston, New York, Philadelphia, Annapolis, Williamsburg, and Charleston by 1836.

These newspapers did little to encourage literature except by increasing the reading public and thus preparing the way for the monthly journals. The first of these, the *American Magazine*, published in 1741 by Andrew Bradford, was quickly followed in the same year by Franklin's *General Magazine and Historical Chronicle*. Both had ceased publication by the end of the year, but the experiment attracted attention, and by 1760 ten other journals had at least continued through short runs in Boston, New York, and Philadelphia. By 1800, the total had swelled to over eighty. The figure is, however, somewhat misleading, for the term of their average life was so brief that there was seldom any alarming competition between them. Among their editors we may count Tom Paine, Mathew Carey, Noah Webster, Philip Freneau, and Brockden Brown. In the encouragement of literature Joseph Dennie was the most successful of them all in his conduct of the *Port Folio* (1801-11). Irving edited the *Analectic*

Magazine from 1813 to 1814, and the first of the successful reviews, the *North American,* made its appearance in 1815. The great age of the *Knickerbocker, Graham's, Godey's Lady's Book,* and the *New York Mirror* was yet to come, when original contributions were in such demand that Poe, Paulding, Willis, and even Cooper turned from books to the periodical press for a chief means of support. The vogues of sentimental poetry and the short story between 1825 and 1850 undoubtedly owe much to this influence.

As we turn the musty pages of the earlier journals, we may wonder how they could have encouraged literature. Even in their own day the small type in double columns and the lack of artistic quality in their borrowed contents must have done little to stimulate reading. No wonder their lives were short; but their influence was far reaching. Although interested chiefly in politics, the editors summoned the ghosts of Addison and Pope to stalk their pages; and dramatic criticism began to appear as soon as there were plays to criticize. The ideal of almost all of them was the establishment of an American *Gentleman's Magazine,* and men and women who could still recall the hardship of breaking a wilderness were summoned to the enjoyment of relaxed indolence in a London club. Flowers of literature may be transplanted from another's garden, but they will be somewhat wilted when they first dig their roots into a strange soil. Borrowing—imitation—creation—these are the normal stages of growth in a transplanted as contrasted with an indigenous national literature. By 1760 the magazines had prepared our reading and writing public for the second of them.

Although a trifle later in maturing, the American theatre had a strikingly parallel growth. Plays had been written or acted in the colonies, chiefly by college students, before 1767. Recorded dramatic performances of one kind or another date from 1713, and Governor Richard Hunter published in 1714 a play which was never acted. Lewis Hallam and his "American" company arrived in 1752 and produced old plays in the principal cities for six years, when his company was reorganized under Douglass. Thomas Godfrey, a college student, doubtless saw them in 1754 when they went to Philadelphia, and was stimulated to write a play of his own. His friend, Francis Hopkinson, adapted *The Masque of Alfred* and produced it with his fellow students in the old English fashion during the Christmas holidays of 1756-57. The first original play to be presented by a professional company was Thomas Godfrey's tragedy of blood, *The Prince of Parthia*, performed "by the American Company, at the New Theatre in Southwark [Philadelphia], on Friday, the twenty-fourth of April [1767]." Williamsburg and Charleston were also early theatrical centers, but censorship in Boston practically excluded dramatic activity from that city during the greater part of the eighteenth century. Even in Philadelphia, a city ordinance caused history to repeat itself by banishing the earliest performance to a new-world Southwark which, like Shakespeare's, was just outside the city limits. From 1774 to 1784 the Continental Congress discouraged all dramatic performances, although the officers of both armies occasionally amused themselves with such diversions. The real history of the American theater begins in 1784 when the younger Hallam returned with his company, and Royall Tyler's *The Contrast*, the first dramatic treatment of an American theme, was produced three years later. Before 1830, William Dunlap, James Nelson Barker, John Howard Payne, Washington Irving, and Robert Montgomery Bird had written plays which were produced by Hallam, Forrest, and others and which are worthy of inclusion in literary history.

Although not strictly a part of this history, the development of the art of painting by Benjamin West and his followers so nearly coincides in date with these other movements that it may be considered a part of the same story, and under Jefferson's inspiration there was a strong classical movement in American architecture. Nor is the sudden increase, about 1760, in the emigration of American students of law and medicine to England for training an unrelated fact. American eyes were at last turned eastward to the traditional homes of wisdom and culture.

With the establishment of these means for culture, the early stages in the development of American literature on our first frontier may be declared at an end. Two decades before they united as an independent nation, the colonies had laid the foundation for a national literature and art. American writers were at last conscious of literary ideals and were eager in their experimentation in literary forms. The Revolutionary War is an incident which first delayed and afterwards stimulated this progress.

This period produced a body of essays, poems, novels, short stories, and plays which bear the unifying stamp of a purely literary movement. Sectional divisions may be considered as of secondary importance; political, social, economic, and philosophical movements may be examined as background rather than for themselves.

The distinguishing characteristics of this movement are that in mode and form it was almost completely imitative of classical and contemporary English and, to a far lesser extent, continental literatures; that it showed a marked interest in tradition, which was balanced by a growing curiosity about the literary possibilities of native materials and ideas; that it developed in the various colonies literary groups of surprisingly similar tastes and ideals; and that it laid the foundations for a romantic movement of primarily native origin and growth. The search for a satisfactory critical term to apply to this movement presents insurmountable difficulties. It might be called a classical period if by that term we mean only a search for standards, a concern with form, and an effort to imitate and adapt rather than to explore and experiment. Certainly its motivating impulses were those of convention rather than of revolt, but so many of the favorite models of these writers were romantic that the traditional uses of these terms could lead only to paradox and confusion. It is probably safer to characterize the period as one of an awakening of literary consciousness through imitation of old forms and exploitation of new material.

English literature in 1760 was at the beginning of a half-century of transition from the most classical to the most romantic period it has ever known. In the distant background were the masters of the past, notably Shakespeare, Milton, and Dryden, the fame of Chaucer and Spenser being for the moment under clouds. In the nearer distance were the masters of the formal essay and poem, of criticism and of satire, Defoe, Pope, Addison, Swift, and their fellows. Among elder contemporaries or recent masters were Samuel Johnson, Goldsmith, and the novelists Richardson, Fielding, Sterne, and the bluestocking ladies. The romantic impulse had already been felt in the poetry of Thomson, Gray, and Cowper and was soon to become more pronounced in that of Blake, Burns, and Wordsworth. In the novel it was creating the mode of Gothic horror in the work of Horace Walpole, Mrs. Radcliffe, and "Monk" Lewis and of manners in Jane Austen. Practically all of these planets had their satellites in the western sky. If we can be satisfied with a division of English writers of the century into neoclassical and romantic schools, we may connect the Hartford Wits and the periodical essayist like Dennie with the former, and Freneau and Brockden Brown with the latter. About the proper classification of the sentimental or picaresque novel, the social comedy, and the political and social satire in prose or verse, we may perhaps be allowed to reserve judgment.

Although Noah Webster sounded the call to arms with his discovery of the American language, doubtless the most satisfactory approach to a study of this literature is in terms of forms. The essay, poetry, the novel, the short story, and the drama each had its brief evolution from anarchy of form and purpose to definition of aims, standards, materials, and structure. The short story alone was in its infancy when Irving began to write during the first decade of the nineteenth century.

Benjamin Franklin was the first notable American apprentice in the art of the essay. A professed student of Addison, he experimented with the periodical essay in his *Dogood* and *Busy-Body* papers, with the Swiftian essay in his political satires like his "An Edict by the King of Prussia," and with the informal essay in his letters like that on "The Whistle." As early as 1736, however, the *Virginia Gazette* had its "Monitor" who, like the "Spectator," commented on the events, morals, and manners of the day, the current drama, and how to give the fair Letitia Tattle a view of his long nose. Letters from Caleb Tenderheart to his friend, Nahab Din, appeared in the *New York Weekly Journal* for April 16, 1739, and a decade earlier Will Pedant was writing saucy letters in the *New England Weekly Journal*. When the weekly, monthly, and quarterly journals were established, they had innumerable Timothy Timbertoes to contribute essays upon characters, manners, fashions, religion, politics, and "The Character and Effects of Modern Novels." Timothy Dwight contributed essays in the "Spectator" manner to Boston and New Haven papers in 1769-70, and Brockden Brown became "The Rhapsodist" in the August to November numbers of the *Columbian Magazine* in 1789. Innumerable as these essays were, the most important of them are probably Joseph Dennie's "The Lay Preacher," "The Farrago," and "An Author's Evenings," in the various journals which he edited. These essays were serious in tone although lightened by an occasional whimsy. Their subjects were frequently American; their pattern and point of view English. It remained for Washington Irving, his brother William, and his friend, James Kirke Paulding, to develop the type into something more characteristically American in *Salmagundi; or the Whimwhams and Opinions of Lancelot Langstaff, Esq.* (1807-08), an independent periodical pamphlet that may almost be taken as the beginning of a national American literature.

The novel and the short story were closely linked to the essay in eighteenth-century England, and they remained so in America. Many of our early periodical essays have as much narrative interest as the de Coverley papers or Goldsmith's *Citizen of the World*. Irving is usually credited with being the "father of the short story," but there was a whole literature of narrative essays before the appearance of *The Sketch Book* with its "Rip Van Winkle" in 1819. The definition of the short story as an independent literary form belongs, however, to the period 1830-1850.

The novel, on the other hand, reached a comparative maturity in the earlier period. Most works of this class bear testimony to the popularity which English stories of sentiment and of assailed virtue must have enjoyed on this as well as on the other side of the water. *The Power of Sympathy* (1789), now believed to have been written by William Hill Brown, is in the epistolary form which had been so popular since Richardson adopted it for his *Pamela,* and it reflected the Richardsonian influence in its theme and mood as well. Mrs. Susannah Haswell Rowson's *Charlotte Temple* (1790) explained its moral purpose most carefully in a preface and then proceeded to a well-constructed tale of seduction that retained its popularity for half a century and suggests many a modern movie story of virtue at war with alluring and cruel vice. The picaresque, or rogue, story, which came to Defoe, Fielding, and Smollet from the Spanish, was transplanted again to America by H. H. Brackenridge in his *Modern Chivalry* (1793-1815) and turned to the purposes of political and social satire, as was *The Algerine Captive* (1797) of Royall Tyler. But perhaps most important of all was the novel of Gothic horror, represented in America by Brockden Brown's *Wieland* (1798) and *Edgar Huntly* (1799). The influence of Godwin's *Caleb Williams* is also to be discovered in Brown's interest in social problems. Practically all other contemporary English vogues, including those of Scott and of Maria Edgeworth, found reflection in one or another of the American novels published prior to 1830.

A similar echo is to be found in the drama of the period. It is not difficult to hear the cry of Lear, first muffled and then shouted through a loudspeaker, when Vardanes, of *The Prince of Parthia*, exclaims:

"Why rage the elements, they are not curs'd
Like me?"

but it is the voice of the "improved" Shakespeare of the eighteenth century rather than of that of the Elizabethan stage. And Charlotte of *The Contrast* similarly recalls the eighteenth-century comedy of manners when she extols the virtues of the bell-hoop for swimming in a minuet before the eyes of fifty well-dressed beaux. Hallam's repertory had included plays by Cibber, Addison, Lillo, Otway, and Steele. The romantic tragedy and the sentimental comedy of the English stage were moved bodily to the American stage, as was the historical tragedy in Dunlap's *André* and the historical comedy in Payne's collaboration with Irving on *Charles the Second*. The scenes and themes of these plays, like those of the novels, were often aggressively American, but their forms, manners, and modes were English.

American poetry of the period provides an even more accurate index to the change in English literary fashions. The objects of the satirical verse of Barlow, Dwight, and Trumbull were American political and theological problems, but its form was usually the rimed couplet and its vocabulary the poetic diction of Pope. Dwight's mild contemplation of nature in the imitative verse of *Greenfield Hill* was modeled on such English poems as Cowper's *The Task,* even though its fantastic scheme and imagery lends it originality, and the churchyard mood of Freneau's *The House of Night* sounds echoes from the work of Gray and Young. The transition from the classic to the romantic mode was telescoped, in New England and New Jersey, to the compass of a few years.

Philip Freneau rises above the other poets of this time in both originality and distinction. His verse forms are imitative and far from perfect in technique, but they are varied and usually successful. His diction adds to the formal vocabulary of English neoclassical writers a freshness which comes from his immediate contact with the life of nature and man. But Freneau was far ahead of his times in poetic understanding, a fact which was recognized by Coleridge and other English poets. His naturalism was not imitative; it came to him from an awareness of natural beauty, a keen perception, and a habit of contemplation. His patriotism has a fervor which carries it above the controversial issues that prompted it. His emotions are deeply stirred and his expression of them is sincere in the best of his poetry. Until the time of Poe, America could boast no poet of greater power.

In spite of imitation, by 1815 American literature was already sending out new roots into the new soil. The romantic movement was born in this country of a strong national pride, an immediate contemplation of nature, an appreciation of the simple elements in the lives of living men, and a search of the past and the present for new forms and themes. These are the elements of romanticism in any age or country.

National pride became vocal soon after 1800 and was belligerent by 1830. America's declarations of cultural and intellectual independence were many during the early years of the century. Challenged by the aspersions of British critics, intelligent Americans suddenly became conscious of the cultural crudity of their countrymen. Indignant protest was one form of their admission of the truth of these criticisms; exhortation to improvement, another. James Nelson Barker, in the Prologue to *Tears and Smiles* (1807), cried,

> But, if some humble beauties catch your sight,
> Behold them in their proper, native light;
> Not peering through discol'ring foreign prisms,
> Find them but hideous, rank Columbianisms.

The campaign was continued by Royall Tyler in his mock travel record *A Yankey in London* (1809), and Charles J. Ingersoll in his *Inchiquin Letters* (1810) made a frontal attack on the worst offender, the *Quarterly Review*. The fight raged merrily for two decades and more, in spite of Bryant's judicious essay on American poetry in the *North American Review* (1818), and Irving's efforts to calm his excited countrymen by his essay "English Writers on America" in *The Sketch Book* (1819-20).

Paulding was perhaps the most bitter of the warriors. In his *Salmagundi* paper on "National Literature," he urged rather mildly that "real life is fraught with adventures" and that the American writer could find in his own country the best material for romantic fiction. His acerbity is marked, however, in his John Bull satires of the subsequent years. Ingersoll's speech before the American Philosophical Society in 1823 was moderate, but it urged the same point: "In the literature of imagination, our standard is considerably below that of England, France, and Germany, and perhaps of Italy. . . . In the literature of fact, of education, of politics, and perhaps even science, European preëminence is by no means so decided." This literature Cooper reviewed briefly in his *Notions of the Americans* (1828), another mock travel record; and Samuel Knapp, author of our first literary history, *Lectures on American Literature* (1829), pleaded for the indulgence of his hearers on the ground that he was "nothing more than one of the pioneers in the great work of redeeming our fame from the foul aspersions of our enemies."

These were a few of the direct answers to Sydney Smith's famous question of 1818: "Who reads an American book?" but

William Ellery Channing, in his belated review of Ingersoll's lecture, wrote a more constructive exhortation for a national literature in the *Christian Examiner* (1830). His text was a definition of literature as "the expression of a nation's mind in writing," a conception which departed from the limitations of the conventional "belles lettres" ideal of the eighteenth century and prepared for Emerson's plea for "man thinking" seven years later.

The conflict between the spirit of nationalism and the sense of value in tradition became most acute in Irving and Cooper. Both started their careers as authors with a feeling of intense Americanism; both felt the lure of Europe and its past; and both, after residences abroad, returned to an incomplete reconciliation with their land and the ideals and manners of its people. In Irving the issue was less acute because he had the milder temperament. He became more completely absorbed than did Cooper in the romantic traditions of Old England and the Continent, and when he returned to Sunnyside to write *The Life of Washington*, he was content to be apart from, rather than in conflict with, the hurried and practical activities of his countrymen. Cooper, on the other hand, reacted violently against all things with which he could not be in accord. The aristocratic social tradition of New York, with its landed patroons and Tory memories, early turned his mind against the leveling forces of democracy. He insisted upon values without realizing that their permanent incorporation in a social pattern inevitably leads to an aristocracy of worth. Like Jefferson, he believed that gentlemen in the old English sense could survive under a popular government, and he took upon himself that role. Critical of the corruptions of European government and society, he was equally annoyed by American crudities and haste. In *The American Democrat* (1838) he defined his social and political ideals; in his *Gleanings* and his European novels he applied them to French, German, and English life and found the Old World civilization wanting in vitality; in his later social novels he applied them to American life and found the New World culture lacking in sturdy roots. In Cooper the spirit of nationalism lost some of its youthful confidence and gained in return the imperfect adjustment of adolescence.

A steady increase of interest in American scenes, people, and problems was the first literary result of this growth of the spirit of nationalism. Although adopting borrowed forms and modes, even Dwight wrote of the "Afric infant . . . to slavery born," Trumbull of "the country clown" at college, and Barlow of a corn husking. The problems of theology and patriotism which occupied most of the poetry of the time were immediate fruits of American social and political history. An election in *Modern Chivalry* was an American election, and the Irishman Teague O'Regan is not unlike the braggard Yankee of later years. A Jonathan who spoke a New England dialect had paced the boards in Tyler's *The Contrast*, and Brown's Indians supplied the traditional horrors necessary to the Gothic novel by the sort of unromantic atrocities described by the early chroniclers.

The Indians and the Dutch were the first Americans to be exploited for their distinctive traits. Brown looked at his primitive neighbors realistically and saw a race driven to extremity by defeat at the hand of the whites, while Freneau meditated philosophically upon their method of burying their dead. Irving wrote of them in *The Sketch Book* with the feeling of the historian he was to become. It was Cooper, however, who first threw over them a romantic glamour. Of the second generation on the frontier, he saw only the remnants of the race and drew upon the missionary Heckewelder for his facts. The result was the glamorous red man who has superseded the actuality in the popular imagination of French, German, English, and American readers of both his day and ours.

The situation was reversed, however, in the case of the Dutch. Cooper knew and admired them as the rightful landed aristocrats of his state, Paulding wrote of them realistically, and Irving began by burlesquing them in his *Knickerbocker's History* (1809) but grew mellow as he wrote and made of their past an American folk legend.

National pride found its principal source of gratification, however, in the contemplation of the grandeur of American scenery and in the habits and peculiarities in forms of life characteristic of this hemisphere. With the calm of a philosophic mind, Crèvecoeur observed the bees and the ants that set up their establishments at his door; but the Bartrams, both father and son, traveled far into the wilderness, the one toward Canada, the other toward Florida, and described the wonders of tree and animal life. Freneau wrote of the "caty-did," the honey bee, and the wild honeysuckle; Bryant of the fringed gentian, the yellow violet, and, less explicitly, a waterfowl; while Drake peopled the Hudson Valley with ouphes and fays. It is to Audubon, however, that we owe our matured and scientific interest in the wild life of the new country. He devoted his life to the observation of the birds and quadrupeds of America, drew them with the hand of an artist, and wrote of them with the feeling of a poet. And before 1820 Meriwether Lewis and Zebulon Pike had begun the second discovery of the West.

The romantic feeling of a Byron was grafted upon this love of native soil in Cooper. He was the first of any race or nation to put the sea into the novel with the passion of the sailor, and he carried with him even to the Alps a mental picture of his beloved Hudson Valley, his inland wooded hills and stretches of primitive wilderness, and the natural marvel of Niagara Falls. His Indians may have been products of his romantic imagination, but the forest trails through which they went were drawn from his childhood memory. A similar love of the soil motivated and colored the work of his contemporaries, Irving, Bryant, and their lesser fellows. The Hudson Valley was the first American scene to provide a native background for the romantic imaginations of our early writers and painters.

Another characteristic of romantic writing which was early evident in the American movement is a concern with the near distance. English writers of the late eighteenth century turned from the classics of Greece and Rome to the middle ages and to Elizabethan times. Early American history provided Barlow and Freneau with themes for patriotic poetry, and the Revolutionary War was scarcely over before it became the subject of historical as well as patriotic poems like Freneau's celebration of the "memorable victory" of the *Bon Homme Richard*, and Cooper's "tale of the neutral ground," *The Spy* (1821). Irving and Prescott turned, however, to Spain, France, and Spanish America when they became seriously interested in history, and even Cooper was lured from his American themes, in his European novels of 1831-33, only to return to them as social historian in the Littlepage and related novels of his later years.

The commanding positions of Halleck and Bryant—particularly the former — among their contemporaries have not stood the test of time. The romantic glamour of Halleck's *Alnwick Castle* and *Marco Bozzaris* now appears rather as a symptom of the age than a sign of genius, whereas the wit of his *Fanny* expresses, in less lofty mood, a gift for social satire in verse. Bryant's early verse brought him almost instant recognition, both because America needed him and because he was a truer poet than any of his immediate contemporaries. In authentic interpretation of nature, in technical maturity, and in moral earnestness, it revealed the steady hand of the master. His essay in the *North American Review* (1818) was the wisest criticism of American literature that had as yet appeared; and his *Lectures on Poetry* (1825) defined an acceptable code: poetry must express not only imagination and passion, but practical understanding, moral purpose, and eloquence as well. This statement of aim, so well illustrated by Bryant's own work, gave authoritative expression to the temper of the times; and under his leadership as editor of the *New York Evening Post* for a half-century, the profession of letters gained in dignity and assurance. Between Freneau and Poe there is no more authentic American poet than this spokesman for the religion of nature; but his achievement as a liberal critic, always and intelligently in accord with the better spirit of his day, provides an even more certain claim to fame.

Except that they tried almost every possibility, the American writers of the early romantic movement show little originality in their choice and development of literary forms. The power of their writers' personalities did much to shape Irving's Addisonian essays, Bryant's blank-verse meditation in *Thanatopsis*, and Cooper's treatment of the long chase and capture into forms which bear some stamp of novelty. The short story alone seems to have developed from the peculiar needs of the American materials and the circumstances of periodical publication, and its maturing must be left to Poe and Hawthorne. For the rest, the second group of American authors was as imitative in the forms which it chose as was the first. Irving had his Goldsmith, Cooper his Scott, and Bryant his Wordsworth.

By 1830, when these three writers had a decade of work behind them and others of greater literary value, like Poe and Hawthorne, had already published their first work, the seat of American literature was ready to move from New York and Philadelphia to Concord and Cambridge and to proclaim the romantic triumph of the early thirties. The national mind of the united colonies had ripened to a state at which the first frontier had begun to produce a culture and a literature distinctively its own.

7 | THE FOUR FACES OF EMERSON

When the time came for me to choose a field of research that would appeal to my deeper philosophic and literary interests, I turned away from the embattled and battling Cooper to the calmer if more rarified climate of Ralph Waldo Emerson.

It is a giant step from the period of awakening of literary consciousness to the actual production of literature of depth and stature, fully expressive of the new culture; and Emerson was its prophet and guide. The American Renaissance was no accident.

From my earliest days, Emerson had spoken to my mind and spirit. When I first had an opportunity to offer a seminar in American literature at Swarthmore, I chose as a topic what Lewis Mumford was then calling The Golden Day, *the period of Emerson, Thoreau, Whitman, Poe, Hawthorne, and Melville. By the time I met the thinking of F. O. Matthiessen through a student of mine who became a student of his, he had thrown Poe out of the plan for his book and had accepted Emerson only because he couldn't escape him. Matty's mind and spirit were more akin to those of Melville and Whitman, but historical logic put Emerson, for both of us, at the heart of the movement. Matthiessen's* The American Renaissance: Art and Expression in the Age of Emerson and Whitman *meant so much to me that I reviewed the book twice, and when its author took his own life, he took part of mine. There seems to be something in an effort to understand the heights and depths of life that makes for either faith and confidence or tragic despair.*

*Emerson knew both; his followers often chose; and the toll has
been heavy.*

*In the mid-nineteenth century, Emerson seemed, as he does
today, to be at a crest in the history of American literature, but
in a totally different context from that assigned to him now by
recent scholarship. One of the most surprising crises in the history of our literature was the almost complete shift in scholarly
interest from a focus on Bryant, Longfellow, Lowell, and the
Brahmins to a general acceptance of the six great transcendentalists (of one kind or another) at the peak of the Romantic
Movement. I remember a conversation I had one day with my
old mentor, Arthur Hobson Quinn, a great teacher and a gentleman of the old school. "Spiller," he said, "you have it all
wrong in your book. You give sixteen pages to Melville and
only six to Longfellow whereas Longfellow has sixteen and
Melville only six in mine." But* Literary History of the United
States *has survived* The Literature of the American People, *in
spite of my guilt for disloyalty to my master.*

*The one thing Dr. Quinn and I had in common was Emerson.
When it came to the moment when the editors of* LHUS *chose
the chapters that they wished to write themselves, I offered to
resign if I couldn't have Emerson; and one of the strongest
influences on my thinking at that stage was the then unpublished dissertation of Stephen E. Whicher, later my successor at
Swarthmore, and the son of my friend, the Emily Dickinson
biographer George F. Whicher.*

*When Steve and I first met to pass on the relay stick, I asked
him what he was working on — the usual social ice-breaker
among scholars. "I have permission," he answered, "to edit a
volume of excerpts from Emerson's unpublished lectures in the
Houghton Library." I tried to cover my dismay when I told him
that William Jackson had given me permission to edit and publish all of those same lectures. The result was a collaboration
that lasted until he too took his own life, and again I wondered.*

*"The Four Faces of Emerson" was also a product of that col-
laboration. When I was asked to discuss Emerson's contribution
to the American character in a bicentennial symposium at
Hampton-Sydney College, I thought immediately of what both*

Quinn and Whicher had taught me; and the many images of
Emerson seemed a problem that I could deal with from all sides.
For Emerson had spoken to my adolescence as he spoke to the
adolescence of the American people, and he spoke to me again
in his ripe wisdom as I was about to marry again and enter the
afternoon of life, remembering his old-age serenity and his
belief that the present is always the eternal.
   The address was included with three others in Four Makers
of the American Mind, *edited by Thomas E. Crawley, Durham,*
N.C.: Duke University Press, 1976. pp. 3-23.

The purpose of this conference, as Dr. Crawley states it, is to
arrive at a better understanding of "the American character as
reflected and/or projected in the writings of Emerson, Thoreau,
Whitman and Melville," and it is my assignment to open the
discussion with some reflections on the way Ralph Waldo
Emerson contributed to shaping that American national
character.

There is some logic in this plan for, by 1850, Emerson certainly stood at the center of American cultural and intellectual
life as the spokesman for that confidence in the integrity of the
individual which inspired Whitman to write *Leaves of Grass* and
has inspired all of us as Americans since to carry the message of
freedom and the rights of man to the oppressed and enslaved
peoples of the earth. What could be more centrally American
than that passage in the essay "Self-Reliance" which we all
know: "Trust thyself; every heart vibrates to that iron string. . . .
Great men have always done so . . . and we are now men,
guides, redeemers, and benefactors, obeying the Almighty effort and advancing on Chaos and Dark."

Somehow we as a nation seem to have absorbed from the zeal
of the early settlers and the great documents of the Revolutionary period the conviction that we, like the Israelites, are a chosen people with a mission to right the wrongs of the past and to
teach the lessons of the future. Even at this late day, I for one
have donned uniform to cross the Atlantic in order "to make
the world safe for democracy," and I have spent much of my
professional life shaping American studies programs here and

in Europe and Asia in the conviction that America has something special to say to the world.

Surely then, when Paul Elmer More, as late as 1917, says in the *Cambridge History of American Literature*, "It becomes more and more apparent that Emerson, judged by an international or even by a broad national standard, is the outstanding figure of American letters," we might expect to learn from him the message of which we are to be the missionaries. But perhaps we should pause, because this is the man who once took as his motto: "A great man is he who answers questions which I have not skill to put." Emerson was a humble seeker after a truth he never fully found and not the Delphic oracle that Whitman thought him. Perhaps we look to him rather because he confronted the confused complexity that our national experience really is and learned a way—not to solve its problems or to preach its message—but to live with it and inwardly to reflect its diverse character.

In this paper I will be speaking on three levels. The first is the obvious one, the experience and teachings of Ralph Waldo Emerson as he passed through the four stages of life from youth to maturity and presented, as we have recently come to recognize, four quite different faces to the world. First he appeared as the young idealist attacking the strongholds of tradition; then as the cosmic sage rising above the battle and maintaining an easy calm of untried authority; then we discovered beneath this surface the disturbed seeker facing the essential tragic issues of life without revealing his distress; and finally he appeared as the wise man who had discovered a balanced way of life for himself and for others in a suspended dualism of the ideal and the real.

The second level of my thinking runs parallel with this but will only be hinted at. It is the level of my own personal lifelong intimacy with Emerson's evolving thought and feeling as I leaned on him in my own progress through much the same curve of life; and the third level—which is more speculative and unprovable even though it is the subject of this conference —the concentration of the whole American experience in the intuitive subconscious of this puzzling man. Mine will be the message of the Devil's advocate. I will be trying to explain why I and Emerson the American Isaiah and the American people themselves seem often to have failed because they asked the right but the unanswerable questions.

You will be hearing more about Whitman later, but I must take him as my springboard because he represented the obvious confident external American man, whereas Emerson was the perplexed and searching prophet of the inner national consciousness. He was, as the psychohistorian Erik Erikson has recently portrayed Jefferson in his book *Dimensions of a New Identity*, equally the representative American man and an index to the inner national character.

Jefferson, Dr. Erikson believes, had to rediscover a sense of identity by becoming "at one with myself" and at the same time establishing his affinity with a new world community's "sense of being at one with its future as well as its history." He achieved this by being a man "centered in a true identity" but able like Proteus to assume a variety of roles or faces behind which his true self could hide, and thus lead the early Americans in their "job of developing an American character out of the regional and generational polarities and contradictions of a nation of immigrants and migrants." The true American is not that written into the Constitution; he is a multi-ethnic mass of restless, seeking, ever-moving humanity in a vast undeveloped continent.

Even though Whitman declared himself the disciple of Emerson as the cosmic heart of man and the voice of the American people, there was little sympathetic exchange between the two poets after the first overenthusiastic response of the latter to *Leaves of Grass* in 1855. Although they could compete equally for the role of the man most representative of the American national character in the mid-nineteenth century, they were at opposite poles of feeling, thought, and action. What we can learn about the American from Emerson may supplement but it does not repeat what we can learn about him from Whitman, or Thoreau, or Melville. Whereas Whitman thought himself the voice of the common man—the democratic mass of humanity — and of the westward-moving frontier, Emerson spoke only the message of that inner frontier of mind and heart which was shaping the experience of a new man in a new world. In 1855, when he greeted Whitman "at the beginning of a great career," Emerson, who was only sixteen years his senior, was nearing the end of a distinguished career of his own. He had delivered his last important course of lectures on *The Conduct of Life* four years before, and he was preparing his last wholly original book, *English Traits*, for the press. Truly this was the watershed of the romantic movement in American literature!

Emerson was descended in an almost unbroken line from the liberal branch of the theological establishment of New England. Born in 1803 of a father who was minister of the First Church of Boston and one of the founders of the Unitarian schism, and of a mother who was descended in a direct line from the Reverend Peter Bulkeley, one of the founders of Concord, he had little choice of his role in life. One of four boys, he was brought up by his pious and thrifty mother after his father's death in 1811, educated at the Boston Latin School and Harvard College, and ordained in 1829 at the Second Unitarian Church in Boston, where he officiated until his resignation three years later. In those few years he lived a full and promising life. Married to a beautiful and delicate girl and minister of a prominent church, he preached over a hundred sermons that showed the strength of his critical mind and the radical questioning of all formulated doctrine. Then, in 1831-32, the whole structure of his life collapsed. His wife died, he resigned from his charge because his conscience would not allow him to administer the sacrament of the Holy Communion as a ritual regardless of his personal feelings at any given time, and he set out alone for Europe in quest of a more open and free base for his developing transcendental beliefs. On his return the next year, he was invited by his cousin George, a leader in the new Lycaeum Movement, to deliver a lecture on science, and a new career as itinerant public lecturer opened before him.

The moment of revelation had come to him in the botanical garden in Paris. "The universe is a more amazing puzzle than ever," he wrote in his journal after this experience. "As you look along the bewildering series of animated forms, the hazy butterflies, the carved shells, the birds, beasts, insects, fish,— and the upheaving principle of life everywhere incipient, in the very rock aping organized forms . . . I am moved by strange sympathies. I will listen to the invitation. I will be a naturalist."

In this doctrine of the exact but mysterious correspondence of the law of nature with the law of God, Emerson had discovered the "First Philosophy" which was to be his substitute for creed for the rest of his life, and an open approach to truth which was to take the place of all systems of received doctrine. When he moved to Concord in 1834 and married Lydia Jackson the next year, he was ready to rebuild his life on the foundations of his own intuitive but fluent convictions.

The first face of the new Emerson is therefore that of a confident and enthusiastic young reformer, driven by his own spirit of independence to defy all truth that rested only on authority and to construct his own message to the world on the truth received directly from intuition and personal experience. The new testament of his faith was the little book *Nature,* conceived on the boat when returning from Europe in 1833 and published three years later, a poem and a guide to life in the prose of revelation rather than of logic. Meanwhile he had been lecturing regularly on the literature and the leaders of thought of the past; now, with his testament in hand, he was ready for a frontal attack on the two entrenched establishments of his own intellectual and moral world: the academic of Harvard College, and the theological of the Divinity School. The twin orations of 1837 and 1838 were the result. After them he stood alone, a new man in a new world of the mind, Adam born again of the inner life.

At this point, what I have so far said and what I plan to say becomes for me a curious mixture of my subject with my own spiritual and intellectual autobiography, for I discovered the Emerson of *Nature* back in my college days of 1914-17 when I threw aside my Episcopal upbringing and my formal schooling to explore the worlds of history, art, literature, and religion in the classroom and in the minds of like curious friends and teachers. Then, after a year in Europe (courtesy of Uncle Sam), I returned to build my own world of the mind in a new and personal commitment to the basic law of self-discovery. Leaving the security of the great university, I chose to teach in a small Quaker college to pick the subjects I needed for the freedom to build my own career. You know the result. Ultimately I came to apply the same principle of integrity to the literary history of my own country that I had found so necessary for myself. I had been taught to think of American literature as a branch of English literature; I now recognized it as the voice of a culture which had evolved from the impact of ancient civilizations on a primitive environment. It must be studied anew from the roots up. I would try to be the American Scholar. Emerson was to blame.

With that, I will leave the personal and return to my subject; but perhaps I have let you in on a secret which will help you to understand why Emerson—at least for me—is the epitome of the American national character, and why, when we came to the point in planning *Literary History of the United States* at which we chose the chapters that each of us wanted to write ourselves, I said, "Give me Emerson and you can deal out the rest."

Emerson appears first to us then in the role of the newborn poet of Nature, eager to rediscover himself and his place in the universe, forsaking the past, challenging the present, reaching out to the future. "Standing on the bare ground—my head bathed by the blithe air and uplifted into infinite space—all mean egotism vanishes. I become a transparent eyeball; I am nothing; I see all; the currents of the Universal Being circulate through me; I am part or parcel of God."

The little book *Nature* which he offered in 1836 had been composed with great care. The task of formulating the new philosophy was one of discovering and defining the place of the self in the cosmic universe where the moral law (the law of God) above was as a mirror to the natural law below, reflecting the truth in a one-to-one relationship at every point.

Emerson had at first planned two books, each dealing with a way of bringing these two together into a realization of what it meant to be. The self could look down to nature and find there the reflection of God, or it could look upward and inward to "the ineffable essence which we call spirit, . . . the organ through which the universal spirit speaks to the individual. . . . Idealism sees the world in God." The mirror reversed—. The first of these books was to be called *Nature,* the second *The Soul.* In the end the two were merged into one, in a rising and falling action which keeps forever fluent within each individual self the ever-changing, ever the same, relationship between God and the world about us.

"Philosophically considered," Emerson first declares, "the universe is composed of Nature and the Soul. Strictly speaking, therefore, all that is separate from us, all which Philosophy distinguishes as the NOT ME, that is, both nature and art, all other men and my own body, must be ranked under the name NATURE, . . . the essences unchanged by man, space, the air, the river, the leaf, . . . as well as the mixture of [man's] will with the same things, as in a house, a canal, a statue, a picture." For Emerson there are four ways in which God is revealed in these things: Commodity, or daily use; Beauty, or the pleasure in contemplation of form and color; Language, or the symbols by which natural facts become spiritual facts; and Discipline, or the power of Reason which perceives and teaches "the analogy that marries Matter and Mind." Once having risen by these means to the plane of the Ideal, the self can be expressed in science, in poetry, in religion—an unending process of teaching and learning.

With his ideological platform thus firmly laid and his tools in hand, the young Emerson was ready to accept the invitation of the Phi Beta Kappa Society of Harvard to deliver its annual address in August of 1837. His subject was assigned, and many learned discourses had been delivered in past years expounding the varieties and the virtues of academic scholarship. It was a time to announce and to discuss the learning of the past and its authority in the present.

"I accept this topic," Emerson began in his usual low key, "*The American Scholar.* Year by year we come up hither to read one more chapter of his biography. Let us inquire what light new days and events have thrown on his character and his hopes." So far there was probably no stir in his robed and sober audience; but then he threw his challenge. The scholar, he announced, is the delegated intellect of a living society: "In the right state he is *Man Thinking*. In the degenerate state, when the victim of society, he tends to become a mere thinker, or still worse, the parrot of other men's thinking." He must use—not merely absorb and pass on—the tools of scholarship: nature, or the world about; books, or the record of the past; and action, or the vocabulary of the present.

Bliss Perry has given us a graphic account of what happened when faculty and students filed out. The repercussions of that moment are felt in the halls of Academe down to the present day.

No less stunning was the second occasion when the students of the Divinity School invited him to address them the next year. One would hardly expect a minister of the radical branch of the New England faith—albeit he had resigned from his own church—to attack Unitarianism in its own stronghold. But the young challenger was unflinching. Received and formulated doctrine, however liberal, could not take the place of a living and functioning Christian life. "Historical Christianity," he said, "has fallen into the error that corrupts all attempts to communicate religion . . . it is not the doctrine of the soul, but an exaggeration of the personal, the positive, the ritual. It has dwelt, it dwells, with noxious exaggeration about the *person* of Jesus. The soul knows no person."

Here was heresy—inexcusable, not to be forgiven. But Emerson clung to his new-found faith in life as function rather than fact, as relation rather than as fixed truth. He faced the lonely path ahead.

With platform as well as pulpit becoming less and less available for his message, he now turned to the printed page. An avid reader of Montaigne and Bacon, the thought came to him that, by cutting, compressing, arranging, and refining the thought he had by now expressed in several series of subscription lectures in the Masonic Temple of Boston and elsewhere, he could perhaps offer a volume of moral essays. By 1841 the project had been completed and the first series of *Essays* appeared in Boston and London.

The effect was almost instantaneous, and the young radical became the cosmic sage. Emerson's second face—behind the mask of print—became that of the wise philosopher, the assured teacher, the secular saint.

But the essays themselves are very difficult to read, a fact which has often worried me as I have leapt from one brilliant phrase to the next but plodded through the long paragraphs which seemed to lead nowhere. The difficulty, I think, lies in Emerson's method of thinking rather than in the complexity of his thought. He was intuitive rather than logical; and language, as he explains himself, was for him the symbol of spiritual insights rather than the conveyer of ideas and facts. His style is still that of the spoken sermon or lecture, even though disciplined by that of the epigrammatic Bacon. Throughout his mature life he kept a journal in which he deposited the nuggets that he dug from the earth of reading and experience—his "savings bank," he called it. His method of composition was first to choose a theme—Self-Reliance, the Over-Soul, Compensation, Love, History—and then to build around it, as a musician might a symphony, a composition made up of the *notes* (the pun is inescapable) he gleaned from his own written words, playing the strings against the woodwinds, the treble over the base, as counterpoint and harmony lead his fugue on through circles of motion to its own climax. To hear a lecture or to read an essay by Emerson is a listening experience of the inner sensibilities rather than a logical exercise of the mind.

Almost all of "Self-Reliance" for example is made up of phrases, sentences, and paragraphs taken from the various journals—some of them as early as 1832 or 1833—and the courses of lectures he had delivered to winter audiences in Boston between 1837 and 1840, themselves composed in the same way largely of journal passages. Yet Emerson wrote, even after the critical success of his *Essays* in England, "I shall someday write something better than those poor cramped arid 'Essays' which I almost hate the sight of," and his revisions in the 1847 edition proves that he tried.

But the *Essays*, with their companion volume of three years later, constitute one of the major classics of American literature;

for their tone is that of mature authority as they open and close
the doors of the spirit, even though their author in the final
essay protests, "Let me remind the reader that I am only an
experimenter, . . . an endless seeker with no Past at my back."
He might have added, "I am the shaper of the new American
gospel, I am the voice of my people and my time." Whether he
would or not, his doctrines of the centrality of the single self,
the all-presence of a pervading over-soul or God, the correspondence of the moral and the natural worlds, and the balanced duality of experience became the creed of a new faith,
and the youthful protester took on the robes of the cosmic seer,
robes which, to the public mind at least, he was never able to
get free of.

Is it stretching the analogy too far to see in Emerson's protests
against conformity to the rigid structure of a present based on
inherited authority and his vigorous assertion of the right of
the individual soul to live its own life a parallel to the Declaration of Independence, the war of the Revolution, and the
founding of a new nation in a new world? And, to carry the
analogy further, can we find in his efforts to formulate his own
"First Philosophy" and to set himself up as lecturer on moral
fundamentals and individual rights a parallel to the making of
the Constitution, the Monroe Doctrine, and the opening of the
West? The Napoleonic wars and the subsequent waves of revolution that spread throughout Europe in 1830 and 1848 were
open invitations to the confident new nation to prove itself by
internal expansion and consolidation and by carrying the
messages of democracy and human rights to the rising peoples
of Europe. The American constitution became in the first half of
the century a model for the political liberation and reform of
the Old World and caused the first major waves of the migration
of the oppressed peoples of Ireland, Germany, and Italy to
assault the harbors of the Atlantic and to push across the plains.

Can we now see Emerson as the philosopher, the interpreter,
the representative man of the American national character in
the first stages of its formulation? At least for the purposes of
this conference may I propose such a thesis as an acceptable
hypothesis if not quite a historical fact? And can we keep this

analogy in mind as I return my focus to Emerson the man and his spiritual life, without making it too specific point for point? And may I also remember, without bothering you with the details, how during my own twenty-four years at Swarthmore I established my own professional and personal orientation to a society rediscovering itself after its first World War, weathering a depression, and gradually taking its place as one of the major world powers? Whether you share this three-level thinking with me or not, I am having fun with it inside myself as I talk.

But to return to Emerson, now settled in the big white Coolidge house on the Lexington Road, building his family, gathering his circle of friends, and stimulating the agencies of the so-called Transcendental Movement: the *Dial* magazine, the experimental agricultural community Brook Farm, and the informal Transcendental Club.

The third face of Emerson should have worn the firm mouth, the wise reserve, the confident eyes of a life achieved and quietly lived, and so it seemed to him and his family and friends when, in December 1840, he wrote to George Ripley of his decision not to join Brook Farm: "The ground of my decision is almost purely personal to myself. . . . That which determines me is the conviction that the Community is not good for me. While I see it may hold out many inducements for others it has little to offer me which with resolution I cannot procure for myself. . . . It seems to me a circuitous and operose way of relieving myself of any irksome circumstances which I ought to take on myself" (Let. II, 325). Thus committed to Concord and to himself at the age of thirty-five, he settled with his growing family into the comfortable home in which, forty-two years later, in 1882, he died.

But the image which he thus assumed of the philosopher-friend was deceptive because, as Stephen Whicher has pointed out in his "inner life" of Emerson, *Freedom and Fate,* the period between 1839 and at least 1844 was actually one of storm and stress equal almost to anything a Byron or a Goethe might experience, but storm and stress held firmly in control.

The strain perhaps began with the death of his beloved brother Charles in 1836, followed by that of his infant son and namesake Waldo in 1842, but the center of tension was inward and not in external events. The Divinity School address of 1839 was his last unqualified statement of enthusiastic idealism, and its reception was devastating to his personal sense of security. Andrews Norton, then the most powerful presence in the Unitarian fold, wrote a systematic and vicious personal attack in *A Discourse on the Latest Form of Infidelity* in the same year, and a factional war of which Emerson was both the cause and the silent center broke out. "Who are these murmurers, these haters, these revilers?" he asked in his Journal. "In the present droll posture of my affairs, when I see myself suddenly raised into the importance of a heretic, I am very uneasy. . . . I shall go on just as before, seeing whatever I can and telling what I see." But his self-confidence had been deeply shaken. "Steady, steady! When the fog of good and evil affection falls, it is hard to see and walk straight."

Perhaps he was speaking of his own efforts at recovery when, in the poem "Uriel," probably written later, he called the challenge of the young God Uriel a "lapse."

> Line in nature is not found;
> Unit and Universe are round;
> In vain produced, all rays return:
> Evil will bless and ice will burn. . . .

And when he had spoken thus,

> A sad self-knowledge, withering, fell
> On the beauty of Uriel; . . .
> And a blush tinged the upper sky,
> And the gods shook, they knew not why.

"Circles," included in the first volume of *Essays*, revealed the same shift from the bold egotism of the Addresses to an acceptance of the principle of learning through an ever-expanding experience. "The eye is the first circle; the horizon which it forms is the second; and throughout nature this primary figure is repeated without end. . . . There are no fixtures in nature. The universe is fluid and volatile. Permanence is but a word of degrees. . . . Do not set the least value on what I do, or the least discredit on what I do not as if I pretended to settle anything as true or false. I unsettle all things. . . . I simply experiment, an endless seeker with no past at my back." "Yes," he is still saying, "trust thyself—even when in the deepest doubt."

The summer of 1841 was apparently the nadir of his spirits. Invited to address the undergraduate literary society at Colby College in Maine, he found it impossible to pull his old thoughts on Nature together again into a coherent statement. Borrowing ideas heavily from articles in the *Encyclopaedia Americana* and elsewhere, and on his own recent and miscellaneous entries in his Journals, he paced the beach at Nantasket where he had gone alone or sought solace in his study. "The Method of Nature" contains some of his best passages but is confused and unconvincing. The fact that his next series of Boston lectures on "The Times" dealt critically with both "The Conservative" and "The Transcendentalist" suggests that he was going through a period of self-analysis and reappraisal of his identity and his deepest convictions.

Committed initially to the doctrine of Transcendentalism, which required that one live by the higher moral law, he was learning the hard way that the doctrine of correspondence between the moral and the natural law on which it was based simply does not work from day to day. In three areas of his private life also he was facing the tragic issue of all time—the realization that what must be, can't be: the areas of money, women, and social concerns.

Although he had a small inheritance from his first wife, the panic of 1837 made the Boston lecture series essential, and when income from these began to dwindle, he responded to the lure of the Lycaeum Movement more and more and began to go on lecture tours, first to neighboring New England towns, then to New York and Philadelphia, and finally to England and the West. His English friend Thomas Carlyle not ineptly called him "the lonely wayfaring man" as he came to spend more and more time away from home.

He was also discovering that Plato was wrong about friendship, especially with women. The vigorous Margaret Fuller and the starry-eyed Caroline Sturgis, as well as others, became increasingly embarrassing as the close relationships that Transcendentalism encouraged became dangerously absorbing. This is a whole story in itself, which can now be more fully told as suppressed letters come to light, but this is probably not the place to go into details, however intriguing. Suffice it that any man who allows his friendships for three or four women at the same time to threaten to cross the line into love may be headed for a nervous breakdown or worse.

And finally, the issue of social involvement, to which I have already referred in the Brook Farm incident and Emerson's decision to go it alone. The first real evidence of a shift of emphasis toward social concern had appeared in his Boston lecture of 1839—40 on "The Present Age" and the omission of the series altogether in 1840—41; but in January of that year he made his first overt statement on social concerns in the lecture to the Mechanics Apprentices' Library Association in Boston on "Man the Reformer."

But it was the slavery question which finally broke down his resistance. As the Abolitionist Movement began to heat up in the thirties, the slavery question had forced itself more and more on literary idealists like Whittier, Lowell, and Emerson. How could the ownership of a fellow human being be reconciled with the basic American doctrines of individual integrity and the rights of man? The answer is that it could not be. Here was the major public challenge to Transcendentalism and the moral law. Whittier and Lowell were easy converts, but Emerson was slower. When he did go over it was to declare, not only against slavery as such but against social evils in general, and the third of his stages of development began to take on a different emphasis with his frontal attack on trade as the cancer of modern society in his 1841 lecture on "Man the Reformer." Even so, it was slavery which finally brought him into the open as the nearest thing to an activist that he ever became. He had been shocked by the murderous attack on the Abolitionist printer Lovejoy in 1837 and he had read an address on slavery at the Concord Church at that time, but he still argued that the answer to social evil lay in the moral education of the individual rather than in concerted social action.

All three of these influences were of course contributory to his depressed state of mind in the third period, but the true core of it was inward and philosophical dismay which is perhaps best expressed in the essay on "Experience" in the second collection of his *Essays* in 1844. Here is perhaps the furthest swing of the pendulum away from his early idealism and self-reliance. He had already stated in an elementary form in the earlier essay on "Compensation" the suspended dualism which was to become his final position. "Everything runs to excess," he concludes in the later essay; "every good quality is noxious if unmixed, and, to carry the danger to the edge of ruin, nature causes each man's peculiarity to superabound." Here for the first time he reached the conclusion that all of life is illusion and that temperament rather than self-reliance is the primary source of individualism. Illusion and Temperament are the first two "threads on the loom of time, these are the Lords of Life; the others are Succession, Surface, Surprise, Reality, Subjectiveness." All of life is relative in actual experience, determined by the quality and the mood of the individual in his special role and circumstance. Relativity and pragmatic acquiescence could hardly go further.

But by 1844, with the birth of his second son, Edward, and the publication of his second volume of *Essays*, Emerson may be said to have passed through what I like sometimes to call "middle-aged adolescence," the reorientation that happens to most people in middle life, and had his feet firmly on new ground. The fourth and mature face of Emerson was beginning to become more clear: the face of a poet-philosopher who had passed from idealism through skepticism into a pragmatic balance, a suspended dualism of irreconcilable opposites which provided both a way to dream and a way to live. To the unknowing, both in his time and in ours, the external calm of the Concord sage seemed unbroken; only those who could reach or listen carefully behind the serene mask and the controlled voice would find the restless flux of thought and feeling, the flow and ebb of life, the eternal questioning and searching that underlay the surface.

Representative Men, first delivered in 1845-46, read in England the following year, and published in 1850, may well have been to some extent Emerson's answer to Carlyle's *Heroes and Hero Worship.* The Great Man, he insists, is not the unique and dominant leader who can impose himself on the masses; he is the best representative of a man's vocation at the highest point of its development, one kind of humanity at its best, like our old friend the scholar, who at his best is "man thinking." These are the men who came nearest to achieving a way of reaching closer to the ideal by best using the gifts which they had in excess but which are within the reach of all. The six Great Men chosen seem to be paired as opposites: Plato, the philosopher who excelled in intellect, is balanced by Swedenborg, the mystic who relied on intuitive insight; Montaigne, the skeptic who questioned all things, is set over against Shakespeare, who stood apart from life and accepted all, judged none; Napoleon, the man of the world who achieved through action, is countered by Goethe, the writer who reported the discoveries of the mind.

All of these Great Men failed to reach the ultimate goal of complete excellence; each revealed only one way to try and thereby offered a possible answer to the question of how to live in the real world while reaching for the ideal. Emerson was now engaged fully in his quest for an alternative to self-reliance.

He next turned from a consideration of the future of individuals to ask what kind of society is possible and acceptable when it deals realistically with existing facts and uses them in its search for the good life. The series of lectures which he delivered on his return from England and which he reworked into *English Traits* in 1856 is a thorough and critical analysis of a modern industrial-agricultural society, almost a portrait and a prediction of what American society could become.

Let me interrupt myself once again to remind you that we are thinking of Emerson as the spokesman for the American national character as well as for himself, and recall that at this time the nation was nearing its own tragic crisis of the Civil War. As it passed through this crisis and moved into a restless peace in which it attempted to rebuild its structure on a new and practical foundation without losing the dreams of the founders, so Emerson became more and more its spokesman, a man "centered in a true identity" but at the same time establishing his affinity with a new world community's "sense of being at one with its future as well as its history." As we approach our own time with its loss of security and identity, he seems more and more to become the representative American man in his relentless searchings rather than in his findings. He was the representative man of a new American national character, reflecting, as Erik Erikson pointed out, "the regional and generational polarities and contradictions of a nation of immigrants and migrants," which we most assuredly still are.

In the last of his major works, *The Conduct of Life*, lectures first delivered in 1851 and published in 1860, the balance between "Fate," or the "given" in life, and "Power," or the ability of man to use his resources productively, was struck. "Let us build altars," he asks, "to the Beautiful Necessity. Why should we fear to be crushed by savage elements, we who are made up of the same elements?" And again, "Who shall set a limit to the influence of a human being? . . . All power is of one kind, a sharing of the nature of the world." The dualism between Mind and Matter is still there, but somehow the order of priority has been reversed. It is in Matter—the laws of the new science—that one must first seek the shaping principle of life. "And so I think," he says in his lecture on "Worship," "that the last lesson of life, the choral song which rises from all elements and all angels, is a voluntary obedience, a necessitated freedom. Man is made of the same atoms as the world is, he shares the same impressions, predispositions, and destiny. When his mind is illuminated, when his heart is kind, he throws himself joyfully into the sublime order, and does, with knowledge, what the stones do by structure." Such complete determinism was possible for the onetime young dreamer of the 1836 *Nature* because this statement was made three years before Darwin's *Origin of Species,* and the then current theory of evolutionary science allowed far more freedom of will and choice than later seemed possible under mechanistic science. Even though natural had superseded moral law as the prime shaper of the universe, the poet could still hold to the ultimate integrity of the individual soul.

"There is no chance and no anarchy in the universe," Emerson concludes. "All is system and gradation. Every god is there sitting in his sphere. The young mortal enters the hall of the firmament; there is he alone with them alone, they pouring on him benedictions and gifts, and beckoning him up to their thrones. On the instant, and incessantly, fall snowstorms of illusions. He fancies himself in a vast crowd which sways this way and that and whose movements and doings he must obey: he fancies himself poor, orphaned, insignificant. The mad crowd drives hither and thither, now furiously commanding this thing to be done, now that. What is he that he should resist their will, and think or act for himself? Every moment new changes and new showers of deceptions to baffle and distract him. And when, by and by, for an instant, the air clears and the cloud lifts a little, there are the gods still sitting around him on their thrones,—they alone with him alone."

This is the Emerson I have always known. For me, he is best enjoyed and used when I recall that he defined the American scholar as "Man Thinking" rather than as "a mere thinker." His is a "Philosophy of Living" in a scientifically determined world rather than a metaphysics, logic, or ethics. In the final analysis he is one of America's major poets, the recorder of the inward experience of a living present. As he has himself described his role: "The poet is representative. He stands among partial men for the complete man and apprises us not of his wealth, but of the common wealth."

8 | THE SECOND AMERICAN LITERARY RENAISSANCE

At this point I must turn back to an earlier stage in my own story in order to set the following address in its proper context.

The period 1939 to 1944 was one of unrest and change for me as for many others, but not altogether for the same reasons. Swarthmore, being a Quaker college, was relatively undisturbed by the war. President Aydelotte resigned in 1939 and was succeeded by another Rhodes scholar, John W. Nason, who continued his philosophy and policy with perhaps less conviction and more of a spirit of inquiry. The college agreed to undertake a naval training program (perhaps more because of a shortage of male students than for any patriotic reasons), but otherwise continued to stress quality liberal education and the now-established honors program. By this time, a Quaker myself, I felt it my calling to keep the aims of idealism alive rather than to take an active part in the war effort. I first became chairman of the Humanities Division and then of a curriculum committee, appointed to explore all the alternatives and methods attendant on the central role of a liberal arts college. It became a kind of faculty seminar on the aims and methods of higher liberal education, with a constantly changing membership and a program of investigation rather than of immediate policy changes. President Nason attended most meetings, and the college emerged from the war strong in its sense of purpose and direction.

But meanwhile my professional life as a pioneer in the field of American literature and culture continued to develop, and I became restless with the limitations of a small undergraduate college. I used to say that I went to Swarthmore for two years before going on to a university but it was so exciting that the two years stretched to twenty-four. I had always thought of myself as ultimately a research scholar in a major university; and now, with a lull in the excitement of a positive and idealistic leader like Aydelotte, I found that my mind was opening to a change before it was too late. I had already been invited to offer graduate courses in a half-dozen or more summer schools from Harvard to Duke and Southern California; and as chairman of the Committee on American Literary History of the American Literature Group of the Modern Language Association, I was a central figure in the movement to rewrite the history of our literature with the aid of the intellectual, social, and cultural historians who were becoming the dominant forces in the revision of the whole field of American history.

After several abortive moves toward other universities, I was surprised one day in 1944 by a telephone call from my old teacher, Albert C. Baugh, then the chairman of the English department of my alma mater, Pennsylvania. "Dr. Quinn is retiring this year," he said, "and we will need someone to join Sculley Bradley in the American field and to work with a literature-history interdepartmental committee in redesigning the course in American Civilization." It looked like the opportunity I was waiting for. "If I do come, Albert, what would you wish me to teach?" "Well," said the scholar who had suggested that I do my dissertation in the medieval drama, "we don't yet have a graduate course in twentieth-century American literature." "Yes," I said over the phone, "I'll come."

As far as I knew, no other university had such a course, and there were few books to guide me. I was already deeply involved in the efforts of younger scholars to redesign American literary history around the two cycles that Norman Foerster for one called "Romanticism" and "Realism," but the fatal flaw in most such plans was that the two terms were confused with the traditional romanticism and neoclassicism of the English Romantic Movement. Wordsworth's emphasis on nature and simple reality had been regarded as an aspect of romanticism and not as its antithesis, neoclassicism, with its emphasis on convention, standards, and forms. American literature in the late nineteenth century was in a state of reaction, but it had developed nothing to match the satire of Swift or the dogmatism of Dr. Johnson. Up to that point it seemed to have experienced only one romantic period, which had been followed since 1870 not by discipline and reaction, but by conventional sentimentality and by what was seen at the time to be a kind of degeneration into the commonplace or morbid realism of Hemingway, Faulkner, and O'Neill. The upsurge of the future was not yet recognized.

I found myself redesigning this antithesis into a period of Transcendental Romanticism and a second of Naturalistic Romanticism, the latter based on the new theories of evolution and depth psychology and on a modern resurgence of the human spirit. Suddenly I realized that there was a second cycle, which rose out of the fin-de-siècle disillusionment to reach a crest about 1915 to 1945. My new course was laid out for me; all I had to do was to read and read and read, and so fill in the picture.

My two-hour lecture course on Saturday mornings grew as I grew, and I soon found that I had more dissertations to supervise than I could possibly handle and that my postponed inner desire — common, I guess, to all research scholars — for professional progeny had helped to produce a new generation of teachers in American literature.

The following, previously unpublished, address was delivered at Kings College, University of London, on February 10, 1959, as an effort to supply the theoretical frame for what was by then obvious. American literary history had reached its second renaissance in the rediscovery of human comedy and tragedy and the forms in which to give them expression.

I

When, back in 1940, I began to think seriously about the need for a proposed collaborative history of the entire story, it seemed to me and my fellow editors that, unless we could discover the shape and meaning of the literary present in the historical development of an American literary tradition, our enterprise would fail. We were confronted by a number of writers in our own time who were becoming recognized throughout the world as a closely related group of original and powerful artists. Obviously they constituted some sort of culmination of a historical process, and it was our task to identify and describe them as a literary movement and then to account for their development. It was not sufficient to call them the "Lost Generation," because they were so obviously not lost. Even when I was myself a university student back in 1914 to 1917, we had spoken confidently of the "Little Renaissance" in poetry, but if there was a renaissance, it was obviously not limited to poetry and it was not "little." Could we by 1940 set up the hypothesis that there occurred, somewhere during the first half of the twentieth century, a genuine literary renaissance in American literature? It took more courage to say so then than it might now, at most two decades later, but even today it must remain an hypothesis rather than an established historical fact. We are too close to the evidence to be absolutely sure of our conclusions.

Nevertheless I am proposing such a hypothesis in order to take you with me through some of the reasoning that gave to our book whatever shape and meaning it achieved. Let us say, at least for the purposes of our argument, that there occurred in the United States between the two World Wars a literary flowering which was both important and characteristically American, with a handful of authors worthy to take their places among the Titans, if not the Gods, of other times and other cultures. Let us also assume that there must be a set of causal and conditioning factors within the American culture to explain this phenomenon and that these factors should lend themselves to scholarly investigation.

It is not hard to date the beginnings of this movement somewhere between 1908 and 1915. It was at that time that Theodore Dreiser republished his first suppressed novel and gained general acceptance; that the first magazine open to the new poetry published the early verse of Frost, Sandburg, and others; and that Eugene O'Neill saw his first one-act plays produced at the tiny Wharf Theatre on the tip of Cape Cod. It was then too—and this is the crux of my argument, that America developed its first vigorous movement in literary and social criticism. I shall be able only to trace the beginnings of this literary cycle, but perhaps I can by so doing indicate why and how it rose to a culmination about 1925 and 1935 and then continued on its arc into some sort of reaction and decline since that time.

II

To set up such a picture of contemporary literary excellence was in 1940 something of a novelty. Our literary history as it had been written up to that time followed a quite opposite line of argument that made the contemporary writers seem a pale and even degenerate afterglow of the Golden Day of Bryant, Longfellow, Lowell, and the other bearded poets of the New England hierarchy. So firmly had the imaginary portrait of the benevolent American democratic gentleman been identified with the national literary ideal that Mark Twain and Walt Whitman had ended their lives in bitterness and defeat, Thoreau and Melville had been conveniently forgotten, and Henry James had turned his back on his native land and settled permanently in England. In 1900, American fiction was struggling along in the polite realism of William Dean Howells, a Trollope without a sense of humor; and the state of the drama, of poetry, and especially of literary criticism, was deplorable.

Perhaps in the lack of a vigorous and fearless critical spirit we may find the clue to this situation. Except for the poetical theories of Poe, which had long since been forgotten, and the mild essays in appreciation of the English classics by Lowell, America had, prior to James's analyses of his own novels, no appreciable literary or social criticism. The habit of looking to the British journals and reviews for critical authority before having any opinion about native writing was so deeply imbedded that a century of protest by American authors had made virtually no impression. American literature was still viewed, by both the journalistic critics and the academic scholars, as a by-product of British civilization and history and subject to the same values, standards, and modes as English literature. What was true in the seventeenth and eighteenth centuries when America was a British colony was assumed to be equally true of the nineteenth and twentieth. After all, the Puritans landed in New England only four years after the death of Shakespeare, and the *Lyrical Ballads* was published only two years after the retirement of the first president of the United States, George Washington. The experience of opening up the western continent was a part of the British spread of empire, and the new civilization was at its start a transplanted British civilization. But Britain did not share in America's conquest of that continent and in the assimilation of perhaps the most polyglot population that has existed in one place since the Tower of Babel. Such a comparatively minor detail as the existence of a written constitution in the cornerstone of the new political structure made a totally different political architecture inevitable. The presence of vast unexploited resources within the national geographical boundaries made the economic development of the new nation almost certainly the opposite in kind from that of a nation dependent so largely on imported raw materials. Even the speech of Americans acquired new rhythms from the open flow of the land and the constant movement of the population; new needs created new words and new meanings for old ones; people of dark skin and alien tongue sought and received the certificate of full citizenship; skyscrapers rose to previously unknown heights and industry pushed toward frightening regimentation of mass production; an unsuppressed proletariat continued to exert full political and social rights without revolution. Whatever it was getting to be, surely this land was not the England of Victoria and George and Elizabeth; nor the Europe of Napoleon and Maetternick, Bismark, and Lenin. If it spoke in poetry, fiction, or drama, surely it would have something quite new to say and new ways to say it.

III

Self-understanding was the first need, and for that a critical movement was essential; but, in 1900, American criticism could discover almost no native literary vitality. This was the year of Edmund Clarence Stedman's *American Anthology*, a garnering of the poetic achievements of the past. "Our afterglow is not discouraging," said this critic in his introduction, after pointing out that the last of the literary masters was now dead. "We have a twilight interval, with minor voices and their tentative modes and tones." Such was the placid state of the American critical mind at the turn of the century, a time when American civilization was in a vast ferment.

The critics who led the revolt of 1910 to 1915 had in common only their impatience with the general stagnation that seemed to have settled on the literary scene. Beyond this initial sharing of a common impulse, they broke up into a variety of schools and of species and subspecies. There was no one positive remedy upon which more than a handful could agree, although some saw "socialism" as a glorious sun on the horizon; nor did many of them think their problems through to a defined and stable position.

The critic who first recognized this ferment as a critical movement was Van Wyck Brooks. Perhaps because of his very lack of connection with existing institutions and interests, he was able to announce the trend that everyone was beginning to feel but no one had as yet defined. His little book, *America's Coming of Age* (1915), created no great stir when it first appeared and has only recently been reprinted, but a search among contemporary documents reveals no better formulation of the critical issues of the day. It can be used to mark the summing up and restatement of the issue between the literary idealism and realism of the late nineteenth century and the announcement of the main action and reaction in the literary movement of the twentieth.

As in all such statements, the central plea in this book is that literature must periodically refresh itself by coming to terms with life in its own time and place. Specifically, Brooks argues that a tradition which he, like Mencken and others, calls "Puritan" has consistently separated America's finest literary minds from the materials of life about them. The pattern of this division between ideals and facts, he believes, was set in colonial days and it persisted throughout the nineteenth century.

This schism between the ideals of the intellectuals and the practices of the people accounts, he thinks, for America's failure to produce major poets and critics from Poe to Lowell and beyond. The moral for twentieth-century literature is that our writers must concern themselves with social ideals and social issues that "catch at the bottom of things, like a dredging machine" (p. 170) before their writings can become vital and authentic. The road was at the fork: in one direction lay social participation and responsibility arrived at through realistic criticism and reform, in the other lay alienation and aesthetic detachment.

Brooks cut the issue sharply for both the artist and his society. He made it clear that the American artist in 1915 must help his society come to terms with itself before he could come to terms with his own art and use it for the expression of eternal verities and values.

IV
Recognition of a problem does not always carry with it the toughness necessary to an acceptance of its consequences. The American people to whom Brooks spoke were not ready to be told that they were lacking in appreciation of the finer things of life, that their civilization was crass and confused, and that their literature had failed to face the realities of their experience. Even the critic himself winced at the full import of his denunciation and, in his later books, somewhat softened his position. In *Letters and Leadership,* three years later, he revealed his impatience with the slow process of assimilation, perspective, criticism, and evaluation that marks the growth from life into art, and in his biographical studies of Mark Twain and Henry James he observed in detail the failure of the American artist to come to terms with his own world. Twain, he felt, never developed fully as an artist because he was too much a part of his environment, and Henry James ran away from the problem by escaping to Europe. Although he had so effectively pointed out the path the new literature must take, Brooks could not accept (as could Mencken, who was made of sterner stuff) the one man who was then cutting his way ruthlessly through to the heart of the problem, Theodore Dreiser. Rather, he chose a less exacting solution by creating his own literary past in *The Flowering of*

New England (1937) and its companion volumes. Even so, the catalytic effect of his criticism did more than anything else to create the situation that he quotes Matthew Arnold as believing to be essential to creative art. "It is the business of the creative power," Arnold had asserted, "to see the object in itself as it really is," and in so doing to create "an intellectual situation of which the creative power can profitably avail itself." The American artist had to learn all over again to see American life as it really had come to be in the twentieth century. No edges could be softened, no vision dimmed. Whatever the consequences and the misunderstandings, the truth about American life must be told.

That there would be misunderstandings, both at home and abroad, anyone could have predicted. If America's dirty linen were to be washed in public, it might be hard for her to retain her reputation with her neighbors as the home of unsullied ideals and moral cleanliness.

This may be the point at which I should interrupt my argument to echo the warning of Carl Bode (then our cultural attaché at London) against accepting the realistic and critical literature of any nation as an accurate source of information about its life and character. Steinbeck's picture of the West, Faulkner's of the South, Farrell's of Chicago, and O'Neill's or even Frost's of New England are almost the reverse of the literal truth.

As a matter of fact, we do not—now, at any rate—have a single novelist of note who gives us an account of the typical American family of our middle class, neither rich nor poor, more materialistic than spiritual but something of both, and living a life of busy routine. . . . In poetry the case is even stronger. . . . I am convinced that the assumption that you can tell about a country—in the sense of forming a proper picture of it—from reading its literature is so false that it breaks down as soon as it is looked at closely.[1]

In other words, the mirror of the critical mind is not enough if it serves only as a mirror. Refraction must follow upon reflection and—to carry the metaphor just one step further without, I hope, overstraining it— the light of truth not only must be accepted in its own terms by the critic, but must be bent as it cuts through the crystal of his aesthetic sensibility and broken into its many colored prismatic elements. Actually, it is the spectrum that tells us the truth about light and not the unaided optic nerve, which sees it vaguely as the opposite of darkness.

In dealing with art, we are in the realm of the imagination, a realm quite different from that of recorded fact. The artist brings to experience his own perspective and values. He is not a mere recorder of life; he is an interpreter, and all the tools of his trade are designed to make it possible for him to present, not the facts as they are, but a deliberate, planned, complex, and often violent distortion of the evidence chiefly through the prisms of comedy and tragedy. If we take the imagination fully into account, we can carry Dr. Bode's warning forward to the conclusion it implies and say: "Not until you know the litera-ture of a people intimately and fully can you understand their inner life and character."

V

For this purpose, of all the creative arts, satire is the closest to direct criticism; yet, by donning the motley, the satirist invokes the comic spirit to protect both himself and his victims from the full sting of his barbs. A Swift can reduce a whole society to the dimensions of pygmies and thereby reveal the pettiness of its leaders and institutions without fear of personal consequences. He can go further and denounce the entire human race for its beastiality, exalting the wisdom of horses in contrast, while the detachment of ironic wit preserves his own aesthetic immunity. A Juvenal, a Voltaire, a Bernard Shaw can heap insults on his fellows and condemn their entire structure of social codes and customs, only to be received with a chuckle of delight by the victims of his attacks. The comic spirit is man's finest invention to protect himself from his own individual and collective fol-lies. To tragedy's total involvement it provides all-seeing detachment.

America has had humor from the start, but until recently has lacked the true comic spirit. From Benjamin Franklin to the *New Yorker*, there has been sophisticated wit on both sides of the

Atlantic, but the characteristic American humor has been mainly the tall tale and the rough dialect of the frontier. Perhaps this is because the sharper barbs of satire require a settled society with manners, habits, and institutions firmly enough entrenched to reveal human folly without risking human survival. America has had such a society only sporadically. The constant movement of the population and the violent conflicts of races and resources within the culture have, at least until recently, prevented the development of an economic and social structure firm enough to offer the resistance to satire that the comic spirit requires.

This situation no longer holds. As the Lynds' have demonstrated in their analytical study of the typical American community *Middletown* (1929), and as other sociologists have repeatedly confirmed, American society today has taken a characteristic and almost universal form in the so-called small town —self-contained, complacent, prosperous, blending its spiritual aspirations with its material accomplishments in a workable union, the embodiment of the "middle-class" ideal that combined the virtues of the farm with the comforts that industry can supply, the rugged individualism of the frontier with the other-directed security that the tight community can provide.

Usually such a town has a population of from one to five thousand. It subsists on the surrounding farms and the factory or two within its limits. It has a railroad station and perhaps an airport. All the chain stores are represented on or near its main street, including the two or three supermarkets dominant in that general area, where are also the town hall or county courthouse, the bank, the firehouse, the grange or social hall, the three or more churches of different denominations, and the elementary and high schools with their playing fields nearby. The surrounding streets are wide, straight, and tree-shaded, with houses ranging from the brick-front solid rows to the comfortable home with its two-car garage and its half-acre lot. There is no class hierarchy in the European sense: no aristocracy, no mercantile class, no working class, although there are well-defined social distinctions and differences in wealth. Such divisions are rather vertical than horizontal in the American system and are determined more by occupation than by family or wealth. The country-club set is composed mostly of the young executives or local representatives of large corporations; there are the Rotary Club and the Business Men's Association, the Women's Club, and perhaps a local dramatic society with a playhouse of its own. The children provide a major social focus, and the Home and School Association, the Public Library, and the Recreation Association are centers of community interest. Each church has its social, as well as its religious following; and, if the town boasts a college or university, the faculty and graduates have their shared intellectual life. There is no middle class in America because American society is not stratified horizontally. The term no longer has meaning because it is all middle, with the pattern of the American community set firmly by institutions, occupations, and community culture.

It was such a society that gave birth, through satire, to America's first genuine discovery of the comic spirit in Sinclair Lewis but, in spite of Mark Twain's earlier efforts, the readers of his day had not yet learned to laugh.[2] Lewis was born to this society in Sauk Centre, Minnesota, in 1885. He went east to Yale and for a time worked in Upton Sinclair's socialist utopia in New Jersey, did hack writing in New York City, and traveled widely over the United States. Success as a writer of fiction bypassed his four early novels and waited until he turned a matured satiric eye on his own home town. The Gopher Prairie of *Main Street* (1920) is Sauk Centre, its people are modeled on the people he knew, his mingled scorn and appreciation for its follies could come only from the local boy who went to the big city and then returned. No one could hate a community so effectively as Lewis does in this book without at the bottom loving it. The material is too close to him to allow a steady flood of the white light of the comic spirit, with its Meridithean ripples of silvery laughter, to illuminate its follies. But the social criticism on every page is as vicious as anything Mencken ever wrote, even as it is projected into Carol and Will Kennicott and presented indirectly as self-revelation. With this tale, the American comic spirit was born, for Lewis had gained in satire a perspective that even Mark Twain and the folk humorists were unable to achieve.

Lewis approached his next book, *Babbitt (1922)*, with a surer hand and a bolder stroke. The story of the realtor "estate officer" of Zenith, Ohio, is more baldly a burlesque of the American junior city. Free now of the sentimental bondage to his own community that had both hampered and enriched *Main Street* (1920), he struck out with ruthless force and point at every phase of American life — its values, its codes, its manners, its instruments of comfort, as well as its fears and frustrations. Only an enraged moralist could have satirized so effectively the materialism and conformity he felt were stifling the best in human nature.

Lewis uncovered the self-delusion and rationalizations that were trying to represent a materialistic, confused, and thoroughly human society as the best of all possible worlds. His satire stung, but it stuck, and "Babbittry" became a word in the American language.

With this book, the pattern of Lewis's subsequent work was set, but he never again succeeded so well in stating and maintaining his ironic perspective. He wrote more bitter books: *Elmer Gantry* (1927), a satire on the evangelical clergy; *It Can't Happen Here* (1935), a timely attack on political complacency in the face of threatening fascism; and *The Prodigal Parents* (1938); an exposé of false values in American family life. He also wrote better novels, as novels: *Arrowsmith* (1925), perhaps his best, based on the medical career of his father and containing his own testament of values as nearly as any one of his books, and *Dodsworth* (1929), a successful treatment of the time-worn theme of the American abroad. But it is as a satirist that his reputation must stand for the testing. Scarcely a facet of American society escaped him: the businessman, the doctor, the lawyer, the career girl, the artist, the clergyman, the family, the school, the race question, the politician, and the theater. He was the first American writer to recognize the true vertical divisions of American society as firm components of the total structure and therefore as fit subjects for satirical attack. Other social novelists — Marquand, O'Hara, Wilder, and Cozzens among them — have followed his lead and have given American literature for the first time a true instrument of the comic spirit. A society that can see its own weaknesses and can laugh is essentially a sane and healthy society. Lucky the court that has a jester.

But Lewis was not at first accepted by the American people and, on the whole, his own life was full of bitterness. Even the award of the Nobel Prize for Literature in 1930 did not salve his wounds. He had rejected the Pulitzer Prize earlier because he felt that it was "cramped by the provisions of Mr. Pulitzer's will that the prize shall be given 'for the American novel published during the year which shall best present the wholesome atmosphere of American life, and the highest standard of American manners and manhood.' " It was just such a scheme of values that Lewis was fighting with all his energy and all his art. The Nobel Prize, however, was awarded for "the most distinguished work of an idealistic tendency" of any author and was interpreted to mean his whole work rather than merely a single volume. This Lewis could accept: he was idealistic and he hoped that his work might be considered distinguished. His speech of acceptance on December 11, 1930, published at his own urgent request in the *The New York Times* two days later and apparently never reprinted, is one of the milestones of American literary history. Not only is it a summary and mainly accurate statement of the spiritual and aesthetic health of American writing at that moment, but it is a generous and acute analysis of the faults in American society that had always frustrated the best literary expression.

Taking as the direct object of his attack an academic critic who had apparently criticized the award, Lewis puts on the gloves and administers a left hook to the chin:

This scholar stated, and publicly, that in awarding the Nobel Prize to a person that had scoffed at American institutions as I, the Nobel Committee and the Swedish Academy had insulted America. . . . I would even have supposed that so international a scholar would have assumed that Scandinavia, accustomed to the works of Strindberg, Ibsen, and Pontoppidan, would not have been peculiarly shocked by a writer whose most anarchistic assertions have been that America with all her wealth and power has not yet produced a civilization good enough to satisfy the deeper cries of human creatures.

The American novelist, poet, dramatist, sculptor and painter must work alone, in confusion and unassisted save by his own integrity. . . . I salute them [the younger writers, whom he names] with all joy as being not yet too far removed from their unconquerable determination to give to the America that has mountains and endless prairies, enormous cities and lost farm cabins, billions of money and tons of faith, the America that is as strange as Russia and as complex as China, a literature worthy of her vastness.

VI

One of the finest things in Lewis's speech is his tribute to Dreiser, his nearest competitor, as he must have known, for the prize which he had received.

> Suppose you had taken Dreiser. Now to me and to many other American writers, Dreiser, more than any other man, is marching alone. Usually unappreciated, often hounded, he has cleared the trail from Victorian, Howellesian timidity and gentility in American fiction to honesty, boldness, and passion of life. Without his pioneering I doubt if any of us could, unless we liked to be sent to jail, seek to express life, beauty, and terror.

It is obvious, however, that even in his enthusiasm, Lewis does not fully appreciate Dreiser's contribution, which was to rediscover, in an American context, the nature of tragedy as he, Lewis, had rediscovered comedy. Without humor and without style, this indefatigable giant from a midwestern German emigrant family hammered his way, as Melville had before him, into the tragic heart of this powerful and prosperous people and found there the eternal and eternally unresolved struggle of man to conquer his inevitable fate.

I realize that any effort to reinstate tragedy in the modern world is doomed to be unpopular because modern criticism of all schools is in seeming agreement that tragedy requires a faith in the dignity of man and the ascendency of deity, neither of which concepts, it is claimed, are tenable today. Arguing from Aristotle's *Poetics*, the critics hold that tragedy must involve the fall of man from high estate through a flaw in character or action and that the resulting unhappy end must cleanse the emotions through the excitement of pity and fear and restore the just moral order of the universe. Almost all the components of this definition, it is argued, are unavailable to an age in which high estate is no longer possible because science has reduced man to little more than an atom or cog in the universal machine over which he has no control or direction. It is paradoxical therefore, to say that Dreiser, the American author who most fully accepted this naturalistic view of fate, rediscovered the spirit of tragedy.

I think, however, that something of the sort can be said if we are willing to forget the formal requirements of classical drama that are so much in the mind of the critic and think rather of the tragic spirit as one of two basic attitudes from which art is created—the other being the spirit of comedy. Dreiser did not write tragedy in the technical sense—nor has O'Neill, Anderson, Williams, or any other modern dramatist in spite of their study of Aristotle—but he accepted as the basic theme of all his work the tragic issue, which A. E. Powell has defined as the demand that what can't be, must be—the old problem of the irresistible force and the immovable object. The two main factors of tragic conflict have always been the unquenchable will of man to prevail over nature and his inevitable defeat by an unbending law of fate on whatever principle of ultimate order the current metaphysic supplies. Empathy carries us with man in his endeavor, we share his ambition and his illusions, but we know that his fall is inevitable. When it comes, we are saved from sharing it by the realization that for us the experience is of the imagination only, and we feel a surge of pity and fear as we return to the security of the accepted moral order.

Dreiser was not a scholar, and he did not think out these problems with the aid of the philosopher or the critic. He was the untutored son of a poor, ignorant, and intensely religious home. What he knew about life, he learned by working on the newspapers of Chicago, St. Louis, and New York. He read, as all intelligent young men were then reading, Spencer and Huxley, as well as the stories that appeared in the magazines. In *A Book About Myself* (1922), written many years later, he tells of the "awe of the grinding and almost disgusting forces of life itself" that his reading brought him and that was confirmed by the "astounding contrast between wealth and poverty" that "gave the great city a gross and cruel and mechanical look." He was struck by "the professed ideals and preachments," contrasted with the harsh actions, of the moralizing *New York World*, on which he was then working, and by the "almost complete absence of any reference to the coarse and the vulgar and the cruel and the terrible" in the work of all the then "assured" American writers. Like Zola, Hauptmann, Hardy, and other naturalistic writers in other countries, he determined to devote his life to a disclosure of the true story of man as Darwinian science explained him and as experience in an urban, industrialized civilization revealed him. Other American writers had already been drawn to the philosophy of mechanistic determinism—Mark Twain, Frank Norris, Stephen Crane—but none accepted the implications of this philosophy so wholeheartedly as did Dreiser. For him it was an emotional commitment that absorbed his whole being in an almost religious devotion. For the basic moral law of the universe he accepted the law of natural selection and for the will of man that of the survival of the fittest. Because he responded, as writers must, to what his heart rather than his mind told him, he could recount with conviction, on the one hand, man's drive for power and mastery over his fellows and, on the other, his inevitable defeat in a mechanical universe that had no care for his individual welfare. Whether his protagonists were weak-willed like Carrie and Jennie and Clyde or strong-willed like Cowperwood and Eugene Witla and Solon Barnes, they shared the same passion for life, which made them challenge fate by overt action at the start of the book and suffer the consequences of that violation of natural law at the end. Each is a tragedy in its fashion; and the paradox of an action, both sides of which are controlled by the same natural law, can be resolved only by tragic irony and not by systematic reasoning.

This paradox became the central theme of all his novels. I could illustrate this from any one of them, but perhaps the best and most thoroughly developed is the novel of his prime, *An American Tragedy* (1925). The early experiences of Clyde Griffith, his ambitions, his jobs, his successes and his frustrations, are largely autobiographical; the central action of the story— his murder of the working girl whom he has made pregnant when another who represents greater wealth, social position, and beauty seems within his reach— is a direct transcription of an actual court case he had clipped from a newspaper. Here, Dreiser seems to be saying, but for an accident of circumstances, am I—or you—or any other American boy. On one level, it is the story of the hopes and errors of a weak-willed, well-meaning American boy; of the evils and distortions of the American industrial system on a second level; and of the tragic irony of life as interpreted by modern science on a third. In this, as so often happens in his tales, Dreiser emphasizes the ironic qualities of his naturalistic fate by a quick twist at the moment of crisis. Clyde has carefully plotted how he will upset the boat in a remote New York lake in order to make Roberta's drowning seem an accident; but, when the moment comes for the execution of his plan, his will fails and events are carried forward as it were of their own momentum so that the drowning, which is really an accident, seems deliberate. Clyde is condemned to death for it and goes to the chair with the passivity he displayed in all other actions in his life. It is also ironic that the district attorney, who wishes to use the case for his own political ends, is forced to plant circumstantial evidence in order to prove it. The culminating irony is that Dreiser repeats in an epilogue the incident of the prologue that set the terms of the tragedy.

One may accept all that has been said about Dreiser's crudity of both concept and style and still not escape from his impelling conviction of truth, his overwhelming human empathy, his massive and harmonious structure of vivid details, and his unqualified acceptance of the world of force and will as modern scientific knowledge has given it to the sensitive aesthetic consciousness. Surely it was he who lighted the lamp of tragic irony and gave American literature of the following generation of writers the rationale in which they have done their greatest work. Like Lewis, they all—O'Neill, Wolfe, Hemingway, and Faulkner—are deeply indebted to him for their freedom from the entanglements of nineteenth-century morality and literary convention and for their steady and profound view of man's predicament in the modern world.

And so, through awakened self-criticism, the American consciousness came to terms with the spirits of comedy and tragedy, and the Second Literary Renaissance was born.

NOTES

1. Carl Bode, *Literary Newsletter* (London: United States Information Service, October 1958), quoted by permission.

2. *From Main Street to Stockholm: Letters of Sinclair Lewis* (New York, 1952), pp. 296-97.

9 | THE MAGIC MIRROR OF AMERICAN FICTION

If I had doubted that American literary history had come full cycle again in the first half of the twentieth century, I would have been convinced when a Fulbright professorship took me to Oslo, Norway, in January 1950. When I arrived, The Death of a Salesman *was playing in the National Theatre and a bookstore on Karl Johansgate was featuring a window display of* The Naked and the Dead. *I was further assured when Professor Sigmund Skard showed me his collection of modern American literature (including a complete Upton Sinclair) in his new American Institute, and I learned that the leading Norwegian publisher, Gyldendahl, had devoted half of his "Golden Series" of translations of the best contemporary foreign authors to American works.*

I soon learned that pretty much the same thing was true of other Scandinavian and European countries. Contemporary American literature was the going thing. But I then wondered why—as I do again now as I think of Carl Bode's warning (cf. p. 133): Was it the emerging political world power of the United States or was it appreciation of literary excellence that made for this popularity with both the public and the scholar?

It was some years before I confronted this question to deal with it fully. My involvement with the Swedish literary committee of the Nobel Foundation had no connection with this earlier Scandinavian visit, but it gave me my opportunity. I met Karl Ragnar Gierow, permanent secretary of the foundation, through a friend when he was worried by the world reactions

*to some of the Nobel literary awards and was planning a confer-
ence of representative scholars in Stockholm to debate the
question.*

*At the last minute, I was unable to present my paper in per-
son, but it was read at the conference and subsequently published in* Nobel Symposium No. 6: Problems of International
Literary Understanding. *It is printed here in this country for the
first time.*

I

Literature, it seems to me, is always some form of comment on
human experience; if it were merely a record of events, it would
not be literature. It is, as the poet Emily Dickinson said, an
author's "letter to the world" rather than the morning newspaper. If we wish to know how a person really thinks and feels,
we should read his poems, plays, and novels; and the same
should be true of a nation. A national literature should be a
record of the way the people of a nation really think and feel (in
other words, their subjective life) and it should therefore be one
of the best instruments of international communication and
understanding.

Unfortunately this is not always the case, because the acts of
writing and reading a work of literature involve two parties to
the occasion, the writer *and* the reader, and the motives of the
two may be very different; in fact, they are often quite opposite.
Especially is this true of the literature of self-criticism, the literature of a people who are trying to define and understand their
own culture. For them this is not a process of merely recording
the truth; the tendency is to exaggerate good qualities and sati-
rize or outright condemn weaknesses. The reader, if he be of
another nation, especially one which wishes for practical and
political reasons to be either friendly or hostile to the nation of
the writer, may get from the book exactly the opposite reaction
from that the author intended because he has no way to identify
either exaggeration or satire and he will assume that what he is
reading is the literal truth, or the way he would like the truth to
be. It is always safer, for example, when a lady says, "I look

frightful today," to tell her that she looks beautiful rather than to agree heartily with her. This may not be one of the most appealing traits of human nature, but it is one of the most nearly universal. And so the acceptance of a work of national self-criticism as an example of realism is a dangerous mistake in international relations.

I approach our problem, therefore, with two very pessimistic premises: The one is that the literature of national self-examination is more likely than not to become an agent of international misunderstanding; and the other is that nations often read the literature of other nations for self-interested and political rather than intellectual and literary reasons. They tend to choose those books which suit the social and political needs and backgrounds of their own culture at that particular time rather than those which might help them dispassionately to understand the culture of the other nation. Both writer and reader are victims of the oblique light of self-interest rather than the direct light of truth, and the two oblique lights rarely come from the same angle of vision.

II

There is probably no modern civilization which has aroused as much curiosity, sympathy, antipathy, and genuine interest as that of the United States from its founding in 1783 to today. Because one of the basic American principles has always been freedom of inquiry and of expression, its culture has been exposed to examination both from within and from without more ruthlessly than would be possible in almost any other nation. Furthermore, during its entire life it has been under more violent pressures for growth and change than other nations because of its heterogeneous population, its vast resources and, in spite of its violent internal conflicts and diversities, its seemingly consistent motivation and national character. One of the main reasons why people of other nations have always been unusually interested in its literature and culture is that the new nation came into existence as a sort of *tabula rasa* on which the peoples of Europe and Asia might rewrite their own histories more as they would like them to be. Or, as

Arnold Chapman has summed up the problem, in another context: "In recent years, the Spanish-American intellectual's reception of United States fiction is in reality a self-appraisal. What he holds in his hand as he reads is a magic mirror that reflects a face that is his and yet not his. It might be his twin brother's or it might be his alter-ego's; but in any case the comfort of the familiar and the disquiet of the strange hit him together." What the European sees in this magic mirror is therefore the reflection of his own ideals of what he might have been combined with the horrible example of what he might become rather than the direct image of what he actually is.[1]

History provides us with three principal distortions of American culture that have appeared in this magic mirror: the image of the primitive American Dream of human perfectibility with equal rights and infinite resources for all; the image of the materialism of industrial capitalism which has corrupted the riches of the New World and will corrupt those of the Old if proper precautions are not taken in time; and the image of a ruthless and imperialistic power that wishes to dominate the course of future world history. I hope that we can agree that all of these images are false; yet all three are widely believed to be true.

Our question then becomes: What contributions have some of our more representative novelists made toward creating, confirming, or denying these false images by their efforts to use their art as an instrument of self-understanding? And the further question: Why have Europeans at times wished to use their writings to establish one or another of these stereotypes as an accurate portrait of the American national character?

Time will allow me to offer only brief and undocumented statements about a few American writers of fiction who have apparently had the greatest influence in shaping the American myth in the European mind. They are James Fenimore Cooper, Mark Twain, Jack London, Upton Sinclair, Sinclair Lewis, and Ernest Hemingway, but I shall also have to refer to many others, including Harriet Beecher Stowe, Theodore Dreiser, Howard Fast, William Faulkner, and John Steinbeck. I did not choose this list; it was chosen for me.

III

Although Washington Irving was the first American writer to be widely read abroad, his popularity rested mainly on his adjustment to European themes and styles; but James Fenimore Cooper won immediate international fame by his brusque and untutored treatment of American subjects in an adapted European romantic style in the 1820s. Cooper's authentic quality, however, broke through the veneer of borrowed manner, and translations into French and German began almost immediately, with simultaneous English and American publication and translations into other European languages before the middle of the century. Greeted first as "the American Scott," he was thought of mainly as a storyteller of the New World, and his Leather-stocking became the prototype of the primitive free American individual on an exciting wilderness frontier, pitting his wits and native skill against the Indians and the perils of wild nature. Considered naive in both style and subject, he seemed all the more young and new and American for that reason, and in most countries he was adapted for children rather than taken seriously by adults. "When we say that he is national," wrote an early British reviewer, "we mean that his characters are the growth of America; that the mountains and streams which he describes, the forests that rustle in his pages, all the phenomena of earth and air are American; that his principles, feelings, and prejudices all lead him to embrace, on every occasion, the cause of America." Nowhere, for almost a hundred years, did it seem to be noticed that the first novel in which Natty Bumppo appears, *The Pioneers* (1823), presents him as a crotchety old man who fails to reconcile the virtues of primitive nature, the morals of conventional Christianity, and the amenities of imported European civilization.[2] Far from being the prototype of the wilderness scout making a new world of morals and manners, he focuses the perceptive reader's attention on the central problem of the new nation and its evolving culture: the irreconcilable differences in the philosophies, particularly with reference to property, of Indian John, Judge Temple, and himself. It was on this problem that Cooper concentrated all his subsequent work and became thereby the first American writer of note to attempt to define and understand the evolving American nation as the latest battleground of primitive vs. civilized man. *Home as Found* (1838) is the direct ancestor of *Main Street* (1920) and is equally bitter, but to his contemporaries abroad Cooper was the writer of romance, the apostle of the primitive, and the celebrator of the virtues of his nation.

The reason for this distortion was that Europe was as yet unafraid of American power, even on the sea, and very much under the influence of the ideals and hopes of the revolutions of 1789, 1830, and 1848. A buoyant, naive, idealistic and somewhat crude cultural image was found because it was needed, not only in the writings of Cooper, but in those of Mark Twain, Bret Harte, the local colorists, and the romancers down to Frances Hodgson Burnett and F. Marion Crawford and even Jack London in Germany, Finland, Sweden, and elsewhere as late as 1920. The American Dream occupied these northern nights long after it had been dispelled by the modern American daylight.

Nor was the romantic concern for the hope of the New World much disturbed by our Civil War, Reconstruction, industrialization, immigration, the closing of the frontier or any of the disillusioning things that the historians tell us happened in the second half of the century. *Uncle Tom's Cabin* ran into many editions, especially in England where it is said to have sold a million and a half copies, but apparently more because of romantic interest in the character of Uncle Tom than because of an aroused concern for the social evil of slavery.[3] Running it a close second in sales was the lachrymose *Wide, Wide World,* and when Mark Twain came to be known in England and on the Continent, it was as a humorist and writer of stories about boys for boys. The pessimist and social critic of *The Gilded Age, A Connecticut Yankee,* and *Pudd'nhead Wilson* was almost unknown. Longfellow and Poe had British and French vogues during these years, but the realistic movement in fiction claimed little attention. Frederic, Howells, and Henry James were very little translated, others were ignored, and even Dreiser was not recognized until *An American Tragedy* in 1925, when a basic shift in the world political position of the United States helped to bring

the now famous American literary renaissance to the attention
of Europeans, and the earlier Dreiśer novels were translated for
the first time, although they had been popular in England.

It is safe to say, I think, that American fiction, whether self-
critical or not, had little effect in Europe during the nineteenth
century and well into the twentieth except as expressions of the
American Dream, which was also luring immigrants in increasing and unrestricted millions from all countries from Norway
to Italy, until the Immigration Act of 1924 slowed the movement to a near stand-still. Of self-critical fictional social documents, only Bellamy's *Looking Backward* (1888) was much
noticed abroad and the effect of such social critics of the American system as Henry D. Lloyd, Thorsten Veblen, Henry George,
and William James was not reflected to any great extent in the
American novels which Europeans read. Yet by 1870 the realistic movement was in full control of the serious American novel
and never before had American writers tried so hard to understand and to portray the truth about American life. While William Dean Howells, Henry James, Howe, Kirkland, and their
fellow realists told what they saw as the truth about American
life and character, the translators turned rather to stereotyped
romances of the American prairies and gold fields to stock the
European bookstalls.

IV

At the same time the American image abroad was going
through a profound though subtle change. The reader of Commager's volume of excerpts from European commentators on
American civilization becomes aware of a new Uncle Sam.
Brother Jonathan has grown up from the innocent youth to the
money-grabbing adult materialist.[4] It was too soon to blame the
change on industrialism and the capitalistic system; that was to
come later, but European travelers, starting with Dickens and
Mrs. Trollope in the 1830s and 40s, were all too anxious to point
out the unhappy change in the American character which they
thought they observed, but for some strange reason the American novels which sought to come to terms with these social
changes were by-passed until Jack London and Upton Sinclair
were discovered just after the turn of the century.

The rise to international fame of this second-rate romancer and this tedious socialistic journalist during the first two decades of the present century is a phenomenon difficult to explain in literary terms and seems, more than any other evidence I have been able to discover, to defend my pessimistic premise that European readers looked in American fiction for the image of their own prejudices rather than for facts. The change was in the European angle of vision rather than in the American novelist's national self-inquiry. Jack London and Upton Sinclair brought exactly the news from the New World that the Old World wanted to hear once the United States had defeated Spain and for the first time had extended her sovereignty beyond her own continental limits. But perhaps even more important was their introduction of the deterministic ideas of Nietzsche, Darwin, and Marx to the growing criticism of laissez-faire capitalistic societies. Americans were developing a guilt complex about their unrestrained exploitation of natural resources and their unregulated economic society, a guilt complex to which Europeans were eager to agree when they saw "Americanism," as they called it, threatening their own more rigid social structures. Even in the 1830s Toqueville had noticed this danger, but a century later it had become so alarming that the French critic Romier could say in 1927: "The debate is between Europe and America: can they join in a common task? Or, if they cannot, which of the two will be responsible for the destiny of the white race?"

There is little doubt therefore that the first impact of Jack London was as a primitive and as a vivid storyteller. His material was the New West, the California and the Klondike which had been opened up to adventure by the Gold Rush, which he shared with such professional hack writers as James Oliver Curwood and Zane Grey, whose novels were as avidly translated as were London's *Call of the Wild, White Fang,* and others of the kind. But underlying London's romancing of dog intelligence was the Nietzschean theory of the superman, the Darwinian stress on natural selection in evolution, and the Marxian attack on capitalism. Basically a confused person, his enthusiasm for all these new ideas at the same time added up to a vigorous attack on American civilization and on capitalism in general. His semiautobiographical *Martin Eden* contained them all, but his only outright fictional advocacy of socialism was the inferior but influential *The Iron Heel* (1907). In other novels he preached an anarchic society based on elemental primitivism and governed by an American type of the superman, more Nietzschean than Jeffersonian.

Upton Sinclair, on the other hand, was a cool and efficient propagandist who early committed himself to a systematic attack on the institutions of American capitalistic industrialism, sometimes directly as in *The Goose-step* and *The Brass Check* but more often in the form of a fictional attack as in *The Jungle* on the meat-packing industry and the exploitation of cheap immigrant labor, in *Oil* on the petroleum monopolies, and in *Boston* on corruption in the judicial system as illustrated in the Sacco-Vanzetti case. His thesis that the moneyed interests controlled the American system from the schools and the press down through all other departments of American life was more negative than positive, a vague socialist idealism rather than a systematic Marxian dialectic, but it was all the more influential abroad because it did not clearly distinguish between that socialism which later took a fascistic turn and that which laid the foundations for communism. But it was Sinclair more than any other American author who gave fictional authority to the materialistic aspects of American civilization and thereby dealt a deathblow to the American Dream. Although a confessed propagandist, his writings seemed to the uninformed foreign reader to be the first authentic and accurate reports of the degeneration of New World ideals and the threat of an anarchistic materialism to Europe's social security. He, more than anyone else, prepared the way for popular acceptance of the award of the first Nobel Prize in Literature, not to himself, because his artistic defects were early recognized, but to his more genuinely literary disciple Sinclair Lewis, who was accepted as a serious artist by Swedish critics from the start.

Granted that it was pretty generally agreed that the award was to be made in 1930 to an American, the only writers well enough known outside of the United States who could be considered were Sinclair, London, Dreiser, O'Neill, Frost, or Lewis, and the choice soon narrowed down to Dreiser and Lewis. The younger generation of Hemingway, Faulkner, Dos Passos, Caldwell, and Wilder, who were in turn to have so profound an international influence, had not yet established themselves firmly enough either at home or abroad to be seriously considered, and Wolfe's and Steinbeck's major works were still to come. London had died in 1916, appreciation of O'Neill was to come later, especially in Sweden, and of Frost not at all except in England where he was first published, and Dreiser could not make a strong claim because he had only just come into full recognition with *An American Tragedy* in 1925 although he had been publishing since 1900 and his first five novels provided the most profound analysis of American society yet to be produced in fiction. His heavy style, however, raised questions about his art, and his naturalism seemed a mode through which most European literatures had already passed. After all, Zola and Dostoevski were no novelties to Swedish intellectuals in 1930.

Sinclair Lewis presented a different case. There was an air of authenticity about his portraits of American character in *Main Street, Babbitt, Arrowsmith, Elmer Gantry,* and *Dodsworth,* all of which had appeared between 1920 and 1929, and a freshness and clarity about his satirical point of view and style which made him seem a better artist than he later appeared. These five remain, after all, his best novels even though he continued to write for another twenty years; and his work, although admittedly satire, seemed at the same time to present a realistic picture of American civilization as the European was coming to visualize it in the magic mirror of twentieth-century political tensions. Here was a kind of Swift or Voltaire who was bringing "news from the New World" of the kind that the Old World was prepared to hear, and his American acceptance (*Babbitt* especially had been a best-seller) seemed to validate the choice. It is the clearest possible illustration of how national self-inquiry may lead to international misunderstanding. The middle-middle-class Lewis, who loved his country and accepted wholly the American way of life, was pained by the weaknesses he saw in the structure of American society and the blindness of

the average American to its true values. With only a modest
skill in satire, he had set out to explore the national weaknesses
one by one in novel after novel.[5] His American readers, because
they shared Babbitt's background and experience, read them as
incidental comments on a fundamentally sound society; but
Europeans, lacking that background and instinctively on their
guard against America's growing power, judged them more
nearly as realistic protraits of a decadent society. It was possible
to recognize Lewis as an artist of power and at the same time see
in his work a confirmation of the American national stereotype
which the European had learned from Sinclair and London to
believe in. Earlier books by the Norwegian Hamsun, the German Schönemann, the French Siegfrid—to say nothing of the
American Harold Stearns' own devastating symposium,
Civilization in the United States, in the same year (1922) as *Babbitt*
—agreed on the threat of American materialism to world culture, while the stock market crash of 1929 seemed to confirm
their worst fears.

V

The vaguely defined dual purposes of the Nobel Prize in Literature, that is, literary excellence and social significance, were
admirably reconciled in the choice of Sinclair Lewis, a fact
which he recognized in his speach of acceptance. After some
deprecatory remarks on the American literary establishment, he
proceeded to introduce to a world public a new generation of
American writers, all of whom except Dreiser, Willa Cather, and
Sherwood Anderson were younger than he; among them were
Wolfe, Wilder, and Hemingway, the last of whom he called "an
authentic artist whose home is the whole of life."

The burst of European enthusiasm for this new group of
American fictionalists had already started by 1925 in many of
the countries of Europe, and it was to reach its height by the
early 1950s when the Nobel Prize went to Faulkner and Hemingway, and later even to Steinbeck. As had happened before in
American literary history, foreign critical recognition served,
between 1930 and 1950, to define and interpret a genuine literary renaissance of which Americans were at that time only par-

tially aware. Europeans were greeting these young Americans individually and as a group and defining their work as a movement in world literature while American critics and literary historians were still lamenting their pessimistic and un-American attitudes, which were taken to indicate the decline of nineteenth-century idealism and gentility into modern decadence and expatriate disloyalty. It was not until almost midcentury that Americans realized that their literature had been passing through one of the high points—perhaps the highest—in its history, whereas the fact had been recognized and dealt with constructively (but perhaps not always for the right reasons), by European literary critics and historians for some two decades. A full analysis of this situation would take another essay at least as long as this one, but it might provide at least some provisional answers to the problem of national self-inquiry as a factor in international literary understanding. All I can do here is to outline the problem in general terms and supply a few of the most pertinent facts.

I can bear personal testimony to the wave of disillusionment and pessimism to the point of nihilism which swept over my generation—we who reached maturity just in time for America's crusading entrance into World War I—when all that had been said about our national materialism and provincialism seemed validated by the breakdown of law and morals under prohibition, the explosive inflation on the stock market, and the failure of the League of Nations partly because of our refusal to join. What Malcolm Cowley and others have said about "the Lost Generation" and its flight to Europe is historical fact, but few of us realized that we were, in this process, reaching a level of cultural maturity and international perspective that had not been dreamt of in our history. The ex-patriots and protesters— Fitzgerald, Hemingway, MacLeish, Wescott, Hart Crane, Dos Passos, Sherwood Anderson, and many others were following the path of national alienation and European cultural education already opened for them by Henry James, Gertrude Stein, Henry Miller, Ezra Pound, and T. S. Eliot, a path which led to London and Paris, where they met Gide, Yeats, Joyce, and the international *avant garde*, as well as the new painters, Picasso

and Matisse, and where they came into contact with the aesthetic and philosophical discoveries of Croce, Freud, Cassirer,
and other spokesmen for the new movements in art and life.
When the currency balance shifted again and most of them
returned to the United States in the early thirties, they brought
with them the makings of the cultural revolution which then
took place.

This migration had been a two-way street, for the Americans
had provided a vitality and naive enthusiasm for violence
which the tired Europeans lacked. By the time Faulkner, Wolfe,
and Steinbeck had joined the movement in the thirties, it had
already been discovered and defined by the literary critics of
France, Germany, Norway, Sweden, Italy, Russia, England, and
other European countries. Blodgett notes a variation of emphasis in two wings of the movement, that which seems to have
centered in England, Germany, and Scandinavia and that which
started in France and moved through Italy and Spain into the
Latin American countries.[6] On the Northern route, he finds
books of broad scope rather than depth, like Wolfe, Dreiser,
Pearl Buck, and the romances; on the Southern, works of more
technical skill and narrower scope like Faulkner, Dos Passos,
Caldwell, and the "hard-boiled school" in general. The division
is not a sharp one, and Hemingway is found equally in both
groups. The roll-call differed slightly from country to country
anyway, but it was essentially the same movement in all. In
France, it was rather sharply limited, mainly by the influence of
Gide and Sartre, to Hemingway, Faulkner, Steinbeck, Dos Passos and Caldwell, "les cinq grands"; the Swedish Thorsten Jons-
sen's list omitted Dos Passos and included Farrell and Saroyan;[7]
Sigurd Hoel's list in the Gyldendal "Yellow Series" included
Bromfield and Wilder among others;[8] the Germans put Thomas
Wolfe high on their rating sheet; and the Russians, for obvious
reasons, gave Howard Fast the number one place among the
American novelists of the new day.[9] From here the various lists
of popular reading and translating shake off in one direction
toward the lesser writers of the "hard-boiled school" like Cain,
Chandler, and even Spillane, and in the other toward the East-
West idealism of Pearl Buck or the pure romance *Gone With the*

Wind, for some years the best seller of them all, in Europe as well as America.

I must apologize for so superficial a rendering of so vast a subject as this, obviously a field for much further research, but I think I am safe in finding two main reasons for European interest in the more serious modern American writers of fiction, the one good and the other not so admirable. Remembering the vogues of Jack London, Upton Sinclair, and Sinclair Lewis, one can hardly escape the conclusion that a main attraction of these writers was their unanimous criticism and rejection of American industrial capitalism and the prosperous and complaisant materialism that seemed to go with it. Where political ideology shaped national destinies, the vogue of these novelists tended to follow closely the official line with reference to the relationships with the United States, but even where the issue was not so sharp, anti-Americanism played a various part. Not all opinion was as bitter as that of Gide's newspaper man in his *Imaginary Interviews:* "If one believes what they are saying, the American cities and countrysides must offer a foretaste of hell," but the vivid and recurring pictures of decay and corruption in American society could, without taking a strict party line, be used to support, as an alternative to capitalism, any vague brand of socialism which involved, as I recall it, state ownership of railroads and utilities, universal state-controlled public education, and equalization of wealth by taxing the rich.[10] On these foundations, almost any form of dictatorship could be erected, and Europeans were not slow to use what looked like an authentic report of American social failure as argument for their own causes. Such a formula did not necessarily require the dialectic of class conflict nor did it necessarily predict a social revolution; that was to come later, and when it came, the group was split into three: those who, like Howard Fast, Michael Gold, Max Eastman, and John Dos Passos committed themselves (probably) to the Communist party and its controls; those who like Edmund Wilson, John Steinbeck, and Ernest Hemingway, at least at times, seemed strongly drawn to communism but remained apparently uncommitted and unaffiliated; and those who like Wolfe and Faulkner praised or attacked American social ideals and institutions but remained uncommitted, although seeming to favor the reactionary alternative if forced to a social or political position.

What confused the Europeans more than anything else was that these writers seemed to be in general agreement in their despair with the American world as they found it and therefore wrote of America with devastating and destructive candor and depth of probing, but they could usually not be tied to any specific political and social system as developed in the various European countries at various times. Their individual reputations went through ups and downs and ins and outs with changing political events, but still maintained a continuous influence. Dos Passos, for example, the almost confessed Communist, was translated in Germany throughout the Nazi period and Faulkner's obvious sympathy for the traditional Southern aristocracy did not exclude him most of the time from the accepted list in Russia.

The only member of the group whose reputation in Europe during these years has been thoroughly studied is Ernest Hemingway, who was made the object of a carefully planned symposium of the European Association of American Studies in 1960. The result of this symposium, which included the reception of these American novelists in England, France, Germany, Italy, Norway, Sweden, Russia, and Spain, reveals how changeable and fortuitous the European reputation of an American writer may be; how often the wrong reasons for interest can bring the most beneficial results; how very closely immediate literary responses are provoked by social and political causes; and finally how, in the long run, a really first-rate author can establish himself in world literature with nearly universal agreement on both his strengths and his weaknesses.

Let me conclude therefore with a summary of the findings on Hemingway, which I think will indicate my second main reason for European interest in American authors, namely their degree of enduring literary excellence. These summaries of the criticism of many nations seem to agree in general that (1) his alienation from his own nation and culture is essentially a criticism of modern man and his world, and is therefore lifted ultimately out of the context of particular political or social ideologies or the destinies of particular nations into a basic comment on life which all nations and all people "in our time" can share; (2) his concern with intensity in living, his fear of death which masquerades as courage, and his limitation to the sensuous level of experience are strengths because of their primitive and universal authenticity, but are also weaknesses because they describe a writer of great power within a narrow range; and (3) his clipped, simple, compressed, and unadorned style, with its heavy use of dialogue, its avoidance of adjectives, and its reliance on implied rather than stated meanings provides a unique model for all modern fiction writers but a model which can be as dangerous and cheap as it is easy when depth of meaning is really absent.

These are conclusions common to the largely unsympathetic and often patronizing British criticism, the response on the level of primitive violence and honest confessional of the Norwegians, and the acceptance of an ultimate meaninglessness of life by the Existential French. Perhaps, therefore, I was wrong in the pessimistic premises with which I started. Although the magic mirror of American fiction gives back to the European a wide variety of distorted images, often the reflection of his own preconceptions and prejudices, this literature, like all literature, can ultimately provide a universal language—if it is good enough, and if it is read as literature and not as mere record.

NOTES

1. Arnold Chapman, *The Spanish-American Reception of United States Fiction* (Berkeley: Univ. of Calif. Press, 1966), p. 2.

2. William B. Cairns, *British Criticisms of American Writings. 1785-1813* (Madison, Wis.: Univ. of Wis. Press, 1918). Studies 2, p. 153.

3. Clarence Gohdes, *American Literature in Nineteenth Century England* (New York: Columbia Univ. Press), 1944, p. 29.

4. Henry S. Commager, *America in Perspective* (New York: Random House, 1947). See esp. Stevens, Gurowski, Munsterberg.

5. Carl L. Anderson, *The Swedish Acceptance of American Literature* (Philadelphia: Univ. of Pa. Press, 1957), p. 63.

6. Harold Blodgett, "American Books Abroad," in *Literary History of the United States* (New York: Macmillan, 1948), Vol. 2, p. 1375.

7. Thelma M. Smith and L. Miner Ward, *Transatlantic Migrations: The Contemporary American Novel in France* (Durham, N.C.: Duke Univ. Press), 1955, p. 18.

8. Roger Asselineau (ed.), *The Literary Reputation of Hemingway in Europe*, with an introduction by Heinrich Straumann (New York: N.Y. Univ. Press, 1965), pp. 129-130, 153.

9. Anne M. Springer, *The American Novel in Germany: A Study of the Critical Reception of Eight American Novelists between Two World Wars* (Hamburg: Cram, de Gruyter & Co., 1960), pp. 88-94.

10. Harold Blodgett, "American Books Abroad," in *Literary History of the United States* (New York: Macmillan, 1948), Vol. 2, p. 1380.

10 | THE CYCLE AND THE ROOTS: NATIONAL IDENTITY IN AMERICAN LITERATURE

When I retired from the University of Pennsylvania in June 1967 at the age of seventy, my first impulse was to write an autobiography; but one informal talk on "Growing up in West Philadelphia" made me realize the law of diminishing returns on the process of total recall. After all, the fact that I once hopped onto the back of ice wagons for refreshment on a hot summer day did not have much to do with my life as teacher and scholar. Instead, I offered seminars in American literature at the Universities of North Carolina and South Florida and finished editing Van Wyck Brooks, Emerson, and a fourth and probably final edition of the Literary History of the United States.

Nevertheless, my professional life seemed scattered as I looked back on it; it was calling out to me to get things in order while I still had time. I began to gather my papers and books and, in a sense, to research my own past for the series of collected essays of which this is the fourth. Instead of writing a single narrative, I focused on aspects of my career that seemed to have produced enduring results: my part in the rise of American literary study in general and in the American Studies Movement; my role as a literary historian and the story of LHUS; the hundreds of book reviews and the travels and lectures in Europe and Asia; but perhaps most important of all, my development of a specific philosophy and architecture of American literary history.

What could be a more suitable subject than this last to offer to the Early American Literature Section of the Modern Language Association for their Bicentennial Conference with the College of William and Mary at Williamsburg in December 1976? As the essays in this volume and its companions are evidence, the theory of the development of an American sense of identity in literature and culture as expression of the whole westward movement had, for forty years, occupied the center of my professional life and thought. At the risk of repeating earlier statements, I decided to attempt a single paper that would strike at the heart of the problem and focus my earlier work on the symbol of organic life and its relationship to man's social and cultural history.

As the present paper was completed too late to be published with the others of the conference, it was held back for the Festschrift *of my lifelong friend and fellow-conspirator Arlin Turner. It appeared in* Toward a New American Literary History, *published by the Duke University Press in 1980. I am glad that what may be my last word on the subject looks to the future as well as to the past.*

I

The recent celebration of the bicentennial of the birth of this country as an independent nation, with parades, pageants, speeches, exhibits, tours, and parties, has made all of us more aware of our formative years and their relationship to what we are today. The seventeenth and eighteenth centuries furnished the wellsprings of our national identity, yet often there seems to be little connection between what we were then and what we are today. I hope to help bridge this gap in our self-understanding by drawing from our colonial and early national literature some general principles of cultural development and then, by applying them to later stages and phases in our evolution, to move toward a better understanding of our complex but nonetheless distinctive national character.

An American national character began to take shape about the time of the American Revolution; that is, between 1763 and 1789.[1] After the fighting was over, the Founding Fathers set to work to create a new nation and to give it voice in a new and self-confident literature.

Why then do we have so many doubts about our national identity today? The authors of the Declaration of Independence seemed to have no such doubts when they state that the colonies were about to "assume among the Powers of Earth the separate and equal station to which the Laws of Nature and Nature's God entitled them," based on the "unalienable rights of Life, Liberty, and the Pursuit of Happiness."

Yet the author of an article on "Recent Interpretations of the American Character" introduces his discussion of some sixty or more books on the subject published since 1960 with the remark: "It is a commonplace that Americans are more concerned with their national identity and spend more time trying to explain themselves to themselves than people of other nations."[2] Why are we thus haunted by our sense of insecurity and inadequacy? Why do we write such books as *The Challenge of Diversity, The Search for Identity, The American Way of Violence,* and *The End of the American Era?* I am not asking what the American identity is, because I do not believe that it ever has been just one thing. I am asking you rather to join me in a rapid look back over our literature and its history in the hope that we may find in it a clue to the complex and changing mystery of our national identity today. For, even if we cannot finally reduce the American character to a single definition, perhaps we can thus discover a way of understanding its unique vitality and virtue.

This may not be as easy as it sounds, for, as recently as a half a century ago, it was generally assumed that there was no such thing as an *American* literature. At that time there were no departments and few courses in American literature as such in our colleges and universities; there were no scholarly societies or journals devoted to its study; the specialists in American literary research could be counted on one hand, and so to announce oneself was virtually to commit professional suicide; and histories of the subject were generally deprecatory and apologetic. Typical is the statement in an elementary school text of 1897: "American literature is an offshoot of English Literature, and shares the life of the parent stock. It uses the same language. . . . The culture of this country is distinctively English in origin and character; the differences are but modifications growing out of the new environment."[3]

Contrast this statement with that of Henry Canby in his introduction to *Literary History of the United States:* "The literary history of this nation began when the first settler from abroad of
sensitive mind paused in his adventure long enough to feel that
he was under a different sky, breathing new air, and that a New
World was all before him with only his strength and Providence for guides."[4] Consider for a moment the fundamental difference between those two statements. The first is mechanical;
it assumes that American literature is a part of English literature
merely because it is usually written in the English language.
The second is organic; it assumes that American literature in
any language is American because it expresses the experience
and culture of the American people. "It is hard to believe
today," comments the psychohistorian Erik Erikson, "—if you
believe we started it in our time—how conscious these early
Americans were of the job of developing an American character
out of the regional and generational polarities and contradictions of a nation of immigrants and migrants."[5] Because the
evolutionary process of creating a national character and then
giving it expression in literature is organic, it is deeply rooted
in the ever-moving, ever-changing experience of a transplanted
and multiethnic people. Throughout our history, the horizontal
movements of migration have tended to come in waves or
cycles of uprooting and rerooting of cultures, and the vertical
growth of new cultures in a new land in each case reenacts the
life cycle of growth from birth, through maturity, into decline.

In this essay I shall not attempt to offer a definition of American identity as the fixed and final shape of American experience, but rather to suggest a method of approach to an
understanding of any specific organic movement at every stage
of its growth and change. This method is based on the principle
of rooting and cyclic growth, which varies only in application
to time and place. It is the task of the anthropologist and the
demographer to study as many as he can of the forces of migration and immigration which have created the American identity; it is the task of the literary historian to understand and to
explain the expressions of the resulting American people in the
arts of writing.

I use the term *culture* in the sociological rather than the aesthetic sense. Culture, in this sense, is the way that people in any time and place have agreed to live together. Toynbee quotes Bagby's definition as being "regularities in the behaviour, internal and external, of the members of a society, excluding those regularities which are clearly hereditary in origin."[6] But again, because they are organic rather than static, such cultural configurations remain fluent and shape and reshape themselves with the movements and growth of experience.

French, German, Italian, Spanish, Scandinavian, and British culture had each, by the seventeenth century, gone through a similar process of evolution and achieved a degree of stability based on language, social structures, and relatively static geographical limits, in spite of political uncertainty and change. The new culture of America, on the other hand, had—with the possible exception of that of the Indian—no such stability. Its chief distinguishing characteristics were its heterogeneous and multiethnic components and its constant immigration and migration for almost three centuries. Mobility and diversity are and always have been the controlling factors in forming the American cultural identity—factors which were not shared to anything like the same extent by the European cultures in the parallel developments in South America, Australia, and New Zealand. The recurring impact of mature cultures on relatively primitive environments and the mingling of one with another provide the keys to the making of a new national identity and are therefore basic to an understanding of the literature of the new nation up to at least 1801 and even well thereafter.

Of course, such cultural conflicts and mergings are basic to all human history and are commonplaces of the ancient world. Why then the sudden explosion of exploration and settlement of the Western hemisphere by the peoples of the Eastern in the thirteenth to the sixteenth centuries? Lewis Mumford has put it in a sentence: "The settlement of America had its origins in the unsettlement of Europe."[7] In other words, the westward movement of European man was but a part of the breakdown of medieval Europe and the explosive forces of the new science, humanism, the Renaissance, and the Reformation. Whether the motivation was scientific curiosity about what lay beyond the horizon and beyond the stars, the search for new trade routes to the rich Orient, the desire for religious and political freedom, or merely the greed for wealth, these were centuries of sudden and powerful mental and physical expansion. We should bear in mind that the thrust of all European peoples was almost as much to the East and South as to the West, but only in the West, on a relatively unexplored and unexploited continent, did the Dutch, Spanish, British, Swedes, and French find open sea and open land ahead. In America at least, the frontier movement of the multiethnic cultures of Europe followed the path of the rising and setting sun for many centuries.

We must also remember that this horizontal westward thrust of the culture, wave on wave, was a continuing and oft-repeated process and not a single historical event. It did not happen in any one period in American literary history nor in only one part of the American continent. Once the impact of a mature culture on a new environment has been made, does the vertical process of evolving a new culture in any one area follow a predictable series of stages, like a growing plant from root to flower? Is the cultural history of colonial Philadelphia parallel in the stages of its organic growth to, say, the nineteenth-century history of Louisville, Kentucky, or modern San Diego, California? When I was lecturing some years ago on colonial American literary history to a graduate class, a brilliant young journalist from New Zealand came up after class and said to me in some astonishment, "Now I understand my country; we have just reached the year 1830!"

We seem to be approaching a cultural model which could be useful in all phases and stages of our effort to understand not only the early but perhaps even the far more complex later American identity in literature. At least there are some questions we can now ask: (1) From our general knowledge of the history of American literature, particularly that of the original colonies as they grew into a unified nation, can we derive a theoretical model of this evolutionary process? (2) Can we next apply this model in detail to the literature of the eastern seaboard from 1492 to about 1800 or 1820 to see how our theory works? (3) Can we then test these results by applying the same model to the settlement and development of the continental nation? And finally (4), is there a possibility that this same model may apply to the complex and multiethnic culture and literature of the later years and today? Thus we can perhaps move from a reasonable certainty through increasing complexity toward a definition of American national identity in literature without doing much more than clarify a series of problems for future study and provide a useful tool for their solution.

II

Two basic factors in the making of a distinctive American culture and its expression in literature may be assumed: first, the constant movement of European cultures westward over a continent new to them; and second, the multiethnic character of this migration. Although each of these factors is repeated an infinite number of times in the course of our history, it is possible to detect in each of them an organic process which remains constant throughout.

The process of westward movement, however, did not result from a single impulse or develop a continuous flow. As I have already suggested, it was varied in kind and time and moved more like the waves on a beach than the current of a river. Each wave was a cycle of its own, with an origin in alien soil, a period of time and a new locale of its own to shape the process of transfer, a crisis of adjustment and new growth, and finally a merging into the composite culture of the New World. Like all human experience, the frontier process consisted of a series of varied and overlapping cycles of growth and change. Each phase of history can be likened to one form of the life of a single organism, and all such life has beginning, middle, and end, even the horizontal movement of people and groups of people across land and sea.

But there is a vertical as well as a horizontal aspect of this cultural evolution, namely the rooting of the new culture in the New World and its growth from the seed planted, through the stages of maturing, to a new form of life, a new flowering. It is a sort of Johnny Appleseed procedure—first the spreading of the seed across the field, and then the nurturing and cultivation of each seed where it has fallen, from sprout to fruit. Does each seed pass through a similar series of stages, and, if we observe one throughout its life, do we understand at least the process of growth of the others, even though the details and mutations may vary?

These two images—the cycle and the roots—have been basic to my thinking throughout my whole career as a literary historian, and all that I have written about the evolution of culture and literature is related in some way to organic nature and the life cycle. I first used the analogy of the plant from roots to flowering as the title of my anthology of early American literature, *The Roots of National Culture,* in 1933, and I first developed what later came to be spoken of as "the two-cycle theory of American literature" in a 1941 address at Fordham University.[8]

The Cycle of American Literature (1955) was an outgrowth of the years of planning and producing *Literary History of the United States.* As a literary history of an evolving culture rather than a history of a national literature, the editors adopted at the start a balanced plan of organization based on the theory of American literature as the expression of two major waves of European culture which moved, first across the Atlantic to settle the eastern seaboard from Maine to Georgia between 1607 and about 1835; and second, across the continent to the Pacific, with the breakthrough of the Allegheny Mountains beginning about 1775 and, in successive waves and counterwaves completing the frontier movement west to the Pacific, north to the Canadian border, and south to Mexico about—to adopt Turner's date—1890.

So much for the westward movement of American culture. The problem of the stages of organic growth in any one place is more complicated, but again, in order to make clear a fundamental theory of American cultural history, I oversimplified the American story in *The Roots of National Culture.* I am now standing still in one place and watching the seed that has been planted grow from first sprout to the final flowering. Experience teaches that each new culture must take its own time in growing and must go through a series of recognizable stages of maturing before it can bear fruit. Therefore, when there is an impact of an alien culture on a new environment, there must be a more or less predictable kind of preparatory expression before a major writer can appear.

I suggest that these stages can be accurately defined and that each new culture passes through them in the same succession. In 1933, I proposed four, and I still find these four to be reasonably accurate, with allowable variations of time, place, and circumstance.[9] Of course, however, it is a continuous process, and someone else might break it down into three, or five, or like the melancholy Jaques of Shakespeare, seven stages.

The first stage is a period of exploration and settlement, which produces narrative and descriptive journals and letters. In the second stage the new settlement creates its own society with instruments of culture such as schools, printing presses, town halls, transportation, and shops, which in turn produce newspapers, broadsides, and magazines, lectures and sermons, book-stores and libraries, and other embryonic means of cultural communication. All of these lead to intellectual activity and even controversy on all subjects, but mainly on politics and religion, as the new community discovers the shape and power of its own mind. This second stage, taken as a whole, can therefore be described as one of Instruments and Ideas. When the time is ripe—and that may be very early in the evolutionary process—all of this leads to a third stage, in which there is a demand for the "leisure arts," especially literature. Even in the sixteenth century, the North American Spanish made a few attempts at producing drama, epic poetry, and fiction—the last a natural outgrowth of their dreams of far inland cities of unbelievable luxury and wealth. But the new society was still too crude to produce its own forms of literary expression for the exciting new experience of conquering and settling a continent. At this point, eyes are turned eastward and, with the importation of books and journals from the homeland, comes imitation of the familiar forms, as the new material is twisted and turned to fit into them, like a farmer's broad-toed foot being pressed into a ballroom slipper; and all this is part of the learning process. Finally, in the fourth stage, new literature steps out with its new experience wrapped about it in natural folds. Only then can the major writer find within him a mature creative power and outside of him an educated and receptive audience.

III

Coming back to our use of the Atlantic seaboard as a model for this evolutionary process, we find the first stage of exploration extended from the Columbus letter of 1493 reporting the "discovered islands" to the King and Queen of Spain, down to Harriot's *New Found Land of Virginia* in 1588 and beyond.[10] The next century was studded with narratives, journals, and even histories of settlement by John Smith, William Bradford, William Penn, William Byrd, and many others.

The second stage, Instruments and Ideas, began in the mid-eighteenth century as the seaboard towns developed into cultural centers with their printing presses, magazines, libraries, and colleges. Benjamin Franklin, with his many inventions and discoveries, is the epitome of this era, while the mind of the new nation was being shaped by the theological wars which culminated in Jonathan Edwards, followed by the political wars between Tories and Rebels and the debates in the Continental Congresses as the Founding Fathers created not only a new nation, but a new kind of nation.

It seems to be a general assumption that the Enlightenment period which followed the Revolution was a time when an organized body of political and social ideas was absorbed by these philosopher-statesmen from the rationalistic thinkers of France and England and written into the Declaration of Independence and the Constitution as a firm platform for a government and an idealistic way of life—a new deal for the Old World. Recent scholarship has questioned this conclusion and has tended to attribute the success of the American democratic system to its ability to absorb and reconcile opposites. As Joseph Ellis puts it: "The dominant metaphors of the age constantly invoked the ideal of balance: the equilibrium achieved by political juxtaposition of opposing interests; the judicious blending of monarchic, aristocratic, and democratic tendencies in a 'mixed government'; the educated man's control over conflicting 'faculties,' with the passions subordinated to the rational faculty and all governed by the moral sense."[11] It was our good fortune, therefore, that the first shaping of the distinctive American character came at a time—the third quarter of the eighteenth century—when at last Western man had learned to live in a flexible intellectual world governed by a reconciliation of contrasts. The contradictions between an absolute moral idealism and a practical common sense are polarized and made flexible and useful in the minds of American literary and intellectual leaders from Franklin to Emerson to William James and down to the present.

Thus this second stage in our paradigm seems to have come to an end in a period of political storm and chaos. When the cloud lifted, Americans were at once ready to enter the third stage of building a new national literature. "The people of the United States," wrote our first professional novelist Charles Brockden Brown in 1802, "are, perhaps, more distinguished than those of Europe as a people of business. . . . When, now that our population is increased, our national independence secured, and our government established, and we are relieved from the necessities of colonists and emigrants, there is reason to expect more attention to polite literature and science."[12]

"Polite literature," to Brown, meant novels in the forms of Gothic horror, psychological perversion, and social problems, but lack of castles and dungeons and our classless society hampered his style, and he turned to the wilderness, to sleepwalking, and to spontaneous combustion for his excitement. An early Poe in many ways, Brown was far ahead of his times, but his novels creak in the joints and are just barely readable, although hardly more primitive than much that we see on TV today.

Our early drama did somewhat better, for, in a torrent of imitations, adaptations, and productions of foreign plays in the theaters which soon sprang up in the coastal cities, we produced at least one good social comedy, Royall Tyler's *The Contrast*. In form and style confessedly modelled on the plays of Sheridan and Goldsmith, it had a central American theme—the contrast between the pseudosophistication of provincial society and the crude honesty of the native American Jonathan.

> Exult each patriot heart! [speaks the Prologue] — this
>   night is shewn
> A piece which we may fairly call our own;
> Where the proud titles of "My Lord! Your Grace!"
> To humble Mr. and plain Sir give place.
> Our Author pictures not from foreign climes
> The fashions, or the follies of the times;
> But has confin'd the subject of his work
> To the gay scenes—the circles of New-York.[13]

But it is at least interesting that the muse again displays her powers by treating the new theme of the contrast between opposite ways of life and the comic balance of tension attained by this very polarity. It is indeed the first truly American play.

The poetry that was written after 1783 exhibits the same balanced dualism. Torn between the desire to put the tremendous American experience into immortal verse and the need to turn to foreign models for form and style, poets like Freneau and the Connecticut Wits met the romantic violence of Blake and Byron on the one hand and the neoclassical rules of Pope and Dryden on the other. Freneau wrote everything from a melancholy dirge on the death of Death to sharp political satire in ironic rhymed couplets. And Joel Barlow, when he decided that the one thing the new nation needed most was an epic great enough to fit its grandeur, turned to Columbus as his hero and found so little to celebrate in the past that his lumbering verse became vague rantings about the future glories of America. "The author rejected," says Barlow, "the idea of the regular Epic form, and has confined his plan to the train of events which might be represented to the hero in vision."[14]

As Lewis Leary has so conclusively proved, this apprentice period in American literature not only did not, but could not produce a major literary artist.[15] What it did produce as typical of the times were such successful mediocrities as John Blair Linn and Thomas Branagan. Great minds like Franklin,

Edwards, and Jefferson did not produce great literature, probably for much the same reasons. When the time had come—after
1820—for a Poe, a Cooper, or an Irving, the wilderness of the
American literary mind was almost ready for the literature of
major tensions and rich balance which produced *The Scarlet Letter, Moby Dick, Leaves of Grass*, and the moving addresses and
journals of Thoreau and Emerson. American literature of the
Romantic period was born of inner conflicts and achieved its
first maturity by the taming of violence which took form in a
balanced polarity of conflicting forces. The fourth stage of our
paradigm did not appear before 1850-55, on the eve of our
greatest national crisis, the Civil War.

IV

And now for the question that I raised earlier: Is this series of
four stages in the development of the early American literature
of the eastern seaboard merely the record of a single period in
American cultural history, or does it provide a model by which
to test the development of all American literary history, a process repeated again and again as the frontier moved west and
the immigrant groups of other cultural backgrounds came over
to settle new parts of the continent?

The subject is far too complicated for detailed study here. All
that can be safely said is that as long as the frontier moved westward across the continent at a reasonable pace, the formula
seemed to work, but as the land spread out flat ahead, it moved
more swiftly and erratically, and as immigration turned into
migration in all directions, the process became more and more
complicated and variable. Yet I am convinced that in all the
phases and stages of American growth toward a national identity, the principle of the overlay of one culture on another or on
an alien environment is basic.

The obvious next place to try out our theory is the Middle
West, or the area between the Appalachian Mountains and the
Mississippi River, in the period from about 1775 when Daniel
Boone, as agent of the Transylvania Company, led a band of
colonists through the Cumberland Gap and founded Boones-

borough, Kentucky. The process of evolution lasted through the nineteenth century and may be said to have come to a climax with the Columbian Exposition in Chicago in 1893.

As in the story of the eastern seaboard, the first stage began with a century of exploration and discovery, this time by French missionary monks, hunters, and traders who, while the British were busy settling the Atlantic coast, explored the region of the Great Lakes and the Mississippi Valley without, in the long run, leaving "a perceptible influence on the growth of European culture in the west."[16]

The period of letters and journals describing the new adventure was comparatively brief because the migrants wrote more to their friends and families in the East than to their more distant relatives in Europe. Boone himself left no record, but the legend of the coonskin cap and the westward trek was preserved in John Filson's biography of him in 1784.[17] Among other narrative accounts are the early records of exploration, like the journals of Lewis and Clark, and the later ones, more strictly limited to the middle western frontier, like those of Timothy Flint (1826) and James Hall (1828).

The second stage—that of Instruments and Ideas—again followed more swiftly and, as in the eastern towns of Boston, New York, Philadelphia, and Charleston, middle western culture began with the permanent settlement of Lexington, Kentucky, in 1799, followed by Louisville, Cincinnati, New Harmony, St. Louis, and ultimately Chicago. Also, this period was characterized by debate in religion, politics, and education, mainly by Methodists and Baptists rather than Calvinists and Quakers. The founding of Transylvania University in 1787 was followed by many other colleges and universities, mostly sectarian, and by 1840 they were the rule in most major towns.

Printing presses and newspapers followed and, by the thirties, the middle western culture was ready for the third stage, with magazines and annuals ready to issue the novels and tales of Flint, Hall, Frederick Thomas, and many others of even less originality and skill, with the ghosts of Irving and Cooper hovering over many of them. Poetry began with reprinting

from eastern journals and homely ballads by local bards long
lost in history, such as "The Michigan Emigrants' Song":

> My Eastern friends who wish to find
> A country that will suit your mind,
> Where comforts all are near at hand,
> Had better come to Michigan.[18]

There were the more vigorous cowboy adaptations of traditional ballads to tell of their lonely and adventurous lives.
Louisville was a center for drama in the early days, but it was
not until the 1870s that the Middle West developed a mode of
its own in the mild realism of John Hay, Edward Eggleston, and
finally William Dean Howells.

By that time, however, the frontier had already swept across
the prairies, leapt the Rockies, and met the Oriental and other
cultures of the Pacific slope and the Spanish-Mexican culture of
the Southwest. The final phase of fully mature achievement in
middle western literature was but a part of the new literature of
the Continental nation with its centers in Chicago, St. Louis,
and San Francisco and its dominant mode the naturalism of
Crane, Norris, London, and Dreiser at the end of the century.
The second cycle of the frontier impact therefore did not pause
anywhere long enough, as the eastern seaboard had, to mature a
regional culture. There was a continual making and breaking of
cultural patterns until Chicago emerged, at the end of the century, as the commerical and cultural center of the Continental
nation as a whole.

That story is fraught with violence and conflict, which had
never really surfaced in the Old Middle West, but had to surface
and then he absorbed in some way before a new national identity could develop. After the Mexican War of 1845-48, the
annexation of huge tracts of new land from Mexico and in Oregon opened, with the earlier Louisiana Purchase, more than
twice the area of the pre-Civil War United States to exploration
and exploitation. We do not need to be reminded of the bloody
Indian wars, the cowboy battles between the cattle and sheep

ranchers, the Gold Rush of 1849, the ruthless mining of the Rockies, the slaughter of the buffaloes, the vast prairie fires, the blazing of overland trails and later of the railroads for thousands of hapless immigrants, all of which were parts of the final rise of the industrial empire of the time of the Robber Barons to complete the commercial triumph of Chicago, Detroit, and St. Louis. Out of such anarchy came the careful accounts, first of Lewis and Clark, and then of John Wesley Powell, Clarence King, and the naturalist John Muir, as well as the regionalism and local color of the Californian Bret Harte and the Mississippian Mark Twain. It was Mark Twain finally who forced the opposites of the genteel East and the raw barbarism of the open West into a still somewhat crude new American mould in which humor triumphed over violence and the comic spirit (mixed with tragedy) again created a major literature. Thus, if we are thinking organically rather than chronologically, the humor of Irving is contemporary in cause and kind with that of Mark Twain because they both were aroused by the incongruities in the frontier situation. By the end of the nineteenth century, however, the polarity of opposites was beginning to reach a precarious balance so that by about 1920 Wolfe, Hemingway, Steinbeck, Faulkner, Frost, Eliot, and O'Neill could join in a second renaissance of American literature between the two world wars.

V

Perhaps my story should end there if we are willing to restrict our theory of the making of an American cultural identity in literature to the westward movement of Old World culture across a new continent. If we are, the basic evolutionary development of literature in any one place in four stages would seem to work if applied with a degree of flexibility. But American culture as we see it and live it today is too complex to be so limited. So far we have only touched on the problem of multiethnicity, as the movement of migration lost its westward direction but remained nonetheless active, and the evolutionary process became more and more the overlay of one culture on another, rather than the movement of a mature culture into a primitive environment as it had been in the days of steady frontier movement. Early examples of this kind of overlay are the blending of the basically English westward migration with the Mexican-Spanish culture of the Southwest and with the French cultures of New Orleans and Quebec.

I realize that, apart from noting the ethnic diversity of the early explorers and settlers, I have paid little attention to the hordes of immigrants that poured into the United States from the non-British nations of Europe during the nineteenth century and up to 1914 when immigration began to be restricted by law. Yet multiethnicity is and always has been one of the principal determinants of the flexibility and strength of our democratic society.

The problem is a complicated one and cannot, of course, be treated adequately in such a brief discussion. We can, however, as a start, distinguish three kinds of ethnic groups which were not parts of the main frontier movement. These are the immigrant groups which came to this country comparatively late; the blacks who were brought to this country under special circumstances; and the Jews who in all their history have mingled with, but rarely become totally absorbed into, any alien culture. All three are of great importance to the American identity today as expressed in its ever-changing literature, but only immigrations from European countries other than Great Britain followed a course close enough to our model to suggest inclusion here, even though the remarkable achievements of the Jews and the blacks in contemporary American literature suggest that—given a slightly different model—their contributions to our culture would lend themselves to similar analyses.

I will conclude, therefore, with a note on the immigrations from European countries other than England. However multiethnic the original settlers of the North American continent may have been, historians agree that by the end of the eighteenth century, British culture and its language were overwhelmingly dominant in that part of it which formed the original thirteen colonies and later became the United States. Other strains like the German, the Scotch-Irish, and the Irish tended to become absorbed quickly into the main cultural stream as the frontier pushed westward; but by the time of the Civil War, the impact of other European ethnic groups had begun to be felt, and it became customary to think of them as "aliens" or "immigrants." Even in the 1820s and 1830s the Scots-Irish and others began to move out of the eastern cities and to take over the lands evacuated by the earlier pioneers in New York, Pennsylvania, North Carolina, and Ohio, and thus were absorbed into the general frontier movement. Concentrated German settlements grew up in Wisconsin and Minnesota where later they were followed by Norwegians and Swedes, who moved quickly westward to Minnesota and then to Oregon. But the main flood of Europeans peaked in the last decades of the century and came from central and southern Europe—Italians, Czechs, Poles, and others who supplied the labor for the rapidly developing industrial revolution.

During the greater part of the nineteenth century, the "melting pot" theory held. It was based on the assumption that the leveling and mixing processes of American society were so great that ethnic cultural differences would wear down in two or three generations at most and all immigrants would merge into one composite American Democratic Man. This theory may have applied when foreign-born immigrants had no permanent settlements of their own to come to, but later the process became more and more one of the coexistence of "cultural islands" within or beside each other, with each preserving a degree of integrity of its own and evolving through our four stages independently and in parallel. Many of the later immigrants tended to concentrate in cities where they set up islands of their own culture and resisted the tendency to merge with the mainstream.[19] Thus there were German, Scandinavian, Italian, Czech, Greek, and many other settlements or urban islands in which the culture retained the language, customs, and inheritance of the homeland, and literature developed from journals and letters through educational, religious, and political institutions and ideas, to fiction, poetry, and drama imitative of a special ethnic tradition. In his pioneering study of the literature of these American-ethnic cultures in 1948, Henry A. Pochmann concluded a rapid survey of such writing with the statement,

"The early desire to cast the Old World into a mythical melting pot has given place to a conviction that the immigrant serves his adopted country best when he is steeped in the traditions of his fatherland; that various and lively regional cultures increase the vitality of the culture of the United States."[20] The study of these literatures in parallel with the mainstream and against the background of their own cultures was brought to a focus with the founding in 1974 of the Society for the Study of Multiethnic Literature in the United States (popularly called "Melus") and with the publication of special studies such as Rose B. Green's work on the Italian-American novel, but our knowledge of many of them is still scant.[21] In his introduction to Rose Green's book, Mario Pei asserts that "there is no question that an Italian-American literature, in English, exists. It has its own distinctive traits and bears its own peculiar imprint." The author then identifies five stages in the evolution of an indigenous literature: (1) explanatory narratives, (2) analysis of this impact as a co-culture, (3) attempts at identification with the native American strain, (4) return to a distinctive ethnic heritage, and (5) the rooting of Italian culture in American soil with the production of a mature literature which is ethnically Italian yet culturally American.[22]

This process has often been accompanied by various kinds of violence, and such violence has been much deeper than the mere physical, as Richard Slotkin has pointed out when he defined American mythology as "regeneration through violence." Starting with the confrontation of the European settler with the dark wilderness and its dark inhabitants, the American myth emerges through various kinds and degrees of conflict and violence into that of the hunter as archetypal American and mediator between civilization and the wilderness.[23] I have tried to trace the evolution of the national identity in much the same terms, but with emphasis on the resolution of violence itself— the violence of cultural conflict—into great literature without so full and specific an analysis of mythology. Behind the comic detachment of an Irving, a Mark Twain, or a Faulkner and the tragic confrontations of a Melville, a Dreiser, or an O'Neill there lie the peculiarly American forms of conflict and growth

—the constant movement and mixing of a nation in the making.

Why, then, do we celebrate our nation's founding if the national identity seems today to have so little of the single-minded moral idealism, individual freedom, and political stability that we are taught to associate with the names of the Founding Fathers? The answer is that this image is itself a myth. Those honorable gentlemen were far more wise, flexible, and fallible than we give them credit for. They did not found the perfect state in which the laws and institutions were so strong that they could resist change and growth under all circumstances and to the end of time. Instead they had the courage to found an open state and society fortified with many internal checks and balances so that conflict, idealism, growth, and decay had a chance to work themselves out to solutions based on human nature and human experience.

In addition to the usual conflicts and tensions that, according to American habits, create violence which may or may not resolve itself into the creative balance of polarity, these multi-ethnic groups suffer the additional conflicts that are created by the interaction of an imported culture with one already entrenched. The problem is complicated and we are not yet far enough into it fully to appreciate its ramifications, but there is no reason to believe that, when cultural equilibrium is achieved by any one group in any one place and time, major literary work might not result. So far that has happened rarely, but at least we can study the early stages.

Through trial and error we learned in our first century, as we opened up and developed the culture of the continent, that the vital mobility and ethnic diversity of our first frontier—the eastern seaboard—had given us a process of cultural evolution which could be carried forward from one experience to the next. As our culture became more complex in the second century we learned to adjust to and absorb new cultures by developing equilibrium rather than resolution of conflicts, without hampering the strength and fluidity of an open and still growing society. This, it seems to me, is the key to our unique national identity as expressed best in our literature.

NOTES

1. Kenneth Silverman, *A Cultural History of the American Revolution* (New York: Thomas Y. Crowell Co., 1976), pp. 3-69.

2. Thomas L. Hartshorne, "Recent Interpretations of the American Character," *American Studies International* 14 (Winter 1975) 10.

3. F.V.N. Painter, *Introduction to American Literature* (Boston, 1897).

4. Robert E. Spiller, Willard Throp, Thomas H. Johnson, and Henry Seidel Canby, *Literary History of the United States* (New York: The Macmillan Co., 1948). Vol. 1, p. xiii.

5. Erik K. Erikson, *Dimensions of a New Identity* (New York: W.W. Norton & Co., Inc., 1964), p. 59.

6. Arnold Toynbee, *A Study of History*, new. edn., rev. & abr. (London: Oxford University Press, 1972), p. 43.

7. Lewis Mumford, *The Golden Day* (New York: Boni and Liveright, 1926), p. 11.

8. "Blueprint for American Literary History," *The Third Dimension* (New York: The Macmillan Co., 1965), pp. 26-36.

9. "The First Frontier," *The Roots of National Culture* (New York: The Macmillan Co., 1933), pp. 1-10.

10. Evelyn Page, *American Genesis: Pre-Colonial Writings in the North* (Boston: Gambit, 1973), 108-10, 208-10.

11. Joseph Ellis, "Habits of Mind and an American Enlightenment," *American Quarterly* 28 (Summer 1976) 164.

12. *The American Review and Literary Journal* (New York, 1802), quoted in Spiller, *The American Literary Revolution, 1783-1837* (New York: Doubleday & Co., Inc., 1967), pp. 32-33.

13. Ibid., p. 27.

14. Ibid., p. 15.

15. Lewis Leary, *Soundings: Some Early Americvan Writers* (Athens, Ga.: The University of Georgia Press, 1975).

16. Ralph L. Rusk, *The Literature of the Middle West Frontier* (New York: Columbia University Press, 1926), Vol. 1, p. 16 ff.

17. John Filson, *The Discovery, Settlement and Present State of Kentucky,* (Wilmington, Del., 1784).

18. Rusk, Vol. 1, p. 307.

19. Marcus Lee Hansen, *The Immigrant in American History* (Cambridge, Mass.: Harvard University Press, 1940), pp. 150-51.

20. *Literary History of the United States*, Vol. 2, p. 693.

21. Rose Basile Green, *The Italian/American Novel* (Rutherford, N.J.: Fairleigh Dickinson University Press, 1974).

22. Ibid., pp. 10, 23-24.

23. Richard Slotkin, *Regeneration Through Violence: The Mythology of the American Frontier, 1600-1860* (Middletown, Conn.: Wesleyan University Press, 1973), p. 23.

III • THE AMERICAN STUDIES MOVEMENT

The American Studies Movement, which produced, among other things, the American Studies Association, is the outward and organizational expression of the ideas I have been discussing up to this point. As I have been associated with the movement at almost every step of its development, the articles I wrote about it from time to time mirror the various stages in its growth, although there is much more to the story than the rather personal account that follows would indicate.

The middle years of my professional life, as we have seen, were devoted first to the preparatory stages of the movement as it related to American literary history and finally to the interdisciplinary national association of which I was one of the first presidents.

I was drawn into American studies through the Modern Greats Tripos of Swarthmore honors work, a blending of modern literature, history, and philosophy. This turned me from the narrow specialization of the philological discipline and into a focus on "area studies," then a widespread movement in higher education. It was inevitable that the cultural "area" to be studied first would be my own, and the progression from American literary history into a search for a more central discipline naturally followed. In this I was part of a general movement, shared by others of my generation, and like them I have often been chided for being overpatriotic or nationalistic almost to the point of chauvinism, a charge that I have vigorously protested.[1] The American Studies Association has always

been engaged in a search for the truth through strictly scholarly activities and, except for special concern at times for the
status of some minority groups, has never become involved in
political or ideological movements.

The scholarly ferment of the early twentieth century of
which it was a part is not too difficult to trace. The founding of
the Modern Language and the American Historical Associations in the 1880s marked the beginning of a trend in American
scholarship toward the study of modern as against classical cultures. By the turn of the century, this revolt had become a revisionist movement among the historians, who moved from the
dominance of the Northeast elite toward a fresh look at the
prewar and reconstruction South and toward the expanding
West. Frederick Jackson Turner led the way in his studies of the
frontier, which, in spite of a widespread reaction against his
central thesis, stimulated a whole generation of scholars to
examine the new approaches of economic, social, and intellectual history, chiefly through the Mississippi Valley Historical
Association and its successor, the Organization of American
Historians.

The literary historians were not far behind in picking up the
realism of William Dean Howells and his fellows, as well as the
humor and folk tales of Mark Twain and other western and
southern writers; but it was not until the 1920s that they broke
the link with a narrowly "English" tradition and joined the historians in a reexamination of American literature in its own
terms.

The second stage in the development of the literary aspect of
the American Studies Movement began with the founding,
within the Modern Language Association, of an independent
American literature group and the appearance of special
degree programs in American literature as such. This was the
era of the "progressive" historians, and a close link with them
developed in many universities.[2] Among them were the
pioneering programs in American studies at Harvard, Pennsylvania, Minnesota, Wisconsin, and many other universities. By
1948 the movement had become so widespread and well
organized that a book seemed called for to sum up the prog-

ress that far.[3] It is significant that the Minnesota program, which was basically interdisciplinary and deliberately synthetic, was offered as the norm for a degree course sponsored by an inter-departmental committee with the requirement of work in American literature, American history, and usually one or two other departments in the fine arts or social sciences. It may also be significant that 1948 was the year of the first edition of *Literary History of the United States,* a summing up and blending of contemporary scholarship in cultural history and historical literary criticism.

The third stage in the American Studies Movement was marked by the founding of the American Studies Association (initiated by Carl Bode and a few others in 1949 and incorporated in 1951) when the concept of a new discipline in American culture or civilization, with borrowings from sociology, depth psychology, and cultural anthropology, was generally accepted. This approach was perhaps worked out in practice most systematically by the American Civilization Department of the University of Pennsylvania.

Finally, the fourth stage in the development came when American studies went international with the cultural exchange programs of the State Department, the Fulbright and American Council of Learned Societies programs, many foundation fellowships, and the forming of American Studies Associations in Germany, the Scandinavian countries, Japan, Canada, and elsewhere throughout the world. Although many of the resulting programs in foreign countries have held to a core of emphasis on American literature or American history, the movement has found its stability in a flexible approach to the study of American culture as a whole, whatever special aspects of American life and ideas may be emphasized.

NOTES

1. Cf. Arthur E. Bester, Jr., "The Study of American Civilization: Jingoism or Scholarship?" *The William and Mary Quarterly,* Third Series, 9 (January 1952): 3-9.

2. Cf. John Higham, *History* (Englewood, N.J.: Prentice-Hall, 1965).

3. Tremaine McDowell, *American Studies* (Minneapolis: The University of Minnesota Press, 1948).

11 | THE GROWTH OF AMERICAN LITERARY SCHOLARSHIP

*When Emerson in 1855 received a gift of a copy of the anony-
mous Leaves of Grass, he sat down and wrote Whitman the
now-famous letter in which he expressed his astonishment at
"the beginning of a great career" which "must have had a long
foreground somewhere, for such a start."[1]*

*It was just such a long foreground to the Literary History of
the United States (1948) that seemed to me a suitable subject
for an address to the Norwegian Academy in Oslo on April 14,
1950, from the Fulbright professor in the new American Institute, founded the previous year by my friend Sigmund Skard.*

*This is the first and preliminary stage in the American Studies
movement, a stage which occupied more than a century; and
this is my most detailed account of the steps in the process
which had by then finally surfaced in a research center at Oslo
for American studies in Europe. I am not sure that the learned
members of the Academy, including the then King Haakon VII,
were as much interested in the story as I was; but they had the
courtesy to publish it in their journal, Edda, the following January.*

*Even though perhaps by now a little out of date, it is
reprinted for the first time.*

We Americans have failed until very recent years to recognize
our own literature as something apart from the other literatures
of the world, a field for study and research in itself. Even today
there are very few departments or professorships of American

literature in the universities of the United States. It was not until 1928 that there was a scholarly journal devoted to research and criticism in American literature, and the *Publications of the Modern Language Association,* the official organ of our largest society of scholars in all the modern languages and literatures, only rarely has published articles on the subject. If we do not recognize the distinctive character of our own national literature, we can hardly expect others to do so. I remember the remark of one of my professors, back about 1917 when I was a student at the university where I now teach. He was referring to one of the pioneering specialists in this field. "My poor colleague!" he told his class. "He has spent all of his life studying the American drama — and there is no such thing as an American Drama!" Such a slight would have had more justification then than it would now for it was made before the coming of Eugene O'Neill, Maxwell Anderson, and Arthur Miller. But it reveals an attitude which is still all too common.

Probably you, as Norwegians, can appreciate this situation rather better than could some other peoples, for you, like we, have been a culturally dependent nation for a considerable part of your history, and you have known what it means to share a language with a kindred but different nation. You have also known what it means to break free and stand alone in comradeship with others rather than dependence upon them. We both have a strong and somewhat self-conscious feeling of literary nationalism. With us, this feeling has its roots in the original settlement of the western hemisphere and in the formation of a new nation in a wilderness by the sheer force of a consistent set of political and social ideals.

To define and to hold to a theory of literary nationalism strong enough to justify the writing and teaching of national literary history, a people must first feel themselves a distinct nation, they must then produce a distinctive literature as a people, and they must finally develop a self-conscious literary criticism on historical principles in order to prompt and to support the definition, research, and evaluation which shapes a scholarly field of study.

The first of these goals was reached in 1783 when the Treaty of Paris chopped off the thirteen original colonies and their westward extensions from Great Britain and permitted them jointly to set up their own government. This was a political fact with largely political causes. The break away of the New from the Old World was more than a disagreement about taxation without representation; it was the climactic chapter in a glorious experiment. America was the stage upon which the great theories of human freedom and perfectibility of the Enlightenment were to be put into practice. It seemed almost a holy experiment to the European revolutionaries of the seventeenth and eighteenth centures whose writings provided a latter-day gospel for the philosopher-statesmen who founded the new nation. Moral idealism embodied in the theory of the perfectibility of man through his own effort, and a practical common sense in shaping the new way of life to the hard facts of wilderness living provided at the start a double drive in the American character which the American people have never wholly lost. Never was there a people with head so serenely in the clouds and with feet so firmly on the earth.

Political idealism had created a nation; but it could not immediately create a culture or a literature. By 1790 there was a healthy group of young writers in the cities of the Atlantic seaboard crying, "Now we have a new nation, we must have a culture and a literature worthy of her high ideals and her unique character." Books and magazines were imported in increasing numbers from England and France as circulating libraries grew, printing presses multiplied and speeded up, roads and postal services were improved, and a copyright law was entered early on the docket of the new Congress. There is something almost pathetically naïve about the Americans' confidence that, by sheer act of will and native energy, they could create a literature and a reading public of their own on demand. The sad fact is that the job took a century and more. Not until almost 1890 was there a solid body of worthy American literature about which histories could be written. But the compelling force of this national pride finally succeeded in creating both a literature and a literary theory which can be said, I think, to be distinctly national and, at the same time, universally applicable. There is a direct connection between the political thinking of 1790 and the studies in American literary history which have appeared since 1920.

That connection may be traced first from the original political ideals of the First Republic to the romantic literary theory of our earliest writers and thinkers. Such preliminary studies of this problem as have been made have demonstrated that the special form of literary nationalism which found first expression in the work of the poet Philip Freneau and his generation, and reached its fullest statement in Emerson's famous "American Scholar" address in 1837, was an American modification of the rhetorical theory of the Scottish rationalists and the poetic theory of the British and American romantic philosophers and poets.

Although there were many shrewd and earlier writers on this subject, the literary situation during the first half century of independence was probably best summed up by the novelist Fenimore Cooper in 1828. Cooper's own literary theory was largely a result of trial and error, but implicitly he adopted the thesis of Madame de Staël, Schlegel, Sismondi, and others, of a close relationship, in the level of ideals, between a literature and its own society. "I think it always interesting," wrote Madame de Staël, "to examine what would be the prevailing character of the literature of a great and enlightened people, in whose country should be established liberty, political equality, and manners in unison with its institutions; there is but one nation in the world to whom some of these reflections may be applied at the present day:—America." Cooper accepts this premise and applies it both negatively and positively as a critique of the literature of his country. On the one hand, he complains that American literature suffers from the poverty of American materials.

There is scarcely an ore which contributes to the wealth of the author, that is found, here, in veins as rich as in Europe. There are no annals for the historian; no follies (beyond the most vulgar and com-

monplace) for the satirist; no manners for the dramatist; no obscure fictions for the writer of romance; no gross and hardy offenses against
decorum for the moralist; nor any of the rich artificial auxiliaries of
poetry.

Here speaks the potential writer of belles lettres rather than
the social historian, the composer of the literature of beauty, of
leisure, of pleasure. And so Cooper, like other American writers
of the day, found that patriotism and literary nationalism themselves might lead back to Europe and to increased dependence
if literature were not closely bound to life. The early American
efforts to overcome this difficulty were often pathetic, sometimes absurd; and the logical fallacy in it still infects those men
of good will who ask today that American literature be not so
ugly and so violent as it sometimes is. American materials of
Cooper's time were too raw and unfamiliar to fit easily into the
sophisticated literary moulds and forms of the Old World; they
had to forge forms of their own in the fires of experience. But
the belles lettres point of view persisted for at least another century. It is basic to the poetry of Bryant, Longfellow, Lowell,
Whittier; it inspired the massive anthologies and cyclopaedias
of Duyckinck, Griswold, and Stedman; and it comes down
almost to our own day in the literary histories of Barrett Wen-
dell and Brander Matthews. Literature, by this theory, is the last
fine flower of a civilization and its relationship with its own
society is that of embellishment.

But Cooper also appreciated the other side of the problem
when he added, "The only peculiarity that can, or ought to be
expected in their (the Americans') literature, is that which is
connected with the promulgation of their distinctive political
opinions." In another place, he adds, "The leading distinctive
principle of this country, is connected with the fact that all
political power is strictly a trust." Thus American literature
must at all times reflect and illustrate the ideals and actions of a
free and sovereign people.

In reflecting such freedom, American literature will, thought
Cooper, differ fundamentally from the European literatures
upon which it is dependent for form. Here he is close to the

romantic doctrine of literary nationalism, but it required the
more philosophical mind of the Rev. William Ellery Channing
to express that doctrine more precisely when he remarked:

> The great distinction of our country is, that we enjoy some peculiar
> advantages for understanding our own nature. Man is the great subject
> of literature, and juster and profounder views of man may be expected
> here, then elsewhere. . . . By national literature . . . we mean the contri-
> butions of new truths to the stock of human knowledge. We mean the
> thoughts of profound and original minds . . . fixed and made immortal
> in books.

And it is only a step from this view of an organic national literature to Emerson's American Scholar, his "man thinking," the
"delegated intellect" of society. "Give me insight into to-day,"
he wrote, "and you may have the antique and future worlds. . . .
The scholar is that man who must take up into himself all the
ability of the time, all the contributions of the past, all the hopes
of the future." Such literary nationalism is at once intensely
specific and broadly inclusive of other times and other places.

By 1840, the romantic theory of literary nationalism had produced in Emerson a doctrine which made it possible to draw
original and profound literary expression from the peculiar
complex of American ideas (now no longer narrowly political)
and experience, and to project it into the wide realm of tradition
and accumulated human wisdom. Thus the writings of Poe,
Emerson himself, Thoreau, Melville, and Whitman achieved, at
their best, the status of world literature because they were so
profoundly and genuinely national in inspiration.

It would be pleasant to record that this theory produced not
only a literature but a body of literary history and criticism as
well. But American literary criticism, before 1920, was negligi-
ble except for Poe and Lowell, and our literary history was
almost nonexistent too. But what there was of the latter clearly
follows the political line and reflects the romantic doctrine. The
first, *Lectures on American Literature* (1829) by Samuel L. Knapp,
deals indiscriminately with expression of all aspects of American life as illustrating "something of the history of the thoughts
and intellectual labours of our forefathers." Knapp's chief inter-

est was in political figures and ideas, and he clearly anticipates Moses Coit Tyler, who wrote a half century later, and who produced the first really great American literary history.

Tyler's history was limited to the pre-national period of the American people, the period from 1607 to 1783, but it was nonetheless a national history because its author assumes an independence of the American mind which was only later to take political form. He was unique among literary historians in that he actually read all the books he discusses, with the result that his projected history ran to four large volumes and reached only the first chapter of the story. Yet his opening paragraph is a classic statement of the method of the national literary historian:

> The American people, starting into life in the early part of the seventeenth century, have been busy ever since in recording their intellectual history in laws, manners, institutions, in battles with man and beast and nature, in highways, excavations, edifices, in pictures, in statues, in written words. It is in written words that this people, from the very beginning, have made the most confidential and explicit records of their minds. It is in these written words, therefore, that we shall now search for that record.

Here, then, in the year 1878, after approximately a century of political independence, is a literary history by Emerson's American scholar. It is, as Tyler elsewhere reaffirms many times, the history of a people; it is the inner or intellectual history of that people; it is the history of the expression by that people of their minds in the written word. Expression is the means; history can be written only about the things expressed, about the experience of a people. The American people were ready to speak.

The appearance of this great work may be taken as a milestone in the study of American literary history, not only because of its intrinsic worth, but because it happens to coincide with the beginnings of systematic academic research in the humanities in America, the founding of graduate schools and special departments, and the forming of learned societies on a national scale. The period from about 1880 to about 1920 saw the growth of universities in the United States from the level of not much more than the high school or gymnasium, to that of the institute for research and for the granting of higher degrees the equal of anything in Europe. In 1880, all professional or specialized education necessitated travel and residence in the great European centers of learning; after 1920, as many European scholars came to America as Americans who went abroad. One might expect that the study of American literary history, after such a start as Tyler gave it, would move forward steadily with the general movement of higher learning. But quite the contrary was the case. It came practically to a complete stop. Almost no contributions of major importance were made to the study or teaching of the subject between Tyler's work and the appearance of the *Cambridge History of American Literature* in 1917-1920.

The mystery of this paradoxical situation cannot, of course, be resolved by the waving of a magic wand, but there may be a clue to its solution in the fact that the first historian of American literature was a member of the history, and not the literature, departments of the universities of Michigan and Cornell, whereas the development of higher study and research in American literature after 1880 was a part of the development of departments of English language and literature. For some forty years—the years in which graduate study was established in the United States—American literature was regarded as a minor part of English literature rather than as the expression, in the written word, of the American people. History departments relinquished it to English departments, and English departments slighted or ignored it.

While history departments, in spite of the Anglophilism, developed methods friendly to the study of American history, departments of modern literature turned to the philological method as a tool to break the hold of classics departments upon the study of literature in our universities. Even the world of the mind has its politics. Philology was the tool of the classicists themselves, further refined by the new theories and discoveries of the Germans in the science of language, and it succeeded in its task of making the study of modern literatures, especially English, respectable. That was perhaps a necessary step toward the further revolt of American from English literature so that the old link between American literature and American social and cultural history once more could be established, but it meant that the study of American literatue itself virtually went underground for some forty years.

Meanwhile there occurred a general revision of the curriculum of the American university. In spite of the practical common sense and modernism of such early American educators as Franklin and Jefferson, the classical and formalistic curriculum of the British universities had triumphed in the American up to the middle of the nineteenth century. Then suddenly the situation opened up at Harvard under President Charles W. Eliot and at Johns Hopkins in Baltimore under President Daniel Coit Gilman. These leaders emphasized two points: education must be modern and suited to the needs of the student, said President Eliot; and education must be scientific and thorough, said President Gilman. The first principle led to a tremendous expansion of the undergraduate colleges and the second to the rapid growth of the graduate schools of higher learning and research in the United States. Eliot's principle led to the subdivision of the curriculum into many more departments in new and practical subjects, while Gilman's led to the development of these "new disciplines" to a higher and higher degree of specialization and to methodologies more and more technical and "scientific." English was modern and new as a discipline but, with the aid of philology, it could be made as difficult as that of the classics. The Modern Language Association was founded and in 1886 began its *Publications,* the official American organ for scholarship in all the languages and literatures.

The first issues of this journal reveal the situation and the attitudes of the early defenders of this radically modern discipline. In the first three numbers there were a total of forty articles. Of these, fifteen dealt with technical linguistic problems and seventeen were efforts to define and defend the higher study of the modern languages. Gradually the controversial articles on method and in defense of modern languages dropped out and literary source studies began to appear. Emphasis on Anglo-Saxon and Middle English topics increased, Elizabethan studies began to appear, and in 1910, with its first article specifically on American literature, the journal finally gave evidence that it was published in the United States. Meanwhile in 1927 the Association altered its official statement of purpose from "the study of" to "research in the modern languages and their literatures," and it was not until the fiftieth anniversary year, 1932, that the then President, John Livingston Lowes, uttered the dissenting warning, "In fifty years our emphasis has gone far towards passing from scholarship for larger ends to scholarship for scholars. Are the humanities by any chance in danger at our hands of ceasing to be humane?"

A similar story is told by the early courses in English literature and language in the universities. Among the major appointments to English departments, as they split off from departments of classical philology, Kittredge of Harvard, Schelling of Pennsylvania, Bright of Hopkins, and Cook of Yale and Hopkins, only Schelling was primarily a student of literature rather than of language, an historian rather than an analytical scholar of texts. These men, probably more than any others, gave shape to the higher study of English in our universities during this half century, and Kittredge, Cook, and Bright were all primarily philologists in the narrow sense of students of language first and of literature only secondarily, of Indo-Teutonic origins first and modern literature only secondarily, if at all. Under such leadership, it is not surprising that courses in American literature increased very slowly during these years, and remained largely elementary, in spite of the phenomenal growth of English departments as a whole, and the rapid increase of research in the field.

Once firmly founded, English departments quickly gained immense power in the politics of American university life. Undergraduate students flocked to them, and the resulting openings for university teaching attracted a large group of advanced scholars to the field. By 1910, throughout the United States they dominated the academic life; because they were relatively modern and free, they crowded the classics into a subsidiary position, only to be challenged, for much the same reasons, in the following years by the even more modern social sciences.

But that is another story. The principles and the ideals of the "English" discipline alone concern us here. As I recall them, here are the dogmas that were impressed upon me long ago as shaping sound scholarship in English (or American) language and literature:

1. It must be objective. No quarter can be allowed to evaluation of any kind. Science is the quest for knowledge, and knowledge is something outside of the mind, to be acquired by it. Subjective impressions and undocumented opinions are outlawed.

2. It must be new knowledge. Old knowledge can be used in the classroom, but the scholar, to justify his position, must constantly search for new facts to add to the sum of those known.

3. It must be difficult so as to discipline the mind.

4. It must deal with early materials, preferably the Anglo-Saxon and comparative Teutonic. Materials as late as 1800 can be reluctantly admitted, but after that date objectivity is difficult or impossible.

5. It must be accurate and complete within its own self-imposed limits. Falsification of evidence, whether intentional or not, or failure to collect all the evidence, are unpardonable offenses.

6. Finally, and most important: Linguistic studies are prior to studies in literature because literature is expression in the written word, and expression in the written word is language. Linguistics is therefore the fundamental form of literary study, and the history of language is the back-bone of literary history. Prosody, symbolism, textual criticism, bibliography, and the circumstances of authorship all may be admitted as extensions of this basic principle and as forms of expression, and therefore of language, but the substance of the thing expressed is a matter for philosophers rather than philologists.

Admirable as most of these principles are in themselves, they succeeded in divorcing literary study from the study of other branches of history by creating for it a vacuum of scientific abstraction; and, by throwing emphasis on early literature, they put American literature under a double handicap, that of being too modern and that of being a mere branch of English literature. In 1920, the young American scholar who dared to declare himself a specialist in the literature of his own nation ran the risk of never advancing in his profession beyond the rank of docent and of failing to find a learned journal in which he could publish his research findings.

There were a few university professors who protested against this situation in the early years of the present century and some even went so far as to offer a graduate course or two in American literature; but the chief revolt came from the young non-academic critics who were active after 1910. These young literary radicals were — and felt themselves to be — parts of a new movement in American literary history itself. They were initiating a movement in literary criticism which ran parallel to that in poetry, fiction, and drama, and which made the twenties one of the richest periods in our literary history. Yet there is in their pronouncement a distinct echo of the literary nationalism of a century earlier. The United States had, after the Spanish War and under the leadership of Theodore Roosevelt, become a world power, really for the first time; and, after the first World War, it was to become one of the leading world powers. The old argument for a national literature was revived by John Macy, Van Wyck Brooks, and, most loud-spoken of all, H. L. Mencken, the bad boy of Baltimore. But these independent young men differed from their forefathers in one important respect. They were basically destructive in their criticism; they declared that American thinking had divorced literature from life and that only by a reunion of the two could either one be whole and healthy again. America has come of age, said Brooks, but it is a blighted maturity for, "those of our writers who have possessed a vivid personal talent have been paralyzed by the want of a social background, while those who have possessed a vivid social talent have been equally unable to develop their personalities." We need a sense of "national culture," "the element in which everything admirably characteristic of a people sums itself up."

So much for the diagnosis; Mencken was the surgeon, cutting sharply into the flesh of American complacency to release the vital energy which he felt was so much needed. For Mencken there were two chief enemies to a free and fresh literature, the "Puritans," by whom he meant all opponents to free expression, and the "Professors," sometimes known as "Schoolma'ams," who were as bad or worse. In 1919, when his study of the American language first appeared, his name was unmentionable in respectable academic circles; by last year, when the second supplement to the fourth edition of that great work was issued, even those who had not learned to like him personally were forced to admit his preeminence as a scholar in the field. He had carried the war to the inner stronghold of the enemy — research in linguistics itself.

John Macy's *The Spirit of American Literature* (1913) may be considered the first step toward a reappraisal of American literature in the terms demanded by these literary radicals. It is as good a point as any to take up again the movement which seemed to have made a real beginning with Tyler in 1878 but then to have lapsed into relative obscurity, the historical study of American literature as the expression in the written word of American life. Macy's social and political radicalism provided the "social background" that Brooks had found to be lacking, for socialism in America was as yet not narrowly Marxian and could still furnish a twentieth-century social philosophy in accord with traditional American principles of democracy. In the perspective of thirty-five years, we can also look back to the work of the neohumanist critics of that day — of such men as Irving Babbitt, W. C. Brownell, and Paul Elmer More — for the other half of Brooks' equation, the renewed feeling of value in personality. Brownell's *American Prose Masters* (1909) may serve as the other foundation post, with Macy, in the new structure.

The materials for that structure were assembled by 1920 in the *Cambridge History of American Literature,* which marked both the end and the beginning of eras in the higher study of the subject. Although itself something of an overgrown appendix to the *Cambridge History of English Literature,* this cooperative work marked the end of the era in which American literature could be taught as a mere by-product of the British literary tradition. The editors opened their doors to anything in print just so long as it was American, and piled chapter upon chapter dealing with travel narratives, newspapers, Puritan divines, patriotic songs and hymns, and popular Bibles. But they were motivated by no consistent view of the American culture and civilization which produced this ill-assorted body of writing. The work, almost unreadable as a whole, performed a great service in disclosing the vast and rich body of American writing that had yet to be studied, and it undoubtedly had much to do with initiating research in the field. But another quarter of a century had to pass before this material could be marshaled into anything like a historical configuration.

Two other books, both published in 1927-1928, helped greatly to develop that historical perspective. These books were *The Reinterpretation of American Literature,* a collection of essays by various hands, inspired and edited by Norman Foerster, and *Main Currents in American Thought,* by Vernon L. Parrington.

Foerster was a neo-humanist, a disciple of Irving Babbitt and Paul Elmer More, a firm believer in the value of personality and in the relationship between literature and life on the level of ethics. He contributed the needed code of personal values to the newly forming concept of American literary history as Emerson had in his day.

> It is time [he wrote] for us to seek, in all simplicity and honesty, a more nearly adequate conception of American literature than has yet existed. . . . All the factors may be comprised under two heads: European culture and the American environment. American history, including literary history, is to be viewed as the interplay of these two tremendous factors, neither of which has been studied profoundly by our literary scholars.

Foerster rightly acknowledged that the historians had developed a far broader and deeper view of American economic, social, and cultural history since Frederick Jackson Turner's classic challenge, "The Significance of the Frontier in American History," of 1893, and he called upon literary historians to apply their wisdom to this less-explored field. But he pointed also, and for the first time clearly, to the parallel development of the romantic movement in American and European literatures, suggesting the interplay of the two worlds of ideas, a field which has not even yet been fully explored.

Almost as a specific answer to this call for a new type of literary history came Parrington's *Main Currents in American Thought.*

> I have undertaken [wrote this obscure professor from a far-western university] to give some account of the genesis and development in American letters of certain germinal ideas that have come to be reckoned traditionally American — how they came into being here, how they were opposed, and what influence they have exerted in determining the form and scope of our characteristic ideals and institutions. In pursuing such a task, I have chosen to follow the broad path of our political, economic, and social development, rather than the narrower belletristic; and the main divisions of the study have been fixed by forces that are anterior to literary schools and movements, creating the body of ideas from which literary culture eventually springs.

This is the spirit of Moses Coit Tyler revived and supplied with a theory of literary history which strikes deep roots into society. It would have been an unequaled instrument for discovering the true course of American literature had Parrington not been somewhat too narrowly limited by his own social view, the product of Jeffersonian democratic agrarianism.

This is, of course, the chief danger for those who would follow the romantic doctrine of a nationalistic theory of literary history; the social or political philosophy to which the literature is related tends to become too narrow and specific. The result may be that what starts out as a broad interpretation of literature becomes merely a special plea for the historian's own dogma. The integrity of Parrington's classic work was not seriously weakened by his propagandistic intent because he was too fine a scholar, but lesser men have become doctrinaire. The extreme instance of this mistake may be found in the Marxist literary histories of V. F. Calverton and Granville Hicks and in the Freudian history of Ludwig Lewisohn. But the ultimate validity of Tyler's theory of the close relationship of literature and society is not destroyed by such misapplication of it.

In more recent times, three historical critics, Alfred Kazin, in a history of American prose which he calls *On Native Grounds*

(1942), Maxwell Geismar in a history of twentieth-century American fiction, the first volume of which appeared in the same year, and F. O. Matthiessen in *American Renaissance* (1941) have demonstrated that it is possible to have firm convictions about American society and to use those convictions as a means for the illumination of literary history without becoming doctrinaire or bending their books covertly to serve the ends of social or political propaganda.

It was the conviction of the self-appointed editorial board of the new *Literary History of the United States,* published a little over a year ago, that the time had come when a group of American literary historians and critics could accomplish together what no one of them had so far been broad enough and deep enough to accomplish alone. "Like man himself," said Sigmund Skard in his recent Inaugural Address in your university,

> literature simultaneously faces Time and Eternity; in the literary creation mass movements with their relatively palpable nexus of cause and effect engage in a continuous interplay with forces of personality, the essence of which will always be fugacious. . . . The tentative description of the poetic mind and the sociological analysis of a broad literary movement are equally indispensable to a scholarship which pretends to grasp the reality of literature in its breadth and depth; and the methods continuously work into each other's hands.

This is Tyler's theory, developed to a point to which Tyler himself never took it because his history did not continue into the era of the great literary artists of the nineteenth century. The dualism of sociology and personality, of institution and idea, of time and eternity, as Emerson so keenly recognized, is essential to the true literary history. With an architectural conception adequate to provide for the horizontal lines of cause and effect and the vertical lines of genius and universality, we undertook in this new *Literary History* the task, not of finding the right facts but of asking the right questions. Only a variety of methods could adequately deal with the causal forces and factors in society and the social mind, with forms and movements as discovered mainly in minor authors and literary groups, and with intrinsic excellence in the works of authors who rose by genius to the level of the universal.

I must admit that critics so far have not always been willing to admit that we actually achieved the aim that we set ourselves, and the editors would be equally hesitant to press the point. But, whether or not this particular book is the final rounding out of the story, the logic of development in American literary history points to an ideal of just such a book as this. And the universities have meanwhile followed along with courses and programs pointing to the same ideal. Since Tyler's day courses and elementary texts in the subject steadily and very slowly increased in spite of official opposition. Even advanced work was offered in some nineteen universities and a total of 133 doctoral dissertations had been produced by 1928 in all universities. It was then that the journal of *American Literature* was founded under the editorship of Jay B. Hubbell. I well remember the smoke-filled room where the decision to publish was reached, as I remember the efforts of Kenneth B. Murdock and myself to prepare a semi-official plan for a Ph.D. degree in American literature and to send it to all the universities in America. Cause and effect here become indistinguishable. Courses, both undergraduate and graduate, increased rapidly everywhere and dissertations so multiplied that counting them would be a labor. By now they run into thousands. In 1948, the development of work in American literature and culture had reached such proportions that two surveys on a national scale were published in the same year. Although there were still few separate departments or professorships of American literature as such, there was scarcely a university of the first or second rank in the United States where it was not possible to take any degree, from the bachelor's to the doctor's, with a concentration in the history and the criticism of American literature. In most cases the degree was still nominally a degree in English language and literature, but the language study had become secondary to the interpretive study of literature, literature since 1800 had far outweighed that of the earlier times, and American literature occupied up to nearly half of the major concentration.

One of the most promising developments out of this progress during the past decade has been the announcement at Harvard, Minneapolis, my own Pennsylvania, Yale, and some other universities, of courses leading to degrees in American Civilization or Culture, as distinct from degrees in history, literature, language, or the social sciences. In all cases so far, these degrees have been administered by inter-departmental committees, chaired usually by the American specialists of the history or literature departments. As one phase of a general tendency in American higher education to view knowledge in larger configurations and to overcome some of the evils of narrow and technical specialization, these courses in American Civilization are exciting widespread interest. As the recent chairman of one such committee, I am even now unprepared to estimate the full significance of this movement or to predict its future course. This year we have at Pennsylvania a young man on a Rockefeller fellowship devoting his full time to planning a course which would serve as an undergraduate introduction to the field but at the same time would help to define that field for the entire program.

We are just beginning to discover ways of exploring the meaning of our own synthetic and heterogeneous, but vital and dynamic culture. The setting up of institutes of American studies at Oslo, Uppsala, Paris, Munich, and elsewhere in Europe is encouraging to our faith in ourselves and our self-exploratory work. We still have much to learn.

NOTE
1. Reproduced from Whitman's own "copy for the convenience of private reading only." *Leaves of Grass* (New York: The Facsimile Text Society, 1939).

12 | THOSE EARLY DAYS: AMERICAN LITERATURE AND THE MODERN LANGUAGE ASSOCIATION

On December 22, 1966, the American Literature Group (now Section) of the Modern Language Association held a joint luncheon with the American Studies Association at the annual convention in New York City, and they invited me — the Grand Old Man of the first and the young promoter of the second — to address them.

This very personal reminiscence tells the story of the first forty years of the movement. It was first published as a "postscript" in The Oblique Light *(1968), from which it is reprinted here in historical context.*

I

It may come as something of a surprise to learn that systematic historical scholarship in American literature dates from the year 1921 and that my invitation to speak was addressed to "the last surviving *active* member from the old days when the Group numbered only a dozen or so." No wonder that I felt like the Ancient Mariner who was impelled to hold the wedding guest with his skinny hand and his glittering eye in order to tell him of that fearsome voyage which he alone had survived. But when I got down to reviewing the vital statistics of the situation, I found that, unlike Ishmael, I had with me other survivors clinging to Queequeg's coffin. So if you think you are listening to a voice from the grave, it will be only the wee small voice of the Acting Secretary of the American Literature Group at its third meeting, in Ann Arbor in 1923, when neither the elected Chair-

man Percy H. Boynton of Chicago nor the elected Secretary
Francis A. Litz, then of Johns Hopkins, were present, and that
old warhorse of the pioneer days, Arthur Hobson Quinn, took
the chair for the second of three consecutive years and asked his
graduate student to take notes.

May I read you those notes? because this is where I came in
and because it contains most of what I would like to say today,
forty-three years later:

(English XII) American Literature. *Chairman,* Professor Percy H.
Boynton. In the absence of Professor Boynton, Professor Arthur H.
Quinn served as Chairman.

Professor Pattee read a paper giving in retrospect the introduction of
American Literature in the College curriculum. The discussion that
followed favored presenting American Literature as expression of
national (historical) consciousness and not as aesthetic offshoot of
English Literature.

In reporting on Problems under Investigation, Professor Leisy called
attention to a list of articles to date in scholarly journals, to theses now
in progress, and to a number of possible subjects for investigation. Professor Pattee suggested rewriting official biographies because of their
prejudiced matter; Professor Hubbell told of teaching literature by
backgrounds; Dr. Mabbott recommended biographical and bibliographical studies of local authors.

A committee, consisting of Professors Hubbell, Mabbott, and Leisy
(Chairman) is to report what theses are completed, what ones are
under investigation, and what special collections are available for
research in various libraries.

About twenty-five persons were present.

Professor F. L. Pattee was elected Chairman and Dr. E. E. Leisy, Secretary.

R. E. Spiller, Acting Secretary

The striking thing about these notes is, I think, that they represent so vigorous and ambitious a response to the presidential
challenge of John Mathews Manly of two years before. Manly,
as chairman of a committee to study and reorganize the diffuse
and boring paper-reading sessions of the Association, had recommended a breakdown into small research groups. "The general impression produced by a survey of our work," he had

charged, "is that it has been individual, casual, scrappy, scatter-ing," but, he continued, "this age is increasingly one of speciali-zation and of organization for the accomplishment of purposes too large for a single investigator."[1] The solution he proposed was for scholars in the modern languages to group themselves for cooperative research and specialized meetings; and Ameri-can literature was obviously one of the subdivisions of the English language segment—specifically English XII.

Up to this time an American specialization was hardly respectable; in fact, it was close to professional suicide. Quinn had spent many years studying the American drama; Cairns had devoted his attention to British criticisms of American writing, and Boynton and Pattee chiefly to the more recent local color-ists of the West. Even the *Cambridge History* editors, to whom everything in print was literature, were predominantly apolo-getic in tone. It was a ragged army of minutemen who assem-bled that day to take stock of the state of scholarship in the American field and to plan the future.

II

It is not surprising, therefore, that the first years of group history, in spite of Quinn's devotion, were still somewhat scat-tered and scrappy. Rather it was to the committee of which Leisy was chairman that we came to look for the thrust that put us, so to speak, on the road. Leisy's surveys, which were subse-quently carried on by Gregory Paine, Lewis Leary, James Wood-ress, and others, have provided us with an essential focus which was lacking in the activities of most of the other early MLA groups, a bibliographical backbone. From that day, we have always known where we stood at any one time in scholarly achievement and have therefore always been ready for the next cooperative move, whereas it was not until 1934 that the Asso-ciation as a whole had a committee on research activities. Most of the other groups, with the possible exception of that on Chaucer, which was already organized and committed to the Manly-Rickert project, kept on their happy-go-lucky way of col-lecting audiences of drifters, different from year to year, and then electing officers from the floor from among those who hadn't been too bored to last out the meeting.

But the American Literature Group had a vitality of its own. It was a combination of the philosophical perspective of Norman Foerster and the tactical generalship of J. B. Hubbell which finally gave it the sense of direction and purpose which rescued us from being merely gentlemen-scholars, like so many of our colleagues, with an overdeveloped taste for the hotel bar and an underdeveloped will to get things done. The elements of organization first appeared in 1925 when Chairman Hubbell and Secretary Leisy were elected to second terms and the critic-historian Foerster, who had just read his classic paper on "The Present State of American Literary History," was made chairman of a newly created executive committee, the body which later became the Advisory Council. This, I think, was the first time a Modern Language Association research group had organized itself as virtually an independent cell within the larger organism and had created the means of continuing activity between meetings and from meeting to meeting over the years. From then on, American literature as a scholarly discipline was on the offensive and the note of apology began to fade.

III

Before looking more closely at Foerster's program, however, I would like to turn to another factor in our history. When the scholars in English literature back in the 1890s broke away from their dependence on Classical philology for the disciplinary core of their studies, they substituted Anglo-Saxon and comparative Teutonic philology for Greek and Latin on the grounds that the Teutonic tradition was more relevant to their subject and that it provided an equally good discipline because it was equally hard. But when the American scholars in their turn attempted to break away from this Old English philological tradition, now become the establishment, and to declare their independence, there was no separate American philological discipline for them to turn to in spite of the efforts of Louise Pound to make American speech academically respectable and of Stith Thompson, John Lomax, and others to substitute American Indians and cowboys for Beowulf and Grendel's Dam. Without an American language with a history and a literature of its own (this was before Mencken became respectable) it is not surprising that they turned to intellectual, social, and cultural history as a way to cut the umbilical cord with Mother England and to relate the American literary tradition more vitally to the tradition of all Western Europe, the tradition which had come down unbroken from the Renaissance and had been imported to the New World by Spanish cavaliers, French priests, Irish farmers, and German Protestant refugees as well as by British immigrants. Foerster's paper became the introduction to the first cooperative effort of the group, the *Reinterpretation* volume of 1928, the year in which the journal *American Literature*, as Hubbell has told you,[2] was initiated.

"The central fact," Foerster claimed.

is that American literature has had its own special conditions of development and its own special tendencies arising from these conditions. Among the literatures of the modern world, its case is unique. The culture out of which it first issued was not a native growth but a highly elaborate culture transplanted to a wilderness that receded slowly as the frontier pushed westward. . . . The three broad problems with which the student of American literary history is concerned are: (1) In what sense is our literature distinctively American? (2) In what ways does it resemble the literature of Europe? and (3) What are the local conditions of life and thought in America that produce these results?"[3]

Foerster's basic approach to the problem as one of the interaction of European (not merely English) culture (not merely literature) and the American environment, and his identification of indigenous romantic and realistic movements in its development were generally accepted at that time as the structural frame for our literary history, from which no later historians have wished to depart to any significant degree.

I wish I could recreate the excitement aroused in some of us by such words as these. Was it really possible for American literary history to make a clean break with historical philology and to share in the vital concerns of the "New History" which was creating such a stir at the other end of the hall in most of the "Old Mains" of the country's universities? For this was the day of James Harvey Robinson, Arthur Schlesinger, Sr., Carl Becker, E. P. Cheyney, Charles A. Beard, and Samuel Eliot Morison. Turner's collected frontier essays had been published in 1920 and Harry Elmer Barnes' *The New History and the Social Sciences* in 1925. These daring new social sciences were apparently developing interdisciplinary concepts and methods which might draw all the traditional disciplines to a new center! Was this the approach we were looking for?

As John Higham has recently pointed out,[4] the revolt of the New History was rather *against* the old order than in favor of a new and consistent one. Provoked mainly by restlessness with the objective reliance on fact and document and by the anti-quarianism of the older historians, these radical few turned to the emerging social sciences for help in dealing with the history of modern man in the living terms of ideas and culture. Vigorously present-minded and speculative, they seemed on the verge of developing a new discipline in economic, intellectual, and cultural history which might fit the facts of American literary development as well. At about this time, the American Literature Group seriously debated the desirability of seceding from the Modern Language Association and joining the American Historical Association, or perhaps the then-emergent Society of American Historians, which has survived as one of the sponsors of *American Heritage*. Fortunately it remained within the fold, for by 1933, John Livingston Lowes was demanding in his presidential address that the Modern Language Association as a whole cease trying to learn "more and more about less and less" and turn to vital and immediate concerns and methods.

Thus when I became chairman of the group in 1930, I found it already virtually committed to the gigantic task of restudying the American past from the point of view of a literary history which was nationalistic without being chauvinistic and which attempted to discover the relationships between the literature actually produced in America and its immediate sources in cultural evolution; while the shift of emphasis from historical philology to intellectual and cultural history opened the way for studies of its indebtedness to the tradition of all of Western Europe rather than exclusively to that of England. There was even a proposal for a new Ph.D. in American literature along these lines, first formulated by Foerster and endorsed by the group under Murdock and Bradley. Meanwhile attendance at its meetings had increased from 25 to 149 and was soon to rise to three or four hundred and more, while its internal organization became increasingly firm, purposive, and effective within the larger association. The masthead of its new journal announced a concern for "Literary History, Criticism, and Bibliography," without reference to "Language," and the early papers which were read to the group or published in the journal followed this program.

IV

Focus for major researches had early been set by Pattee on the restudy of individual biographies with the aid of the new psychological and sociological insights and by Hubbell on the redefinition of the special characteristics of regions with the help of frontier and ethnological discoveries. Murdock had reexamined Increase Mather, and with him the whole history of European and American Puritanism; Williams was at work on the definitive biography of Washington Irving with special reference to his Spanish sources; Melville had been exhumed from oblivion by Weaver, Thorp, and others; Rusk was beginning to collect the letters of Emerson in preparation for his masterly biography; Quinn and Mabbott were putting the elusive Poe into a believable world from which the Rev. Rufus Griswold had been finally exorcised; and McDowell was discovering a very American Bryant, while Randall Stewart was at work, with Norman Pearson, on the task of eliminating the gentle Sophia from the notebooks of Hawthorne in preparation for a three-dimensional story of his life; Bradley had resurrected Boker, not only as a respectable playwright but as a love-sonneteer honest enough to make Longfellow shudder; Harry Clark was dividing his time between the radical Paine and the genteel Professor Lowell of Harvard, while I was at work taking James Fenimore Cooper and his Indians away from the kiddies.

There were more general studies also. Howard Mumford Jones was discovering that the Europeans, particularly the French, brought deviltry as well as divinity in their baggage when they emigrated to this continent, while Pochmann was doing much the same thing for German culture; Hubbell was reassessing the special features of the literary culture of the Old South, Rusk of the Middle West, Quinn of the Middle Atlantic States with special reference to the theater, and Murdock, Jones, and later Perry Miller, of colonial New England in a plan to rewrite Moses Coit Tyler in three volumes. Walter Blair was taking American humor as his province, Clark and Hornberger American science, and Arthur Christy the Oriental influences; but the most emphatic as well as the least expected revisionist document of them all came out of the West in 1927 when V. L. Parrington launched the first two volumes of his *Main Currents in American Thought*, which Murdock reviewed for the group at an animated meeting and which left many of us wondering whether we had gone too far in our flirtation with the historians and social scientists and had become outright political economists ourselves.

There were also many studies undertaken to determine the exact conditions under which the American writer worked. Magazines and newspapers were reexamined by Frank Luther Mott, gift-books and annuals, publishers and bookshops, libraries, literary clubs and theaters all had their histories written, and contemporary reviews were scanned for evidence of reader-reception of American works.

V

My own chief concern during all this time was moving toward the problem of the philosophy and structure of American literary history taken as a whole, toward accepting the challenge of Foerster and Pattee to attempt a single and total synthesis along new lines, but the way was not yet clear. Chairing that 1930 meeting was a task like that of the old woman who lived in a shoe. The business of the group had moved forward on all fronts and we had so many projects that we did not know what to do. Reports were heard on the progress of the journal, now two years old, and on the Columbia-based Facsimile Text Society, on the committee on manuscript resources, on the historical *Dictionary of American English* and the *Linguistic Atlas of the United States*, and on the *Dictionary of American Biography*. That was the first year of a double session, with a luncheon and business meeting between, and a letter was drafted to the executive council of the association asking for more autonomy as well as more direct representation of the group in its higher echelons of power. Even a sharp slap on the wrist at the council's meeting of 1932 (and as I *now* read the record, probably a deserved one) did little to curtail the brash energy of this prodigious infant!

By 1939 at the New Orleans meeting, the group's committee on a cooperative literary history and bibliography, which had been appointed at Columbia the year before, was authorized to sign a contract for a multi-volume work and to set up the machinery for its execution. I have often wondered what would have happened if we had taken that charge literally, but caution intervened and action was postponed. Instead, at the 1940 meeting at Cambridge this committee's revised and more specific recommendations were withdrawn in the face of mounting resistance from those who felt that the time was not ripe for such a group undertaking. The papers prepublished in *American Literature* and then discussed made clear the general conviction that there was so much "spade-work" still to be done that any attempt at an authorized synthesis would be premature. The solution of the issue — that the group as such should continue this spade-work by undertaking a nationwide survey of manuscript and other resources, leaving the field open for individual and unsponsored attempts at synthesis—was unquestionably a wise one. It established a policy of sponsored research for factual compilations and symposia while encouraging individual initiative in works of interpretation and synthesis. The recent launching of a five-volume short history of American literature under the general editorship of Quentin Anderson, without group sponsorship, tends to confirm the continuing soundness of that policy, while the group itself has officially authorized the symposia on *Transitions*, edited by Clark; and that on *Criticism*, edited by Stovall; the bibliography *Eight American Authors*; the checklist volume on *American Literary Manuscripts*, edited by Joseph Jones and others; Leary's lists of aritcles on American literature; the *Bibliographical Guide*, edited by Gohdes;

the several dissertation lists; and now the annual volume on *American Literary Scholarship*; to say nothing of the Center for Editions of American Authors, which was initiated by the group and is still informally controlled by it.

This last stupendous project, which has for the first time attracted major financial support from outside sources, is the greatest test to which the American Literature Group—or rather, now Section—of the Modern Language Association has been submitted. Have we the cooperative energy and vision to carry it through, even with the help of the parent Association? And have we the perspective which will allow us to sponsor a cooperative project without infringing on the prerogatives of the individual scholars involved? This review of our past experience, I hope, will help us to move ahead confidently with the guidance of our accumulated experience and a working sense of what *can* be done in the world of humanistic scholarship by cooperative effort and what must be left as always to the vision and energy of the individual scholar. Let us not merely imitate the scientists and learn to depend too heavily on government foundations for the support of cooperative research. For as humanists we must always remain a free society of scholars rather than a committee of management or, even worse, a computer. The Center, so far, has been true to this ideal under the wise leadership of its director and executive committee; may it continue to be so and may the American Literature Section move on to the initiation of further and even more ambitious projects of both individual and cooperative scholarship.

VI

Before I close, I would like to add a word to the members of the American Studies Association who may have wondered where they fit into this history. I was tempted to broaden my range today to include you, but I decided to respect the limits of your patience. Suffice it to say that, when the group about 1950 began to move with the fashions of the times to an increasing emphasis on analytical and textual criticism and away from literary and cultural history, its old concern for the relationship between literature and culture was largely taken over and developed by the new Association, to the benefit of both. But as that is in itself a complicated story, which others are perhaps better qualified than I to tell, I will conclude as I started, as one of the few surviving of the ancient sages who can cull from the past what he believes to be the wisdom of hard-earned experience, but which may well be little more than fragments of memory. Take it for what it is worth, and let's get to work on the next chapter in the history of American studies, literary and otherwise.

NOTES

1. *Publications of the Modern Language Association* 73 (December 1958): 35.

2. Jay B. Hubbell, *South and Southwest* (Durham, N.C.: Duke University Press, 1965), pp. 22-48.

3. *The Reinterpretation of American Literature*, edited by Norman Foerster (New York: Harcourt Brace and Co., 1928), pp. xi-xii.

4. *History*, edited by John Higham and others (Englewood Cliffs, N.J.: Prentice-Hall, 1965), pp. 104-16.

13 | UNITY AND DIVERSITY IN THE STUDY OF AMERICAN CULTURE: THE AMERICAN STUDIES ASSOCIATION IN PERSPECTIVE

The decade following my return to Pennsylvania in the fall of 1945 was the happiest and most productive of my life. Not only was it an academic homecoming and an opportunity to teach mature and professionally oriented students, but it was also the first time that I had been able to blend on a regular basis my commitment to higher liberal education with my scholarly concentration on American literary history and civilization.

It wasn't long before things began to happen. The first was the sowing of the seeds of a national association for American Studies. The four of us who shared the chairmanship of the new department soon began to gather together scholars in subjects other than history and literature from colleges and universities from New York to Washington into a very exclusive occasional dinner club (limited to thirty-five members), which met at the Franklin Inn Club in Philadelphia for an afternoon and an evening session of both philosophical and practical problems. We called it "The Society for American Studies" (SAS), and for several years it furnished wonderfully stimulating meetings of diversified and well-stocked minds—literary and art historians and social and intellectual historians of many kinds, as well as sociologists, economists, and philosophers—all drawn together by the one adjective, "American."

The SAS, however, soon was challenged by the American Studies Association (ASA). Carl Bode came up one day in the fall of 1949 from Washington and suggested that we go democratic and national. The SAS held firm, but many of its members recognized the value of Bode's suggestion and helped him

216

form a much less concentrated group that met in the Library of Congress as the "Chesapeake Chapter" of a new American Studies Association, which then began its history of fanning out into other regional groups—northern New York, New England, southeastern, midwestern.[1] By 1953, when I became the ASA's fourth president, it was recognized as a "learned" society by admission to the American Council of Learned Societies.

It was then that John Gardner, president of the Carnegie Corporation, invited me to lunch with him in New York to discuss what his foundation might do for "American studies." The result was a generous grant that made possible a paid executive secretary for the association and many small conferences from the Atlantic to the Pacific coast. By the end of Louis Rubin's very short term in that post, there were eighteen regional societies, or chapters, and a membership of two thousand. Further grants to the programs at the Universities of Minnesota and Pennsylvania led to a national office at Pennsylvania and the founding of the American Quarterly at Minnesota (later moved to Pennsylvania). The American Studies Association was on its way.

During this time I was Chairman of Penn's American Civilization Department much of the time, with my historian colleague Thomas C. Cochran, and helped to expand its program with the Carnegie grant. We introduced a new program of scholarships and fellowships, including an annual visiting professorship by a foreign scholar. At the same time a grant from the Rockefeller Foundation made possible a two-year research fellowship to help define the department's role.

The first holder of this fellowship, Anthony N. B. Garvan, led to a fundamental change in direction for the department's policy. For some time there had been a growing split between the Minnesota approach of bringing two or more disciplines to bear on every problem, course, or dissertation in American Studies, and the sanguine hope expressed by Henry Nash Smith that a single method might develop out of this ambiguity.[2]

We at Penn had already elected to search for a central definition of a national culture and to shape our program—as it were, from the hub rather than from the rim of the wheel—around a *single concept. Garvan was given this assignment and, in an adaptation of the Yale program in cross-cultural studies, developed an undergraduate course in American civilization around which the rest of our program took form, with much modification by the test of experience. The result has been a sharp division, both at Pennsylvania and in the American Studies Association at large, between these two approaches (which I here call the "synthetic" and the "holistic"), a division that I attempted to resolve in this article. This address at the Third National Convention in the Association in Washington, D.C., in 1971 was published in* American Quarterly *25 (1973):611-18.*

The founding of the American Studies Association in the early 1950s was but one event—a major one—in the history of the American Studies movement in the United States, but in order to understand and evaluate it, we must see it in relationship to the awakening of a self-conscious cultural nationalism which had roots in the early years of this century.

This was a time when the United States was emerging into the role of a world power and the stirrings of cultural nationalism were beginning to be felt in the universities in practically all of the academic disciplines except perhaps those in pure science; and even there, American technology gave to scientific disciplines something of a nationalistic flavor. Looking back at the founding, in the early years of this century, of various learned societies, particularly in economics, political science and the behaviorial sciences, and at the increasing emphasis on American history in history departments, American literature in English departments, and American art and archeology in art departments, we can see now a common drive or movement which was not as obvious at the time as it is today, and which came to some sort of fruition just before and after World War I, or between 1915 and 1925.

The common question which was being asked individually by all these academic disciplines at that time could be phrased something like this: Has the time come when the people of the United States can accept as a fact the maturity of a total and autonomous American culture, distinct, as Greek or Germanic culture might be thought distinct, from the cultures of other peoples in other parts of the world, and suitable for higher study and research on its own terms?

The reorientation of American academic thinking around this question began to be obvious in the twenties; it gained force in various departments of our universities—but primarily in those of history and English literature— during the next quarter-century; it reached a kind of climax in the early fifties when the American Studies Association was founded; and it has gone through various permutations since that time, at one moment seeming to crystalize its thinking into the terms of a new discipline, at another to dissolve back into its component parts and re-merge with the disciplines of its origin. There are those who think that the question itself was not valid; and there are those who think that it was crucial for the time it was asked but that it has done its work and no longer need be considered. Both these groups would like to see the American Studies Association dissolved; but there are also those who have been trained by departments and programs to perform within the context of a total and autonomous American culture and who will carry through life, like a tattooed figure on the chest, the symbol of the Ph.D. in the new discipline. The justification and the continued growth of the American Studies Association is essential to a validation of their commitment.

I am not sure just how clear the founding fathers were in their formulation of this question or in their answers to it, but I can assure you that we tackled the problem as though we knew what we were about. We said by our actions if not by our words: There is now in existence a well-formed total and autonomous American culture and it is our business to find out just what it is, how it came into being, how it functions, and how it should be studied, researched and taught.

Probably a good deal of our feeling during this formative period from 1920 to 1950 was negative: a revolt against the way things were rather than a positive movement for reform. Why, we asked, should we be the exception to all other peoples who boast national cultures? Why should we have a history that the British think of as a dark chapter in the story of the British

Empire, graphic arts that are not much more than an eclectic conglomerate, literature and language that are a debasement of a noble Anglo-Saxon heritage? Was it radicalism in us to demand that Americans take a second look at their own history and experience, and re-evaluate it in its own terms? If so, we were radicals and proud of it; for what is radicalism but a getting at the roots (radix: root, foundation, origin) and not necessarily a reform or change. Radicalism by definition can be the highest form of conservatism: the rediscovery of the root-truth and its implementation.

But the American culture we then knew was shattered into fragments, each taught in our universities as a part of some other culture or discipline; American literature as a dialect of English literature; American art as a denigration of the great tradition of the art of Renaissance Italy; American history as a branch of the great mercantile explorations of the 15th and 16th centuries; American political theory as a product of British and French rationalism; American economics as a re-enactment on the frontier of the European war between agrarianism and industrialism; American society as a corruption of the pure white Anglo-Saxon Protestant tradition by "foreigners." American civilization, or culture, as a thing in itself did not seem to exist.

Against this background the recognition of a genuine American culture was not easy, yet it was essential. Actually, there never was such a thing as an ethnically, geographically and temporally pure culture; nor was there ever a culture that was not made up of an infinite number of variations and subcultures; but such qualifications of the concept of total culture do not invalidate it where the gestalt is clearly enough defined to overcome the problems of inner diversity and conflict. It is not hard, for example, to recognize the validity of the concept of a Greek or Roman culture, an Indian or a Chinese, a French, German, British or even a Mexican or Australian. Such cultures are composed of basic political structures, economic conditions, and social instruments and patterns of behavior, on which are built, in an ascending scale of values, developments and configurations of language and literature, philosophy and religion, architecture and the graphic and plastic arts. No scholar is expected to master all aspects of any one of these cultures, but in specializing in one or a few aspects of it, he is expected to think in terms of the frame of the whole. To be sure, there have probably been Greek archeologists who never heard of Homer, Pericles or Praxiteles, but if so, they worked under severe handicaps and their results could be validly questioned. But in general, Greek culture stands as a viable premise for all of its component disciplines.

Until very recently this has not been the case for American culture. American experience has been that of a transplanted rather than a native growth; it has been characteristically heterogeneous rather than homogeneous, agglomerative rather than organic. The controlling ideas of political and religious liberty, economic abundance and racial tolerance have none of them been strong and enduring enough to overcome the difficulties of too great fluidity and diversity in its history, particularly in recent times. Yet a distinctive American national character has long been recognized by Europeans in fiction and in fact, and the identity of the American nation and its people has for long been accepted throughout the world as a political, economic and cultural reality. Why were we so long in coming to a self-recognition? Our cultural colonialism survived our achievement of political independence by more than a century.

I have said that the founding of the American Studies Association in 1951 was the climax rather than the origin of a widespread movement, mainly in humanistic scholarship, to define and implement the concept of a total and indigenous American culture. The laboratories in which this movement had been subjected to tests and experiments were the various courses, programs and departments of American Studies and American Civilization, both in Europe and the United States, which were documented by the studies of Sigmund Skard of Norway and of Robert Walker in the United States, in 1958. Attempts to evaluate the findings of these two scholars, to bring the story down to date, and to predict a future for the movement have been many, and I shall not now attempt another. Instead, I shall be content with a few generalizations which grow out of my own experience, both in this country and in Europe, Japan and India. To oversimplify the situation, let me therefore give you my general impression (I cannot call it a reasoned conclusion from evidence) that there have been two principal approaches to the problem of defining and implementing the movement, which I shall call the *synthetic* and the *holistic*. Sometimes these two approaches have appeared separately, sometimes in collaboration, sometimes in rivalry, but both have achieved victories and have contributed to the clarification and strengthening of the movement as a whole.

The synthetic approach has been the more general and influential of the two, perhaps because it is the more obvious. It has been called the Humpty-Dumpty technique because it is based on the observation that American culture is fragmentary, with the need for all the king's horses and all the king's men to put it together and set it up on the wall of academic respectability, if not as a separate department, at least as an interdepartmental committee with varying degrees of power, from the creation of a minor area of study to the awarding of the Ph.D. As Tremaine McDowell points out in his classic definition of this approach in 1948, it was influenced by and closely related to the strong post-World War II movements in general education, area studies and interdepartmental programs. The normal structure in most programs, both undergraduate and graduate, McDowell found, was the major with two or more minors and an emphasis on American aspects of all subjects. This plan allowed for a concentration in American subjects in from three to six departments while retaining control of a student's upper-class or graduate program by the department of the major. The Minnesota program was perhaps the outstanding example of this approach, but Princeton, Yale and Harvard and a few other institutions had already offered interesting variations. I remember sitting down with Sculley Bradley when I went back to Penn in 1945 and checking through the catalogue all courses that contained the adjective "American" in their titles, much as they are now doing with courses in Afro-American Studies. By that time we had a "History, English, and Others" committee, and we limited the interdepartmental freedom of the candidates for our degrees; but I have to admit now, in looking back at our thinking, that we retained the force of an academic discipline in one of the "Old-line" departments—usually History or English—with cooperation from the others and miscellaneous assists from outside. The Humpty-Dumpty that we tried to set up on the wall was at best held together by Elmer's glue and Scotch tape. A subject-matter concentration does not constitute a new discipline, and the danger was that our degree-holders would be mere smatterers, ill-equipped to teach advanced work or to do research on the university level. It was perhaps the fact that the experimental nature of the course attracted enough strong and unconventional students to float it that saved us from complete disaster.

In recognizing the superficiality of most of these programs, however, we should not forget that we admitted at the time that they were experimental and we usually protected our degree candidates by giving them sufficient grounding in a conventional major to equip them for regular positions in established university departments. In fact, the specialization in interdepartmental American subjects often made them even more attractive to institutions which were also experimentally minded, and we had less difficulty in placing our products than did many of the conventional departments.

More important, however, for the future of the American Studies movement was the education of the academic mind in the concept of an indigenous American culture. During these years, specialization in American subjects and increase of American dissertations and Americanist faculties was phenomenal. I do not need to cite statistics to prove that soon there were almost as many dissertation candidates in American as in all of English literature, the American faculties increased from a single pioneer in 1920 often to three to five tenured appointments by 1950, and the journals of *American Literature* and *American Quarterly*, as well as the annual reports of current research, came into being to meet the overflow of new scholarship in the subject. The reforms and the progress in American Studies should be measured, during these years, not by the development of a single discipline that could be called by the American name, but by the sharp separation of each aspect of the American cultural whole from its false colonialist and traditionalist bondages. American literature specialists now could head English departments, American history, and American concentration as such came to be respectable in the social sciences, philosophy and the arts. By 1950, the existence of an indigenous American culture with a history and a definition of its own was a generally accepted fact even though still broken down into its various aspects by the traditional organization of academic departments. Scholarly societies, however, and specialist journals did not need to safeguard the participant or to demand too comprehensive a mastery of subject matter from him, and could therefore draw together into a common endeavor specialists in all aspects of American Studies who were interested in the relationship of their studies, not only to their own discipline, but to others and to the concept of a total American culture. The American Studies Association and the *American Quarterly*—not to mention other Americanist associations and journals abroad and at home, of which there have been many—were called into existence because they were needed. In these areas the synthetic principle proved to be valid because groups of scholars could work in specializations and at the same time struggle to bring their results together into an integrated whole, while individual scholars would still have to restudy the roots of their American specialization in their own respective disciplines and relate their special aspects of a culture to the whole by tying it to manageable parts from other fields. That these years did not produce a generally satisfactory American Studies or American Civilization discipline or generate a new scholarly method of research does not mean that the movement had failed in its primary objective of identifying and reexamining American culture in all of its various manifestations.

Nor does the success of the synthetic approach mean the total failure of its supplementary and alternative—what I have called the holistic—approach. As one of the earliest to recognize the need for this kind of thinking, I should be the last to declare it invalid. For me the acceptance of the principle of a loose synthesis of American aspects of traditional disciplines for practical purposes does not preclude the need for constant experimentation with new ways of studying any culture as a whole, and American culture in particular. I would like at least to mention four such ways in which I have been involved and can therefore speak with some confidence. They are:

(1) The application to the American field of new concepts, materials and methods of cultural and comparative-cultural study in the disciplines of sociology and cultural anthropology. Such study might involve artifacts, values, social institutions, roles, behavioral habits, concepts or any other factors that form meaningful cultural configurations when limited and defined by an area and a period of time. The mass media provide an obviously rich source of material for such study.

(2) The application of advances in depth psychology, folk and popular expression, and the archetypal myths and faiths of traditional religion, supernaturalism and imagination to modern literature and art. Archeology, anthropology, and the histories of religion, tribal customs and philosophy all contribute to such study, and the culture is finally defined in terms of man's dreams, illusions and the realities of his non-world.

(3) The development of a special field of intellectual history or the history of ideas which, in itself, cuts across many areas and involves a number of traditional disciplines without limiting itself necessarily to any one culture such as Greek, British, or American. This approach has, in a number of cases, given depth to historically oriented programs which are presumably economic, sociological, or even political or constitutional in their primary emphasis, and so given them an interdisciplinary and holistic orientation. Recent histories of American culture by Boorstin, Barker, Lerner, and others are cases in point.

(4) And finally, my own specialty: the development of a philosophy and practice of literary history and historical criticism, particularly American, which starts with the aesthetic examination of the highest form of an individual work of art and attempts to relate it, causally and circumstantially, first to its creator by thorough biographical and psychological study and then to the basic culture and history of the people who produced it in a given time and place. Thus literary study becomes

holistic when it is involved in the history of thought and manners, as well as in psychology, sociology, philosophy and the
interrelationship of the arts.

Each of these approaches leads in its way toward a satisfactory
gestalt for the definition of any culture, and can therefore be
applied to a new field of American culture with a degree of
integration unattainable by the synthetic approach I have earlier described.

There are probably other holistic approaches to the study of
American culture which are now in various stages of experimentation but with which I am not familiar. Nor do I pretend to
have mentioned the variations within each of the kinds of holistic approach with which I am to some extent acquainted. And
rather than develop the philosophies, methods and degrees of
success or failure of any one of them, I must conclude with some
generalizations which are common to them all and so relate
them as a group to my hopes for the future of the American
Studies Association and American Studies as a field of specialization.

The holistic approach, like the synthetic, posits a concept of a
total and autonomous American culture, separate from but
related to and comparable with other cultures. It differs from
the synthetic in that it attempts to define a method of dealing
with this culture which is distinguishable from the methods of
other humanistic and scientific disciplines. In doing so it nar-
rows the area of aspects of American culture that can be dealt
with in these terms. Larger in range and freer in experiment
than most of the older disciplines, it must nevertheless in the
end become one more unit in the synthetic process. An American Studies program based on one or another of these holistic
systems will not take the place of American specialization in the
older disciplines, but it may help immeasurably in providing
chemical rather than physical mixtures among such disciplines.
These experimental programs provide the cutting edge of the
whole movement and may create new disciplines which can
take their place in the whole system of humanistic studies,
without a limitation to American subject matter. For example,
the cross-cultural studies of the Department of American Civili-

zation at Pennsylvania have invaded the whole museum and national park areas and tie into experimental research in ecology, modern archeology, ethnology and many other fields. Other similar developments must be taking place elsewhere. We cannot afford to allow any one of these advances to rule out the others as irrelevant or distracting movements to take our minds off the scholarly business at hand. Both the synthetic and holistic approaches are essential, each in its place. The American Studies Association has always been open to new ideas and experimental methods. There is no reason for it to be any the less so in the future.

NOTES

1. Carl Bode, "The Start of the ASA," unpublished memorandum written in 1960 and deposited in the files of the American Studies Association of the University of Pennsylvania.

2. "Can 'American Studies' Develop a Method?" *Studies in American Culture: Dominant Ideas and Images,* edited by Joseph J. Kwiatt and Mary C. Turpie (Minneapolis: University of Minnesota Press, 1960), pp. 3-15.

14 | AMERICAN STUDIES ABROAD: CULTURE AND FOREIGN POLICY

I was hardly settled in my new office at Penn when visitors from abroad began to arrive. The Rockefeller Foundation had sent its representative to Europe to seek out professors of English who were moving into American literature to fill the gap created by the war and the Nazi regime. Among those to appear in these early days were Professors S. Liljegren of Uppsala, Sweden; Maurice LeBreton of the Sorbonne; and Hans Galinsky, of Mainz, Germany.

One of the first, however, was Sigmund Skard, of Oslo, Norway. One afternoon in the fall of 1946 the telephone on my desk rang and a voice from Washington, D.C., said, "I am Sigmund Skard, and I would like to come up to Philadelphia to consult you about an offer I have received from my University of a new chair in 'Literature, Chiefly American.' " It turned out that he had been a professor at Oslo before the war. At the time of the German occupation, he had escaped with his wife and four young children across Siberia and the United States to Washington, where he took a post in the Library of Congress and travelled widely over the United States for the next few years. Here was a distinguished scholar in classical and comparative literatures who knew our country at first hand better than most of us did, but had almost no knowledge of American literature as such. I advised him to accept because he had a Rockefeller grant for 1947-1948 for study, travel, and the purchase of books.

He came to Pennsylvania in September of the next year, and by spring he went home with a mind well stored with his new subject, a host of American academic friends, and books enough to found an American Institute in Oslo. My return visit on a Fulbright professorship to Oslo in 1950 was matched by one at Pennsylvania for him a few years later. Our mutual friendship and interdependence has lasted through the years and has been at the heart of all my Fulbright and other involvements in American studies abroad.

The Fulbright program that soon followed the Rockefeller initiative was the result of the original Fulbright Act (P.L. 584, 79th Congress) and the Smith-Mundt Act of 1948 (P.L. 402, 80th Congress). It was administered by the Board of Foreign Scholarships through its Committee on International Exchange of Persons (CIEP) and an American studies subcommittee. During the next decade I made frequent trips to Washington in order to sit at policy and award-granting sessions of these committees, and I had many telephone conferences about specific problems and appointments. I became immersed in the exciting world of international cultural exchange, made many foreign friends, and learned to know a whole new scholarly world.

As the program developed, it began to show weaknesses: low stipends for grantees to match salaries of the countries of visit, insufficient provision for their families and, most serious of all, too little attention to the need for a real two-way exchange that would bring Europeans to America. The Fulbright-Hays Act of 1961 (P.L. 256, 87th Congress) was designed to remedy all of these weaknesses, and for a time it seemed to be working; but by 1966, when I addressed the American Academy of Political and Social Sciences on the subject, it was apparent that the promise to solve all problems had failed of realization because Congress did not implement its provisions by providing adequate funds. In 1970 I expressed my disappointment in a report to the CIEP, a disappointment shared by Truxten Russell, Executive Secretary of the American Studies Committee. Further, he pointed out that the Committee itself and the American scholars involved in the program's administration had also failed because they did not recognize that the goal of an exchange of scholars in American studies is to persuade other peoples to train their own scholars and to establish autonomous programs in American subjects. It was chiefly a realization of this failure that prompted my article.[1] We had been sending too many Americans abroad as missionaries, and we had not helped enough by bringing here for advanced research those young men who could grow to professorial status and speak for us in their own lands and in their own languages.

Meanwhile, I had become further involved in what, in some ways, was a competing effort in the American field. Skard and I and some others early appreciated this situation and convinced the Ford Foundation in 1960 to make a five-year grant of $2,500,000 (renewed several times later) to the American Council of Learned Societies to right this error. I was asked to chair the first policy and fellowship committee to allocate this vast sum to individual European scholars for advanced study and travel in the United States, together with funds for supporting libraries and chairs of American studies in European universities to greet them on their return. The success of this program speaks for itself and for the competence of its director, Richard Downar. It was not long before there were chairs of American literature and history in most of the major universities of Germany, England, Scandinavia, and other countries of Europe and Asia, and American Studies Associations or research centers in the Nordic Countries, Germany, France, England, Japan, and India.

I realize now that a second Fulbright professorship to London in 1957 to 1958, with courses at Kings and Bedford Colleges and lectures in the Scandinavian countries and in the Rhine Valley from the Netherlands to Switzerland, as well as work with the Fellowship Committee of the American-Scandinavian Foundation and a trip around the world in 1962, with its conference with forty Indian professors at Mussoorie in a high pass of the Himalayas, were all undertaken not for myself, but to help others in international understanding. A German honorary degree, an Indian festschrift, and the translation of my books into a dozen or more foreign languages suggest that I have been heard.

The following article was part of a symposium presented at the annual meeting of the American Academy of Political and Social Sciences held in Philadelphia, April 15 -16, 1966. The audience was composed largely of invited delegates from associations and organizations here and abroad, and it represented a wide spectrum of interests and backgrounds. I therefore included a good deal of factual information that seemed necessary for so diversified and, at the same time, so qualified a group. It was published in the Annals of the Academy *366 (July 1966): 1-16.*

NOTE

1. "The Fulbright Program in American Studies Abroad: Retrospect and Prospect," *American Studies: International* 9 (Autumn 1970): 10-16. Reprinted in R. H. Walker, *American Studies Abroad* (Westport, Conn.: The Greenwood Press, 1975), pp. 3-9.

I

To discuss the effectiveness of a program of cultural exchange in developing good international relations is to raise at once the basic question of whether familiarity breeds love or contempt, and the evidence—at least the superficial evidence—of human experience would make it seem that all too often the better we know each other, the less we find to respect in each other. Perhaps we might revise to our purpose the classic paraphrase by Tom Brown of the thirty-third Epigram of Martial:

> I do not like thee, Dr. Fell,
> The reason why I cannot tell
> Unless it be, I know thee well,
> I do not like thee, Dr. Fell.

Certainly the attempt of the British over many years in India, of France in Indo-China, and even of the United States in Cuba to acculturate an alien people in the interest of mutual economic and political benefit have not been reassuring. Perhaps their motives were impure, and the more recent foreign policy of the United States has been pure, but, in any case, the decision of our government after World War II to add a program of cultural exchange to its military, economic, and political commitments overseas deserves close scrutiny at a time when the chant, "Yankee Go Home" is echoing from Djakarta to Havana and from Tokyo to Santiago and when American libraries and cultural offices are being attacked and often closed because of economy budgeting at home and worsening relationships abroad. Perhaps we should admit failure and quit, blaming human nature rather than our own ineptness.

But the policies of the Kennedy and Johnson Administrations fortunately do not suggest this course of action. Both by executive recommendation and by legislation enacted and at least partially implemented by Congress, we as a people have been enabled to persist through the last twenty years and more in a consistent but modest expansion and development of our agencies for international and cultural exchange, both at home and overseas. Public Law 87-256 of 1961, the so-called Fulbright-Hays Act, broadly liberalized the provisions of the earlier Fulbright and Smith-Mundt programs and led to the setting up of the United States Advisory Commission on International and Cultural Affairs. This agency has been effective not only in advising the President and Congress on policies and implementations of the program, but also in sponsoring at least three widely influential survey reports: *A Beacon of Hope: The Exchange of Persons Program* (1963); *American Studies Abroad*, by Walter Johnson (1963); and *A Report on the Strategic Importance of Western Europe*, by Walter Adams (1964). And it has more recently inaugurated what will probably become a quarterly journal of its own. Add to this development the involvement in these areas of the Agency for International Development, the United Nations Educational, Scientific, and Cultural Organization, the Institute of International Education, and other international agencies, both public and private, devoted primarily to the broader aspects of international cultural relations, and the task of an amateur and outsider such as myself in finding his way through this jungle of activities and reports and then shaping up something new and pertinent (or impertinent) to say on this subject becomes almost insuperable.

Let me at once confess, therefore, that I do not plan to discuss the new International Education Act of 1966 or President Johnson's message on it; nor shall I consider, as such, the problem of the expansion of educational and cultural, along with economic and military, aid to the "developing" as contrasted with the "developed" countries; and I shall become involved only incidentally in the broader problems of how to screen and then handle the increasing numbers of foreign students who come to our colleges and universities. Finally, I do not expect to ask you to write immediately to your Senator or your Congressman urging his support for any part or all of this program. I am primarily concerned, as is Mr. Charles Frankel in his recent and lively book on this subject, with how to make human nature, rather than mere governmental agencies, behave rationally and effectively in this cause.[1]

We must start, therefore, right or wrong, with the assumption that if we get to understand the language and culture of other peoples better and other peoples get to understand ours better, the world will be a better place in which to live, and we must not relax our efforts in this direction even though we have no way of judging the value of present action in terms of ultimate results. We are surely in for surprises both ways if we live long enough. For example, my own university was host to the recently deposed Nkrumah of Ghana in his student days, and many similarly ruthless dictators have learned much of what they knew (the past tense is appropriate) of political and educational manipulation and control in our universities. On the other hand, there is little question that American friendship with Great Britain has been immensely stimulated by the fact that so many American intellectual leaders are, in part, British-trained as Rhodes Scholars, and there is even less doubt that the maintenance of cultural relationships with nations which border both East and West, from Norway and Poland in the North to India and Thailand in the South, has provided a far more effective wall against totalitarian expansion during the Cold War than could have been built by arms and arguments.

There is one more limitation that I must impose on myself, and then I am through with preliminaries. Although educational and cultural exchange is and must always be a "two-way street," my experience has been pretty much limited to the American cultural impact abroad, and my topic today must follow suit. I will therefore try only to formulate a philosophy of cultural exchange based rather on general principles of human nature than on any political or sociological data, and then test its relevance to the specific problem of the development of American studies abroad, both past and future. I shall rely mainly on my own United States Educational Foundations and Commissions abroad, and the Conference Board of Associated Research Councils (a private association of scholars which cooperates with the State Department in the administration of the Fulbright program of professorial exchanges), and direct contact through the American studies movement with native efforts of people in various parts of the world to undertake a more thorough study of American culture on their own initiative. Scattered and impressionistic as my evidence will be, its validity must rest on the insights it may provide into basic human nature and upon a faith in the universal similarity of human responses to common needs and situations, rather than on measurable data. If I seem to dwell too much on Norway, England, Germany, India, and Japan, it is because I know these countries from at least some firsthand experience.

The primary purpose of this aspect of American cultural foreign policy can therefore be said to be the shaping of the American image abroad. Probably the central desire of all human beings is to be liked by others for what they think they really are, whether their opinion of themselves is accurate or not. Nations are not too different from individuals in this respect; whatever the facts may be and whatever the accepted stereotypes abroad of any national character, a cultural foreign policy is always and inevitably directed toward correcting or at least ameliorating the attitudes of other nations, so that the national self-image and the opinions of other nations may be brought into closer agreement. In any such policy there will always be two factors: (1) the effort toward truth with the correction of false attitudes and assumptions, and (2) the effort toward amelioration with the softening of antagonisms and the improve-

ment of friendship. The image of our national character that our
cultural foreign policy will therefore wish to foster and develop
should not only be an accurate portrayal; it should be as
favorable to us as, within honesty, we can make it.

II

The first and most superficial phase of such a cultural foreign
policy is what is usually known as "information," and the
agency that we set up to deal with this phase is known as "The
United States Information Agency." By this term we do not
really mean information in the strict scientific and objective
sense, but rather selective data, ideas, and attitudes which we
would like others to accept concerning ourselves. Our methods
of persuasion may not go quite as far as those of the Madison
Avenue gentlemen who point out that smoking a particular cig-
arette will bring about a change of season and a glandular resto-
ration of youth, or who portray languishing nymphs of
flickering lashes and a come-hither drawl: "When you use
Tiger after-shave lotion, *be kind.*" But our approach may be, if
not that of telling the whole truth, at least of telling nothing but
the truth. We need not deliberately misrepresent, but we may
select our evidence. We may photograph our skyline from one
of the surrounding hills rather than down the canyon of slum
tenements, and if we are providing a list of books for translation
into Hindi or Arabic, we may select a history which stresses our
gift of independence to Cuba rather than our intervention in
the recent arms crisis. And if we are choosing only one recent
novel, we may prefer the mature character analysis of Bellow's
Herzog to the abnormal violence of Mailer's *An American Dream.*
But this does not mean that all our historians should imitate
Parson Weems or even George Bancroft and that all our novelists should remain as harmless as Horatio Alger or Louisa May
Alcott. I have been concerned with a number of the activities of
the USIA, and I have been impressed always, under a succession
of administrations (and one of the weaknesses of Washington
bureaucracy is the rapid turnover of personnel), by the persistence of the idea that freedom of speech and right of criticism must always be emphasized as cardinal qualities of the

American national character and, as such, as qualities which must be not only preached but practiced in our cultural foreign policy. If we do not allow our representatives the freedom of criticism, we cannot claim that we believe in the freedom of speech. In a recent list of recommended readings sponsored indirectly by a branch of the USIA, we find represented such a wide range of opinions as Lerner's *America as a Civilization* and Rossiter's *The American Presidency*, Handlin's *The Uprooted* and Kirkland's *Industry Comes of Age.*

A shrinking from overt propaganda, with an unwillingness to be aggressive, have been characteristic of the American overseas cultural effort from the start. An admirable trait, it has, I think, been an important factor in the success of that effort, but it makes it difficult to estimate the extent and nature of that success. The recent closing of the USIS (it becomes a Service rather than an Agency in the field) libraries in London and Paris and of many of the Amerikahäusern in Germany and similar agencies alsewhere has seemed to many people, in the words of Jerome Beatty, Jr., of the *Saturday Review,* "one of the screwiest moves this government has made"; but before giving in to our legitimate dismay, perhaps we should ask if there are any more encouraging factors in the situation. Lack of adequate congressional appropriation which forced measures of economy was certainly the chief reason for the move, but there may also be compensating circumstances. In our distress, we may at least take some comfort in the thought that this particular kind of service may not be as much needed now as it once was. When I went to Norway in 1950 as Fulbright Visiting Professor at Oslo, I found the American USIS library an invaluable resource to supplement the scant book collections at the University, but at present the library of the Amerika Institutet is housed, with its 11,000 volumes (one of the largest collections in Europe), in new seminar rooms on the Blindern campus of the univeristy, with magazine and microfilm collections and other resources that would make any American professor in an American university jealous.

The American library in London, which I knew well and used in 1958 when I was lecturing at King's and Bedford Colleges, was one of the best of its kind and, for appointments, service, and collections, it was a credit both to its librarian of many years, Miss Margaret Hafert, and to the United States government. But, again, the growth of the British Association for American Studies (BAAS); the creation of important teaching posts in various American subjects in the colleges of the universities of London, Oxford, and Cambridge, most of the "Red Brick," and all of the newly founded universities, especially Sussex, Keele, Hull, and East Anglia; and, finally, the establishment by the BAAS of an American Institute and Research Center in Central London under the direction of Professor Harry Allen of University College—all of these developments make the maintenance of a public library at the Embassy far less essential as a government-sponsored activity than it was ten years ago. There is no doubt that the United States government has deliberately sacrificed an important means of communication with the British people by taking this step, but I think that there is also no doubt that, at least on the academic level, the acceptance of the books from this library by London University creates a new center which is not shadowed by the eagle on Grosvenor Square and which can, if properly housed, staffed, and kept up to date, become an even more effective, if less immediate and conspicuous, means of communication in the future.

In fact, I am inclined to believe that the less conspicuous activities of the USIA and other cultural arms of the State Department are the most important ones, even though less easy to observe. From my own experience with the "Voice of America," the translation division, and the agency which sponsors the University of Pennsylvania certificate examinations in American studies and the University of Michigan examinations in the American-English language, I get a sense of a constantly expanding and consolidating program of behind-the-scenes and in-spite-of-the-deficit, but very effective cultural promotion. I wonder what has been the experience of others when I realize that my own books have been translated into German, Urdu, Bengali, Arabic, Brazilian Portuguese, and Yugoslavian—by or with the aid of government subsidies to foreign publishers—as well as privately into Italian, Swedish, Japanese, and Korean; and I have had the experience of lecturing one evening on tape on the radio and the following morning in person in a hill station in India. I have also received a Christmas card this year with the inscription: "I have enjoyed your book so much all this year that I am dead sure you deserve a Christmas card from your unknown Chilean student." I tried not to remember his name so that I would not be prejudiced when his examination, with others in his USIA class, reaches us, probably this spring.

Such scattered evidence leaves me personally impressed, as well as humble, for I know that, even if they cannot be counted, my experiences world-wide are far from unique. And I know also that I have other "unknown students" in Israel, Turkey, Iran, Brazil, the Argentine, Bombay, Athens, and many other places, because I read their examinations in American language and literature. I wish I knew to what extent we are conducting similar activities in at least the more independent of the Communist countries, but here there is less feedback and hence no satisfactory way for the layman to estimate what is being done. I do know, however, that when I received from my publishers not long ago a substantial check for an edition of 3,500 copies of one of my books, to be printed and bound in Yugoslavia for circulation abroad, presumably in some of these countries, I was talking to many people whom I was very happy to reach, even though I could not hear their replies.

This is enough perhaps on the "informational" level of our cultural foreign policy, although much more could probably be said.

III

The second level, which we may call the "exchange" program and which centers in the so-called Fulbright procedures, is only semiofficial; in fact, it is ostensibly not official at all but is operated by a committee of scholars and administrators cooperating with government agencies and is financed by the Congress with special appropriations under the Fulbright-Hays Act of 1961. At this point, the intricate relationships between various branches and agencies of the United States government, private and semiofficial agencies sponsored by the government or appointed by the President, and foundations and other agencies working on their own becomes too complicated for explanation in so cursory a survey as this. But the assumption that the government as such operates a structured policy of international cultural exchange is far from the truth.

It has not always been understood, for example, that the original Fulbright Act (Public Law 584) of 1946 was drafted in the interest of the individuals of an exchange rather than in that of the countries involved. It was designed to offer worthy students or teachers an opportunity for foreign study in their own disciplines. For this reason, the stipend was set at the customary low figure of a scholarship, and application was made voluntary and competitive.

This plan was fair and worked well for the genuine student, but the act also allowed awards to teachers for posts of Visiting Professor in major universities, and research students often found themselves lecturing to popular audiences and even offering courses on invitation from universities. The exchange of high-level teachers was further encouraged by Public Law 480 and by subsequent legislation, administered at first by the State Department, often in unintentional competition with the Conference Board and its Committee on International Exchange of Persons. What a built-in package of potential misunderstanding!

The presence of "resource persons," as the jargon has it, was soon appreciated by those administering USIS and other cultural programs abroad, and a state of benevolent anarchy developed in most countires, with the official and unofficial United States cultural agents competing and cooperating alternately in an important extension of the "information" program to the use of exchange persons in the national interest. The exchange scholars and teachers found themselves, in many cases, performing professional services for their own nations in a difficult foreign setting with inadequate tools, ridiculously low compensation, and general misunderstanding of their role and function on all sides.

It is not surprising that the numbers and quality of applicants sank so rapidly that major policy changes were indicated in order that the quality of the appointees might be maintained. Slightly higher remuneration for teaching awards, recognition of some of the costs of dependents, and a cautious policy of recruitment finally led to a basic change of orientation of policy more in line with the cultural efforts of the United States under USIS and other programs abroad. This change was made official by the Fulbright-Hays Act of 1961 when the role of the Visiting Professor of American Studies in foreign universities was finally and officially acknowledged and implemented, if not adequately subsidized even yet. The creation of the American Studies Advisory Subcommittee of the Committee on International Exchange of Persons which followed, with its quarterly publication, *American Studies News*, was a belated recognition of the part which the Fulbright Visiting Professor had played between 1946 and 1961 in making the United States cultural effort abroad effective against discouraging obstacles, and a hopeful offering of support and guidance for the future.

But in many important respects the aid was *post facto* because the period of crisis had passed and what could be done had already been done under emergency circumstances of hardship, a condition that in the course of human affairs is not always to be deplored. The crucial work of shaping postwar attitudes and programs, particularly in the previously enemy countries of Germany, Italy, and Japan, had already been done by private agencies and individual effort working through the existing government cultural agencies and programs and by the occupying forces themselves. So great and obvious was the need for immediate action that Americans abroad on an "exchange" status were drawn willingly into "informational" activities, and a consistent middle policy was evolved from what seemed confusion. A debt that no one will ever be able to measure is undoubtedly owing to Francis A. Young, Executive Secretary, and his Committee on International Exchange of Persons, during most of these years, for clear heads and gently discreet hands in formulating and guiding the policy of the Fulbright exchange program between government cultural agencies and private supplementary resources.

Those who would cling to the original Fulbright point of view might argue that scholar exchange on a competitive basis is a better instrument of foreign policy than the development of American studies programs in universities overseas, and that the latter was a misuse of Fulbright funds and therefore should not expect to be successful. This argument is, I think, beside the point because of the success of *both* aspects of the developed policy, unless it is needed as an explanation of some of the difficulties and inconsistencies that arose. At the center of this success was the Fulbright Visiting Professor, whose role was as ambiguous as that of the American cultural officer which Mr. Frankel has described so aptly:[1]

> He would be an intellectual with gregarious instincts; a warm-hearted communicator between two cultures and yet a hard-headed negotiator; an administrator of a large staff and program who keeps his staff and program in hand while he spends most of his time out of the office; a faithful bureaucrat who nevertheless can deal with the temperamental idiosyncracies of professors, musicians, athletes, and VIPs.

I will not attempt a similar portrait of the temperamental professor who was trying to be faithful to his intellectual commitments and at the same time to help this mixed-up bureaucrat to an accord with the politics-ridden world of European academia. He was misunderstood even by his fellows.

For example, in 1964, a distinguished American professor lectured on American literature in a number of German universities and brought back a very critical report on what he thought to be the low quality of Fulbright appointments in American studies and on the poor reception they were receiving from German academics. At the same time, the health of American studies, as such, was reflected by the German professors of American literature, history, and other subjects who were holding their own annual conference of the Deutsche Gesellschaft für Amerikastudien and were carrying forward, under their own momentum, a vigorous program of research, teaching, and publication. After twenty years, the kind of help that the United States Embassy and Educational Foundation had offered in the early stages of German-American rehabilitation apparently was far less needed, but the habits of procedure were hard to break. The cultural- as well as the economic-assistance policies of the United States had, like the work of a good doctor, been so successful that they had almost put themselves out of business!

And I understand that there were similar developments in Italy and Japan. The mouse had roared for cultural understanding as well as for economic rehabilitation of the defeated nations, with the result that high-level American cultural studies, as well as economic stability, had achieved the first and firmest footholds abroad in the nations that needed them most: America's former enemies. But exactly the same process was taking place in the nations which had fought along with us, even though, perhaps, not in so obvious and sensational a manner.

Much credit must go to the Rockefeller Foundation for initiating and providing most of the techniques subsequently used in developing the interest of foreign scholars in American subjects. Immediately after the war, this Foundation sent Mr. John Marshall to Europe to invite a selected group of scholars in Scandinavian, French, and other universities to come to this country for short visits of the kind which later became known as leadership grants. In this first group was Professor Sigmund Skard, a Classical and Renaissance scholar of philology who had just accepted a new chair of "Literature, Chiefly American," in the University of Oslo. Professor Skard's grant allowed him opportunity to visit widely in the United States, to confer with American specialists in American literature, to compile a bibliography of ultimate needs for a new American Institute in Norway, and to purchase and ship home the first consignment of books. On his return, he worked alone until, in 1949, the first Norwegian Fulbright grants enabled him to ask for the assistance of a Visiting Professor from America. For the first few years he asked for, and received, men of full academic standing, but it soon became apparent that he could, with the aid of his Norwegian colleagues, carry the main burden of teaching American literature and civilization, but that he could use the help of an American assistant of lower rank to supplement his offerings. Further grants from private and official Norwegian and American sources have by now resulted in one of the best centers for the higher study of American literature and related subjects outside the United States itself, a center which is now wholly supported by Norwegian funds, with occasional special grants from other sources.

The experience of the University of Oslo is not unique and may be instructive, for its general pattern is fairly common in other countries. Similar institutes or seminars have developed at Kiel, Freiburg, and Frankfurt in Germany; Zurich and Lausanne in Switzerland; Innsbruck and Vienna in Austria; Rome, Florence, and Milan in Italy; and elsewhere—to mention only a few from a long and growing list. Note the techniques of cultural policy which this development involves: a leadership grant to an influential and interested national for a preliminary trip to the United States; a Chair or other teaching post in an American subject in a foreign university, often subsidized for one to three years from American sources; a fund for the purchase of a scholars' library and the use of a USIS library in the interval; a visiting Fulbright professor for a few years to give academic dignity to the new subject, followed by Fulbright aid of a lesser sort for as long as needed but not longer, and by other incidental American aid from both foundations and government as asked for and allocated by the foreign university or professor.

In the case of Scandinavia, similar developments led to similar results in Sweden, Denmark, Finland, and even Iceland, and American subjects are now regularly taught, usually by nationals with the assistance of Americans, at least in Uppsala, Lund, Gothenburg, Stockholm, Copenhagen, Aarhus, Oslo, Bergen, Trondheim, Helsinki, and Turku. The first conference of the Nordic Association for American Studies was held in Sigtuna, Sweden, in 1961, and the publication of its proceedings under the title *Amerika och Norden* in 1964 bears testimony to the momentum that has brought Scandinavian scholarship in American studies to a self-supporting, cooperative, and academically productive level. One can only ask whether all this would have happened as soon or as effectively without the incentives provided by the earlier Fulbright, State Department, and foundation efforts, however scattered and inadequate they may have seemed at the time. And one can only hope that this experience may be useful as we move into the far more complex tasks of developing American studies in India, Japan, Australia, South America, and Africa, where, in many cases, the native scholarly resources are not as rich and available as they were in the countries of Europe. But already, particularly in India and Japan, it has become apparent that the same combination of information, exchange, and self-help will prove effective.

IV

I have now moved into my third stage of development from the "informational," through the "exchange," to what we may call the "continuing support" or self-help stage of a progressive foreign cultural policy. This is the hardest kind of program to plan or to budget because it depends so largely on the response and initiative of those who are to be encouraged and aided. But the main lines of such a policy have surely been indicated by what I have already said.

Perhaps this is the point at which I should pause to define the term "American studies" which I have been using so constantly. In the strict sense it refers to a movement which began in the 1930s to bring together study and research in the history, institutions, literature, art, and other aspects of American culture in an effort toward the definition and better understanding of our national character. Beginning usually in the academic departments of English literature and of history, it took a leaf or two from the book of foreign area studies and programs which had become increasingly important during World War II and developed its own academic curricula, departments, national scholarly association and specialized journal. Maintaining its subject-matter focus and its interdisciplinary methods, it normally is administered by an interdepartmental committee, but occasionally it develops its own departmental structure.

It is only natural that the concept of a total and unified national character and culture which could be described, documented, and presented in a single package to our potential friends in other lands would appeal to the informational branch of our government. This is the concept which underlay the USIS library, lecture, and conference programs which were so successful in the early postwar years, and it even extended into some of the first efforts to establish American Institutes attached to European universities. It is instructive to review the history of the American Institutes at Oslo and at Munich in this light. The first was modestly established on the initiative of a Norwegian professor who was aided, as requested, by American resources in men and money; the second was established outright on an interdisciplinary plan and manned in the first instance by top-bracket American scholars. I should not, perhaps, discuss the Institute at Munich because I do not know it at first hand; all I should say, therefore, is that its progress toward full integration into the German academic system has been extremely difficult and for long unsuccessful under a series of directorships, while, at Oslo, American literature and culture is now a fully accepted, even universally required, area of study. The difference would seem to be that of cultivating a natural growth versus that of imposing an alien pattern of procedure from the outside.

As Professor Skard has pointed out in his survey of American studies abroad,[2] the study of American literature, history and other subjects had a long, if spotty, record going back to the beginning of the nineteenth century and even before. With World War II, however, progress was slowed or halted in most countries, but with the peace of 1945, many Europeans became aware for the first time of the importance of the United States in the cultural as well as the political and economic future of Europe. European universities soon began to show signs of receptivity to the idea of introducing American subjects, but they were unable to accommodate an interdisciplinary or area-study approach to the problem because of the differences between the American and European systems and structures of higher education and research. In the United States, the basic organization is in terms of departments and schools; in Europe it is normally in terms of Chairs and Faculties. The difference is far more than one of terminology, but even a glimmering of understanding of the subtleties involved will help to explain why European universities began, soon after 1945, to appoint professors or lecturers of American literature to their Faculties of Philology or the Humanities and professors or lecturers of American social science to their Faculties of Law, but found it extremely difficult to merge the supporting libraries of the two appointments or to allow the same students to take work in the two subjects. The vertical channels of specialization were dug too deeply to allow horizontal patterning of academic or professional programs without fundamental reorganization of the whole system of higher education. Such reorganization is unquestionably taking place in many countries, but the development of American studies in foreign universities has been most successful where it has adjusted to existing systems of higher education rather than demanding reforms as the price of adjustment to the new subjects and new ideas.

What has happened is a widespread development, usually in the Faculty of Philology at the initiative of the Professor of English Literature, of American Institutes, with much of the interdisciplinary approach of the American studies movement injected as necessary background and collateral study to the study of literature. To a lesser extent in most countries (Great Britain is the outstanding example) professors of history have found it easy to develop the study of American history on a broad platform which includes intellectual and cultural, and even literary, facets of American civilization. The cautious transfer therefore, of USIS library collections to the American Institutes of universities at the stage at which they have developed out of their narrow subject-specializations into something more nearly resembling an interdisciplinary resource begins to make some sense.

The full history of this movement would be instructive, but it has not yet been written. It would also be useful to our policy as we expand it into other parts of the world. How will we use, for example, the resources of the Indo-American Foundation proposed to Prime Minister Indira Gandhi if it becomes a reality? In many Asian, South American, and even African countries, the formulae and basic patterns of the European higher educational procedure (whether the English, German, or French, which differ in subtle ways even from each other) have been deeply rooted for several generations by nineteenth-century colonial policy. In such areas the opportunity as well as the technical problems of adjustment are increased by the fact that American studies, by sheer osmosis, tend to take the place of receding European influence, especially in such countries as India where English is a universal language in educated levels of society.

From what I have said, it would be easy to conclude that our educational and cultural foreign policy has, so far, been a jungle of errors and misunderstandings, but quite the contrary is, in fact, the case. The British Empire survived on a policy of "muddling through" during many crises in which a firm and unbending policy might have spelled its ruin. Perhaps the same kind of thing is happening to us, and perhaps, with caution, we should let it happen. The fact is that the American-studies movement overseas is in a relatively, and perhaps unexpectedly, healthy condition. The situation almost everywhere has been favorable for the universities to pick up avidly the resources supplied by the USIS, the Fulbright program, and other foreign cultural efforts, however slight, and to take the initiative in their development.

Where this opportunity has been understood and supported, the results have been truly phenomenal. There are now centers of research under local and national initiative in Rome, Hyderabad, and Tokyo, to mention only a few. There are courses, and often chairs, of American literature or history, or both in most of the universities of Great Britain, Scandinavia, the Low Countries, Germany, France, Switzerland, and Italy, as well as India and Japan. There are national professional societies of American studies in Japan, Germany, Great Britain, the Scandinavian countries (the Nordic Association), and Europe at large—the highly effective, though small in numbers, European Association for American Studies (EAAS)—and regular publication of news notes and learned papers in all of these countries and some others. In short, the American-studies movement has become well-rooted in Europe, Japan, and India during the past two decades and is beginning to have an increasing influence in Australia, New Zealand, Latin America, and even Africa. It is this spread into new and relatively "undeveloped" areas, as well as the wise fostering of the movement where it is well entrenched, that should command our attention from now on.

I realize that, in making this suggestion, I am ignoring the problem of differences between different nations. Efforts made so far to establish American-studies centers and professorial chairs in Latin America have been many, but relatively unsuccessful, while in India and Japan there are plenty of teachers anxious to move into the American field, but not enough jobs for those already qualified. But these variable circumstances should not deter us from using our European experience to respond to aroused interest elsewhere by setting up seminars and conferences along the lines of the pioneering Salzburg Seminar and other binational conferences of American studies such as have been common in Europe throughout the entire postwar period. Many summer conferences and seminars at Nice, Tokyo, Kyoto, Mussoorie, Oxford, the Hague, Groningen, Oslo, Bonn, and elsewhere have become established annual or periodic events for school and university teachers. Such conferences help to discover and to nourish the incipient interest of the foreign scholars in American problems and traditions. The next step is to invite these people to the United States for visits and preliminary study, and at the same time to offer them assistance in books, salaries, and American visiting personnel to consolidate a center of foreign study of American culture. The final step is to offer substantial fellowships, such as those now administered by the American Council of Learned Societies in Europe, Japan, and "down under" to younger scholars so that they may become trained research specialists in American studies when they return to their home universities. From then on, the role of an American cultural foreign policy is a continuing receptiveness to requests for aid and support without any accompanying acts of control. We will be understood best by people who are sufficiently interested in us to study our culture thoroughly and dispassionately. If the final result is that we are feared more than we are trusted, hated more than loved, perhaps the trouble is not in our stars but in ourselves and we should look for reform in our domestic rather than in our foreign policy.

NOTES

1. Charles Frankel, *The Neglected Aspect of Foreign Affairs: American Educational and Cultural Policy Abroad* (Washington, D.C.: Brookings Institution, 1966). See also Walter Johnson and Francis J. Colligan. *The Fulbright Program: A History* (Chicago: University of Chicago Press, 1965).

2. Sigmund Skard, *American Studies in Europe: Their History and Present Organization* (2 vols., Philadelphia: University of Pennsylvania Press, 1958).

BIBLIOGRAPHY OF THE WRITINGS OF ROBERT E. SPILLER

Titles have been divided into five categories: books, original and edited; articles and chapters in books; articles in journals; forewords and introductions; and miscellaneous. The following types of material have been omitted: early articles on technical problems in higher education, book reviews, poems, and juvenilia. Titles are listed chronologically within these categories.

BOOKS, ORIGINAL AND EDITED

The American in England During the First Half Century of Independence. New York: Henry Holt and Co., 1926. Reprint. Philadelphia: Porcupine Press, 1976.

Gleanings in Europe: France. By James Fenimore Cooper. New York: Oxford University Press, 1928 (edited text with introduction). Reprint. New York: Kraus Reprint Co., 1970.

Gleanings in Europe: England. By James Fenimore Cooper. New York: Oxford University Press, 1930 (edited text with introduction). Reprint. New York: Kraus Reprint Co., 1970.

Fenimore Cooper: Critic of His Times. New York: Minton, Balch and Co., 1931. Reprint. New York: Russell and Russell, 1963.

The Roots of National Culture: American Literature to 1830. New York: The Macmillan Co., 1933. Revised (with Harold Blodgett). New York: Macmillan, 1949. (A period anthology with introduction and notes.)

A Descriptive Bibliography of the Writings of James Fenimore Cooper (with
    Philip C. Blackburn). New York: R. R. Bowker Co., 1934.
    Reprint. New York: Burt Franklin, 1968.

James Fenimore Cooper: Representative Selections. New York: American
    Book Co., 1936 (edited with introduction, bibliography, and
    notes).

English Institute Annual, 1939. New York: Columbia University Press,
    1940 (edited with introduction, pp. 1-14). Introduction reprinted
    as "Science and Literature." In *The Third Dimension*, 1965.

Literary History of the United States (with Willard Thorp, Thomas H.
    Johnson, and Henry Seidel Canby). 3 vols. New York: The
    Macmillan Co., 1948. (A cooperative literary history with multi-
    ple authorship. Vols. 1 and 2: History; Vol. 3: Bibliography). See
    also, "Articles in Books."
        Revised second edition in one volume (with Postscript and
    Readers' Bibliography). New York: Macmillan, 1952.
        Bibliography Supplement No. 1. Edited by Richard M. Lud-
    wig. New York: Macmillan, 1959.
        Revised third edition. 2 vols. New York: Macmillan, 1963
    (Vol. 1: 2 vols. in one, with Postscript and Readers' Bibliogra-
    phy; Vol. 2: Bibliography, with Bibliography Supplement No.
    1).
        Bibliography Supplement No. 2. New York: Macmillan, 1972.
        Revised fourth edition. 2 vols. New York: Macmillan, 1974
    (Vol. 1: History, with new section and Readers' Bibliography;
    Vol. 2: Bibliography, with Bibliography Supplements No. 1 and
    2).
        Translation. 5 vols. Illustrated. Milan: Casa editrice I Saggia,
    1963 (Traduzione di Georgio Braccialargha e Fedora Dei Scat-
    tole).
        Translation. Mainz: Matthias-Grunewald Verlag, 1959
    (German translation of second edition, Vol. 1, History only).
        Translation. Moscow: Progress, 1977. 3 vols., without bibliog-
    raphy (Russian translation by a committee of the Moscow Insti-
    tute).
        Reprint. Belgrade: United States Information Agency, 1948.
        Reprint. New Delhi, India: Amerind Publishing Co., Pvt. Ltd.
    1972 (Vol. 1 only of third edition).

Changing Patterns in American Civilization (The Benjamin Franklin Lectures, No. 1). Philadelphia: University of Pennsylvania Press, 1949. Reprint. Philadelphia: University of Pennsylvania Press, 1962.

Five Essays on Man and Nature. By Ralph Waldo Emerson. New York: Appleton-Century-Crofts, 1954. Reprint. Arlington Heights, Ill.: AMH Publishing Co., 1974.

The Cycle of American Literature: An Essay in Historical Criticism. New York: The Macmillan Co., 1955.
    Reprint New York: New American Library (A Mentor Book), 1957.
    Revised. New York: Macmillan (Free Press), 1967.
    Reprint. Belgrade (Jugo-Slavia): United States Information Agency, (1955).
    Translation. Tokyo: The Hokuseido Press, 1956 (translated into Japanese by Mataki Matsutori).
    Translation. Buenos Aires, Argentina: Editiones La Reja, 1957 (translated into Spanish by Cora Bosch).
    Translation. Seoul, Korea: Dong Shin Pub. Co., 1959 (translated into Korean by Prof. Beonzoheon).
    Translation. Beirut, Lebanon: Al'assassah Al-Ahliah, 1959 (translated into Arabic by Tarvfik Sayegh).
    Translation. Rio de Janeiro, Brazil: Editoro Fundo de Culture, 1961 (translated into Portuguese).
    Translation. Storia della Litteratura Americana. Florence, Italy: Sansoni, 1962 (translated into Italian by Persio Nesti).
    Translation. Stockholm, Sweden: Walstrom and Widestrand, 1968 (translated into Swedish by Karin Thorén-Hribar).

The Early Lectures of Ralph Waldo Emerson. Vol. 1 (with Stephen E. Whicher); vol. 2 (with Stephen E. Whicher and Wallace E. Williams); vol. 3 (with Wallace E. Williams). Cambridge, Mass.: The Belknap Press of Harvard University Press, 1959, 1964, 1972 (edited from manuscripts in the Houghton Library, Cambridge, Mass.).

Social Control in a Free Society. By Loren C. Eiseley, Carl G. Hempel, Gilbert Seldes, George J. Stigler, and Willard Hunt. The Benjamin Franklin Lectures No. 6. Philadelphia: University of Pennsylvania Press, 1960. Reprint. Westport, Conn.: Greenwood Press, 1975.

American Perspectives; The National Self-Image in the Twentieth Century (a symposium, with Eric Larabee). Cambridge, Mass.: Harvard University Press, 1961. Translation Tokyo, Japan: Kobundo, 1961 (translated into Japanese).

A Time of Harvest: American Literature, 1910-1960. New York: Hill and Wang, 1962 (United States Information Agency broadcasts by R. E. Spiller and others. Issued first on tape and in separate pamphlets).
   Translation (translated into Japanese, 1961; and into Arabic, 1961).
   Translation. Buenos Aires, Argentina: Editorial nova, 1962 (translated into Spanish by Gerardo Meyer).
   Translation. Rio de Janiero, Brazil: Editora Letras e Artes, 1963 (translated into Portuguese by Francesco Rocha Filbo).
   Translation. Seoul, Korea: Tangu Dang, 1966 (translated into Korean).
   Translation. Dacca, Pakistan: Zeenat, 1966 (translated into Pak-Bengali).
   Reprint. Bombay, India: Vora and Co., 1966.
   Reprint. Madras, India: Higginbothams, Ltd., 1968.

James Fenimore Cooper (University of Minnesota Pamphlets on American Writers No. 48). Minneapolis: University of Minnesota Press, 1965. Reprinted in *Six American Novelists.* Ed. Richard Foster. Minneapolis: University of Minnesota Press, 1968, pp. 10-44. Translation. Bangladesh, n.d. (translated into Bengali).

The Third Dimension: Studies in Literary History. New York: The Macmillan Co., 1965. Reprint. New York: Collier Books, 1966. Translation. Tokyo, Japan: Tuttle, 1975 (translated into Japanese by Hajimu Sasaki).

The American Literary Revolution, 1783-1837. New York: New York University Press, 1967. Reprint. New York: Doubleday and Co., Inc. (Anchor Books), 1967. (An anthology of early statements on literary nationalism, edited with an introduction and notes).

The Oblique Light: Studies in American Literary History and Biography. New York: The Macmillan Co., 1968. Reprint. Bombay: Popular Prakashan, 1970.

The Van Wyck Brooks-Lewis Mumford Letters: The Record of a Literary Friendship, 1921-1963. New York: E. P. Dutton and Co., Inc., 1970 (edited with biographical commentary).

The Mirror of American Life: Essays and Reviews on American Literature. Tokyo: Eichosha, 1971 (annotated, in Japanese, by Yukio Irie).

Nature, Addresses and Lectures. Vol. 1 of the *Collected Works of Ralph Waldo Emerson* (with Alfred R. Ferguson). Cambridge, Mass.: The Belknap Press of Harvard University Press, 1971.

The Philobiblon Club of Philadelphia: The First Eighty Years, 1893-1973. Philadelphia: Bird and Bull Press, 1973 (printed for the Philobiblon Club).

Milestones in American Literary History (with a foreword by Robert H. Walker, contributions in American Studies No. 27. Westport, Conn.: Greenwood Press, 1977.

ARTICLES AND CHAPTERS IN BOOKS

"The Arts and Crafts," In *An Adventure in Education: Swarthmore College under Frank Aydelotte.* By the Swarthmore College Faculty. New York: The Macmillan Co., 1941, pp. 171-83.

"The Making of the Man of Letters." In *Literary History of the United States.* Ed. Robert E. Spiller, Willard Thorp, Thomas H. Johnson, and Henry Seidel Canby. Vol. 1. New York: The Macmillan Co., 1948, pp. 122-30.
"Art in the Market Place." In ibid., Vol. 1, pp. 228-41.
"Ralph Waldo Emerson." In ibid., Vol. 1, pp. 258-87.

"Toward Naturalism in Fiction." In *ibid.*, Vol. 2, pp. 1016-38.

"Henry Adams." In ibid., Vol. 2, pp. 1080-1103.

"The Battle of the Books." In ibid., Vol. 2, pp. 1129-56.

"Theodore Dreiser" (with James T. Farrell). In ibid., Vol. 2, pp. 1197-1207.

"End of an Era" (with Willard Thorp). In ibid., Vol. 2, pp. 1392-1411.

"Benjamin Franklin: Promoter of Useful Knowledge." In *The American Writer and the European Tradition.* Ed. Margaret Denney and William H. Gilman. Minneapolis: University of Minnesota Press, 1950,pp. 29-44.

"Second Thoughts on Cooper as a Social Critic." In *James Fenimore Cooper: A Re-appraisal.* Ed. Mary E. Cunningham. Cooperstown, New York: New York State Historical Association, 1954, pp. 172-90.

"Henry James." In *Eight American Authors: A Review of Research and Criticism.* New York: Modern Language Association, 1956, pp. 364-418. Reprint. New York: W.W. Norton and Co., Inc., 1963.

"American Studies, Past, Present, and Future." In *Studies in American Culture: Dominant Ideas and Images.* Ed. Joseph J. Kwiatt and Mary C. Turpie. Minneapolis: University of Minnesota Press, 1960. pp. 207-20. Revised as "Values and Methods in American Studies." In *Jahrbuch für Amerikastudien,* Vol. 4 (1959). Reprint. *American Personality and the Creative Arts.* Ed. Joel C. Mickelson. Minneapolis: Burgess Pub. Co., 1969, pp. 1-15.

"The Use of Old Sources in New Ways." In *The John Carter Brown Conference.* Providence, R.I., 1961, pp. 19-28.

"Literature and the Critics." In *American Perspectives: The National Self-Image in the Twentieth Century.* Ed. R. E. Spiller and Eric Larabee. Cambridge: Harvard University Press, 1961, pp. 35-58. Reprinted as "The Critical Movement in the Twentieth Century." In *The Third Dimension,* 1965.

"The American Literary Dilemma and Edgar Allan Poe." In *The Great Experiment in American Literature.* Ed. Carl Bode. New York: Frederick A. Praeger, 1961, pp. 3-28. Reprint. London: Heinemann,

1961. (An earlier version was published as "New Wine in Old Bottles." In *The Third Dimension*, 1965).

"Literary History." In *The Aims and Methods of Literary Scholarship*. Ed. James Thorpe. New York: Modern Language Assn., 1963, pp. 43-55. Revised. Second edition. New York: M.L.A., 1970, pp. 55-68. Translation (Japanese), 1972.

"Tragedy and Romanticism in Modern American Literature." In *The Third Dimension*. New York, 1965, pp. 172-88.

"A Letter to American Literary Historians." In *The Third Dimension*, 1965. Reprinted in *Milestones in American Literary History*. Westport, Conn.: Greenwood Press, 1977, pp. 139-43.

"After the Romantic Movement." In *The Third Dimension*, 1965, pp. 103-22.

"Ralph Waldo Emerson, 'The American Scholar,' 1837" In *An American Primer*. Ed. Daniel Boorstin. 2 vols. Chicago: The University of Chicago Press, 1966, Vol. 1, pp. 283-301.

"The American in Europe, Then and Now." In *USA in Focus: Recent Interpretations*. Ed. Sigmund Skard. Oslo, Norway: Universetetsforlaget, 1966, pp. 174-88. Reprinted in *The Oblique Light*, 1968.

"The Mirror of American Fiction: A Study of the Novel of Self-inquiry as an Instrument of International (Mis)Understanding." In *Problems of International Understanding*. Ed. Karl R. Gierow. Proceedings of the Sixth Nobel Symposium. Stockholm, 1967. Stockholm: Almqvist and Wiksell, 1968, pp. 23-36.

"Those Early Days, A Personal Memoir." In *The Oblique Light*, 1968, pp. 257-68. (Address at the luncheon of the American Section of the Modern Language Association and The American Studies Association. New York, December 27, 1966).

"The American Literary Declaration of Independence." In *Literatur und Sprache der Vereinigten Staaten*. Ed. Hans Helmke and others. Heidelberg: Carl Winters, 1969, pp. 62-73 (based on prefatory material from volume of the same title).

"The Four Faces of Emerson." In *Four Makers of the American Mind*. Ed. Thomas E. Crawley. Durham, N.C.: Duke University Press., 1976, pp. 3-23.

"Einheit und Vielfalt im Studium der Amerikanischen Kultur." In *Die Amerikanische Literatur der Gegenwart, Aspecte und Tendenzen*. Herausgegeben von Hans Bungart. Stuttgart: Philipp Reclam, June 1977, pp. 263-70.

"Time Present: Amerikanische Literatur seit 1945." In ibid., pp. 18-27. "The Cycle and the Roots: National Identity in American Literature." In *Toward a New-American Literary History*. Durham, N.C.: Duke University Press, 1980, pp. 3-18.

ESSAYS AND ARTICLES IN JOURNALS

"The English Literary Horizon, 1815-1835." *Studies in Philogy* 23 (January 1926): 1-15. Reprinted in *The Oblique Light*, 1968.

"Brother Jonathan to John Bull." *South Atlantic Quarterly* 26 (October 1927): 346-58.

"A New Biographical Source for William Cowper." *PMLA* 41 (December 1927): 946-62.

"The Mind and Art of Nathaniel Hawthorne." *Outlook* (August 22, 1928): 650-52, 678. Reprinted in *The Oblique Light*, 1968.

"The College, Past and Present." *General Magazine and Historical Chronicle* (April 1928): 3-20.

"The Verdict of Sydney Smith." *American Literature* 1 (March 1929): 3-13. Reprinted in *The Third Dimension*, 1965.

"Cooper's Notes on Language." *American Speech* 4 (April 1929): 294-300.

"Fenimore Cooper: Critic of His Times: New Letters from Rome and Paris, 1830-31." *American Literature* 1 (May 1929): 131-48.

"Cooper's Defense of Slave-Owning America." *American Historical Review* 35 (April 1930): 375-82.

"A Case for W. E. Channing." *New England Quarterly* 3 (January 1930): 55-81. Reprinted in *The Oblique Light*, 1968.

"Fenimore Cooper and Lafayette: The Finance Controversy of 1831-32." *American Literature* 3 (March 1931): 28-44.

"Major in English." *English Journal* 20 (January 1931): 37-42.

"Ten Years of Outside Examiners." *English Journal* 22 (April 1933): 310-19.

"Fenimore Cooper and Lafayette: Friends of Polish Freedom." *American Literature* 7 (March 1935): 56-75.

"The Task of the Historian of American Literature." *Sewanee Review* 43 (January-March 1935): 70-79. Reprinted in *The Third Dimension*, 1965.

"War with the Book Pirates." *Publishers Weekly* 133 (1937): 1736-38.

"Biography of the American Scholar: An Address Read at the Opening of Honors Work at Swarthmore College, September 24, 1936." *English Journal* 26 (October 1937): 637-47.

"John Woolman on War." *Journal of the Rutgers University Library* 5 (1941): 60-91.
"Benjamin Franklin: Pragmatist." *General Magazine and Historical Chronicle* (University of Pennsylvania 44 (1941): 48-61.

"Higher Education and the War." *Journal of Higher Education* 13 (June 1942): 287-97.

"What Became of the Literary Radicals?" *New Republic* 64 (1946): 664-65. Reprinted in *The Third Dimension*, 1965.

"Critical Standards in the American Romantic Movement." *College English* 8 (1947): 344-52. Reprinted in *The Third Dimension*, 1965.

"Sidney Lanier: Ancestor of Anti-Realism." *Saturday Review of Literature* 31 (January 10, 1948): 6-7, 24. Reprinted in *The ObliqueLight*, 1968.

"The Function of Literary Research, A Reconsideration." *College English* 10 (January 1949): 201-09.

"The Myth of Materialism." *Pennsylvania Literary Review* (University of Pennsylvania) (Fall 1951): 13-19.

"The Growth of American Literary Scholarship." *Edda* (Norway) (January 1951).

"Franklin on the Art of Being Human." *Proceedings of the American Philosophical Society* 100 (1956): 304-15. Reprinted in *The Oblique Light*, 1968.

"Nobel preisträger Eugene O'Neill und die Weltliterature unsern Zeit." *Universitas* (Stuttgart) 12 (1957): 1277-80.

"Blueprint for American Literary History." *Pennsylvania Literary Review* (University of Pennsylvania) 8 (1957): 3-10. Reprinted in *The Third Dimension*, 1965.

"The Influence of Edmund Wilson: The Dual Tradition." *Nation* (February 22, 1958): 159-61. Reprinted in *The Oblique Light*, 1968.

"American Literature in British Universities." *Bulletin of the British Association for American Studies* 9 (1959): 21-25.

"From Lecture into Essay: Emerson's Method of Composition." *Literary Criterion* (Madras, India) 5 (Winter 1962): 28-38.

"Is Literary History Obsolete?" *College English* 25 (1963): 345-51. Reprinted in *The Third Dimension*, 1965.

"American Studies Abroad: Culture and Foreign Policy." *Annals* of the American Academy of Political and Social Science 366 (July 1966): 1-16.

"The Fulbright Program in American Studies Abroad: Retrospect and Prospect." *American Studies International* 9 (Autumn, 1970): 10-16. Reprinted in *American Studies Abroad*. Ed. Robert H. Walker. Westport, Conn.: Greenwood Press, 1975, pp. 3-9.

"Emerson and Humbolt." *American Literature* 42 (1971): 546-48.

"Faces on the Wall: An Address at the . . . Franklin Inn Club (Phila.)." Philadelphia: *Franklin Inn Club Membership List* (1972): 3-10.

"Unity and Diversity in American Culture: The American Studies Association in Perspective." *American Quarterly* 25 (1973): 611-18.

"History of a History: A Study in Cooperative Scholarship." *PMLA* (May 1973): 602-16. Reprinted in *Milestones*, 1977.

"How to Grow Old." *Pennsylvania Gazette* (University of Pennsylvania) 72 (1974): 36-41.

"The Impossible Dream: Adventures in Editing American Literary Texts." *Library Chronicle* (University of Pennsylvania) 13 (Winter, 1978): 83-97.

FOREWORDS AND INTRODUCTIONS

Letter to Gen. Lafayette, by James Fenimore Cooper; and Related Correspondence on the Finance Controversy. New York: Columbia University Press for the Facsimile Text Society, 1931.

The Lake Gun. By James Fenimore Cooper. New York: William Farquhar Payson, 1932.

Satanstoe. By James Fenimore Cooper (with J. D. Coppock). New York: American Book Company, 1937.

Esther. By Frances Snow Compton [Henry Adams]. New York: Scholars Facsimiles and Reprints, 1938, 1976. Reprinted as "The Private Life of Henry Adams." In *The Oblique Light*, 1968.

Tahiti (Memoirs of Arii Taimai E). By Henry Adams. New York: Scholars Facsimiles and Reprints, 1947, 1976.

The Malady of the Ideal: Obermann, Maurice de Guerin, and Amiel. By Van Wyck Brooks. Philadelphia: University of Pennsylvania Press, 1947. First American edition.

The Last of the Mohicans. By James Fenimore Cooper. New York: E. P. Dutton Co. (Everyman's Library), 1951.

Crumbling Idols. By Hamlin Garland. Gainesville, Florida: Scholars Facsimiles and Reprints, 1952, 1957.

The American Democrat, or Hints on the Social and Civic Relations of the United States of America. By James Fenimore Cooper. New York: Vintage Books. 1956.

Notions of the Americans, Picked up by a Travelling Bachelor. By James Fenimore Cooper. 2 vols. New York: Frederick Ungar Pub. Co., 1963.

The Pioneers. By James Fenimore Cooper. New York: New American Library (A Signet Classic), 1964.

Selected Essays, Lectures, and Poems of Ralph Waldo Emerson. New York: Washington Square Press, Inc., 1965.

The Pathfinder. By James Fenimore Cooper. New York: The Heritage Press, 1965.

The Autobiography of Benjamin Franklin. Boston: Houghton, Mifflin Co., 1966.

MISCELLANEOUS

Indian Essays in American Literature. Papers in Honour of Robert E. Spiller. Ed. Sujit Mukherje and D. K. V. Raghavacharyulu. Bombay: Popular Prakashan, 1967.

American Quarterly, 1967 (Supplement, summer 1967): 291-302. Dedicated to Robert E. Spiller. Essays by Russel B. Nye, Sigmund Skard, Anthony N. B. Garvan, and Louis D. Rubin, Jr.

James Fenimore Cooper (Film). Wilmette, Ill.: Encyclopedia Britannica Films, Inc., 1949.

Great American Writers (Casette Tapes). Deland, Florida: Everett/ Edwards, Inc..
1. The Republic, 1783-1840: Franklin, Irving, Cooper, Poe.
2. Renaissance, 1840-1860: Emerson, Thoreau, Hawthorne, Melville.
3. The Nation, 1860-1910: Whitman, Mark Twain, Henry James, Dickinson.
4. Second Renaissance, 1910-1945.
5. Prospects, 1945-?

INDEX

263

About the Author

ROBERT E. SPILLER is Felix E. Schelling Professor Emeritus of English at the University of Pennsylvania in Philadelphia. He was the editor of the *Literary History of the United States*. His other books include *The Cycle of American Literature, The Third Dimension, The Oblique Light,* and *Milestones in American Literary History* (Greenwood Press, 1977).